REMEMBERING JEWS IN MAGHREBI AND MIDDLE EASTERN MEDIA

Remembering Jews in Maghrebi and Middle Eastern Media

EDITED BY BRAHIM EL GUABLI AND MOSTAFA HUSSEIN

The Pennsylvania State University Press
University Park, Pennsylvania

Library of Congress Cataloging-in-Publication Data

Names: Guabli, Brahim El, editor. | Hussein, Mostafa, editor.
Title: Remembering Jews in Maghrebi and Middle Eastern media / edited by Brahim El Guabli and Mostafa Hussein.
Description: University Park, Pennsylvania : The Pennsylvania State University Press, [2024] | Includes bibliographical references and index.
Summary: "Explores Maghrebi and Middle Eastern communities reckoning with the loss of local Jews over the past seven decades through literature and film, creating a new conceptual framework through which Jewish-Muslim relations can be studied"—Provided by publisher.
Identifiers: LCCN 2024024553 | ISBN 9780271097558 (hardback)
Subjects: LCSH: Arabic literature—20th century—History and criticism. | Arabic literature—21st century—History and criticism. | Jewish-Arab relations in literature. | Loss (Psychology) in literature. | Jews—Africa, North—Migrations. | Jews—Middle East—Migrations. | Motion pictures—Arab countries. | Jewish-Arab relations in motion pictures. | Loss (Psychology) in motion pictures.
Classification: LCC PJ7519.J4 R46 2024 | DDC 892/.093529924—dc23/eng/20240625
LC record available at https://lccn.loc.gov/2024024553

Printed in the United States of America
Published by The Pennsylvania State University Press,
University Park, PA 16802–1003

The Pennsylvania State University Press is a member of the Association of University Presses.

It is the policy of The Pennsylvania State University Press to use acid-free paper. Publications on uncoated stock satisfy the minimum requirements of American National Standard for Information Sciences—Permanence of Paper for Printed Library Material, ANSI Z39.48–1992.

To our respective families with a lot of gratitude

CONTENTS

List of Illustrations (ix)

Foreword (x)

Acknowledgments (xvii)

Introduction (1)

1 Generative Absence: Jewish Loss as a Catalyst for Literature, Film, and Thought (25)
Brahim El Guabli

2 On the Wrong Side of History: The Jews in Algerian Literature (48)
Abdelkader Aoudjit

3 Literary Representations of Jews in Twenty-First-Century Arabic Literature in Egypt (69)
Mostafa Hussein

4 *Al-Zaman al-Gamīl* Refigured: Jews and Re-Narration of the Nation on Egyptian TV (93)
Iskandar Ahmad Abdalla

5 Death, Burial, and Loss in Ali al-Muqri's *Al-Yahūdī al-ḥalī* (The Handsome Jew) (113)
Sarah Irving

6 Bearing Witness and Resurrecting Kurdish-Arab-Jewish Memory in *Mādhā 'an al-sayyida al-yahūdiyya rāḥīl?* (135)
Stephanie Kraver

7 Documenting and Debating Turkey's Loss (154)
İlker Hepkaner

8 Exile in a Contemporary Artistic Project in Morocco: Jewish Memories in Form and Concrete Territories *(171)*
Nadia Sabri

9 Narrating the Homeland from Exile: Iranian Jewish Writers Writing on Their Departure, Identity, and Longing *(190)*
Lior B. Sternfeld

List of Contributors (211)

Index (214)

8.1. The main door of the Museum of Moroccan Judaism in Casablanca, located in the Oasis neighborhood *(172)*
8.2. Mustapha Akrim, *Now, in Exile*, 2016 *(173)*
8.3. *Safarad IV*, exhibit of Josep Ginestar *(174)*
8.4. Ulrike Weiss, Untitled, 2016 *(179)*
8.5. Ulrike Weiss, Jewish woman of Debdou *(180)*
8.6. Ulrike Weiss, Untitled, 2016 *(181)*
8.7. Mustapha Akrim, *Now, in Exile*, 2016 *(184)*

FOREWORD

In 2014, the Iraqi novelist Ahmed Saʿdāwī won the International Prize for Arabic Fiction for his gothic novel *Frankenstein in Baghdad*.[1] Its 2018 English translation was widely reviewed, garnering critical acclaim. Set in Baghdad of 2005, the novel borrows Mary Shelley's icon to depict the nightmarish reality of Iraqi life in the aftermath of the US war. In Saʿdāwī's retelling, a grubby junk dealer and raconteur stitches together an assortment of body parts from anonymous victims of the bombings then consuming the city, thereby creating the titular monster. After it miraculously comes to life, the "Shesma" (Whatsitsname), as the monster becomes known, embarks on a killing spree that it explains to its followers as the discharging of "justice"; eventually, it becomes evident that the monster is killing Iraqis at random simply in order to survive.[2]

Much has been written about this novel, generally in appreciation of its allegorical elements: at one point in the story, the multisectarian monster is dubbed the "first true Iraqi citizen."[3] Critics have also heeded the novel's setting in al-Batāwīn (Batawin), once a heavily Jewish neighborhood of Baghdad and a location that, perhaps more than any other, symbolizes Baghdad's vanishing and suppressed multiethnic, multireligious heritage. Indeed, Batawin, as Hani Elayyan writes, is "almost a character in the novel"; it "boasts complex layers of history from Jewish, to Christian, to Muslim, that have contributed to the make-up of the Iraqi national identity."[4] In the novel, Batawin's layers of history are worked into the narrative in a quite literal form. The Shesma is first fabricated by Hādī the junk dealer in a decrepit house known as "the Jewish ruin." The corpse is then inadvertently brought to life by Elishva, a senescent Assyrian woman who lives next door. When Iraqi authorities in pursuit of the monster ransack Hādī's home, they destroy an old plaster icon of the Virgin Mary attached to a wall. Hādī then makes an unexpected discovery: behind the smashed icon, literally hidden inside a cavity in the wall, is a wooden engraving of a Jewish menorah adorned with Hebrew script: "he immediately thought this, too, was something he could sell."[5]

That the menorah, symbol of the historic Jewish presence in Baghdad, is a trace concealed by a Christian façade within an abandoned Jewish house occupied by a Muslim Iraqi (who sees it as a potential commodity) attests to Saʿdāwī's deployment of the lost Iraqi Jewish past in the novel. As Booker and Daraiseh point out, "*Frankenstein in Baghdad* makes numerous references to the fact that Jews had once played an active role in Iraqi culture. But all of these references are to ruins and traces. There are, in fact, no Jews at all in the book, just as there are essentially no Jews left in current-day Iraq."[6] Yet, I argue, Saʿdāwī is doing more than depicting the absence of Jews from the Iraqi national body (itself personified by the Shesma): the loss of Iraq's Jews metonymically alludes to fragmentation of the nation that culminated in the cataclysm of post-2003 Iraq. As if to drive this point home, Saʿdāwī offers us a heavy-handed metaphor, which he places in the mouth of an Assyrian deacon who is encouraging the elderly Elishva to emigrate: "The whole country's starting to look like the Jewish ruin next door."[7]

But if in *Frankenstein in Baghdad* Batawin is a site of loss and ruins, in Iraqi Jewish literature and memoirs this same neighborhood plays a diametrically opposite role. Batawin in those works is a newly built neighborhood, the epicenter of a vibrant Jewish community embracing modernity and enjoying the opportunities afforded by citizenship in the nascent Iraqi state. Batawin enjoys an outsize presence in Iraqi Jewish memory; even in the final years of Jewish life in Iraq, it was the location of Baghdad's last functioning synagogue (now closed). Any of the numerous Iraqi Jewish authors who have written about Batawin of the 1930s and 1940s would be hard pressed to identify the Batawin of the 2000s depicted in Saʿdāwī's tragicomic novel. It is almost as if there are two separate Batawins, performing opposing functions within two different literary economies of loss that intersect only through their shared resonances of Jewish presence. Reading *Frankenstein in Baghdad* in conversation with the memoirs of Jewish Baghdadis such as Sasson Somekh and Naim Kattan, or with the fiction of Sami Mikhael, Eli Amir, Samir Naqqash, and Shimon Ballas, one cannot help but see Saʿdāwī's Baghdad as a grotesque epilogue to an aborted history, an epilogue that inevitably invites questions of "what if" and fantasies of alternative realities.[8]

Iraq, of course, constitutes but one thread among several in the fabric of Middle Eastern and Maghrebi Jewish communities whose presence has migrated to the realms of stories, memories, and traces. As the editors of this volume rightfully note, each such Jewish community has its own situated history formed through an intimate relationship to place—its own "Batawin," so to speak. Moreover, each community has its own story of the "break" from the homeland, in some cases more voluntary, in others more traumatic. The particular circumstances of departure, the nineteenth- and twentieth-century histories that preceded the departure, and the degree of Jewish integration into non-Jewish society, all influence the way both Jews and non-Jews remember Jewish life in the nation of origin. Yet what all these Maghrebi and Middle Eastern Jewish communities share is the stunning finality and scale of their collective dissolution. As the editors write, "for a vibrant and fully integrated religious community to move swiftly over the course of twenty years, leaving hearth and home without impending danger to the lives of the majority of its members, is an unprecedented phenomenon"—one that not only froze the Jewish emigrants' memories of their former homes in the amber of the past, but that also irrevocably transformed the social composition of those cities, town, and villages for the non-Jewish friends, neighbors, and co-citizens whom they left behind. The belated responses to the latter in the form of television dramas, novels, feature films, and documentaries form this book's point of departure.

Today, the discourse of Maghrebi and Middle Eastern Jewish memory is multifaceted and intermedial.[9] There is of course the ever-growing archive of novels, stories, poems, memoirs, and films made by the Jewish émigrés and their children, memorializing their erstwhile homelands and seeking to recover the lives and memories of prior generations; music constitutes an additional medium of memory and cultural preservation as well as renewal. As this volume demonstrates, that considerable archive is now complemented by the creative work of non-Jews in situ reimagining (and often instrumentalizing) their own lost Jewish pasts in literature and film. For over a decade now, there has also been an active discourse of memory at play in the digital realm, with numerous dedicated Facebook groups (e.g., "Jews of Egypt"; "Iraqi Jews"; "Jews of Lebanon") in which both Jewish émigrés and non-Jewish members of the former homelands reunite, discuss memories, share photographs, relate experiences and return visits, translate for one another, and help decipher official family documents, with these written interactions taking place in Arabic, French, and English.

The unique capacity of the digital sphere to host Maghrebi and Middle Eastern Jewish memory became powerfully evident with the founding of Diarna (the Geo-Museum of North African and Middle Eastern Jewish Life)[10] around 2008. Diarna, meaning "our homes," is a virtual museum of Jewish heritage sites primarily in the Maghreb and Middle East with, at the time of writing, seventeen "exhibits" that are searchable by country. Several of these exhibits, in turn, feature multiple sites documented by Diarna, in some cases from throughout the region, or in other cases from a single country. Some of those sites, such as the famous Eliahu Hanavi (Jobar) synagogue in Damascus, have since been destroyed. As Dara Horn writes, "The flagship project of the nonprofit group Digital Heritage Mapping, Diarna is a vast online resource that combines traditional and high-tech photography, satellite imaging, digital mapping, 3-D modeling, archival materials and oral histories to allow anyone to 'visit' Jewish heritage sites throughout the Middle East, North Africa and other places around the globe."[11] Thus, Diarna allows people of all nationalities and faiths to visually access Jewish sites of memory along with key contextual information. The researchers associated with Diarna—an interfaith team—insist on its political neutrality. But, as Horn points out:

> The choice to present these Jewish sites is itself a statement, one that underscores an undeniable reality. "The Middle East is becoming more homogeneous," says Diarna's lead research coordinator, Eddie Ashkenazie, himself a descendant of Syrian Jews. "We're pointing out that the store next to your grandfather's in the market was once owned by the Cohen family," he tells me. "Whether they got along or it was fraught with tension is going to vary depending on the time and place, but it testifies to a society that had other voices in it, that had minorities in it, that was heterogeneous. Today you have whole societies that are only Libyan Muslims, or only Shiite Arabs. But they used to be incredibly diverse. All Diarna is trying to do is say that Jews once lived here."[12]

Another important virtual resource, the Iraqi Jewish Archive,[13] encapsulates the various themes and questions that animate this volume. The ambiguous relationship of the Iraqi Jewish past to the Iraqi national future is best illustrated by the bizarre story of this archive. In May 2003, US troops seeking weapons of mass destruction waded into the basement of Saddam Hussein's secret police (*mukhabarat*) headquarters, which had flooded with sewage water when they bombed the building. They found not weapons, but an enormous cache of over twenty-seven hundred books (many of them in Hebrew) along with thousands of manuscripts, documents, and photographs covering all aspects, religious and secular, of Iraqi Jewish life. The soldiers immediately realized they had stumbled across a treasure whose survival now hung in a very soggy balance. Inquiries revealed that these were private materials pilfered from the Jewish community. The materials were initially dried outside in Baghdad's humid climate, leading to mold, a preservationist's nightmare. They were subsequently loaded into a freezer truck to prevent further damage. With the agreement of Iraqi officials, the materials were transported to the United States for a decade-long process of cleaning, preservation, and documentation. The archive was stipulated to be returned to Iraq once preservation and digitization efforts were completed, with a formal return date of 2014. The US National Archives and Records Administration, in collaboration with numerous other organizations, restored the materials and created a searchable database for the collection with 3,846 entries; it also created a traveling exhibit. When I visited the exhibit in December 2013 during its debut at the National Archives in Washington, DC, I chanced to see Edwin Shuker, a prominent Jewish Iraqi based in London, declaiming before a rapt audience; his sixth-grade report card, once confiscated by Saddam's secret police, was displayed just above his head on the exhibit wall.

However, despite the State Department's repeated assurances of repatriation to Iraq, the archive still remains in the United States. Why? Unsurprisingly, the question of the archive's permanent home triggered a heated dispute over patrimony and access. Beyond its clear cultural and historical significance, the collection—which contains, inter alia, both antique manuscripts and the personal items of living individuals, such as Shuker's school records—has tremendous emotional purchase. As such, its fate has been hotly contested ever since its arrival on US soil. Jewish and pro-Israel groups supported by US legislators lobbied to delay and ultimately prevent the previously negotiated return to Iraq on the grounds that the archive should remain housed in a stable environment accessible to the descendants of Iraqi Jews. The heads of the Babylonian Jewry Heritage Center in Israel have claimed the archive for their own museum, arguing that its contents are the rightful property of the Iraqi Jewish community, whose members and descendants are concentrated largely in Israel. As for Iraqi officials, they have made it clear that they view the archive as an important part of Iraq's cultural patrimony. In January 2010, Sa'd Eskander, the director of the Iraqi National Library and Archives, told the Associated Press that the archives are needed to "show . . . our people that Baghdad was always multiethnic," and to help them come to grips with their complex history.[14] The fact that the collection was expatriated from Iraq during the American occupation also rekindles sensitive memories of colonial plunder throughout the region.

To whom do these relics now belong—if not legally, then morally? To the descendants of the Iraqi Jews, from whom they were confiscated and whose personal and communal histories they so richly document? To the Iraqi state, from which they were removed by an occupying power under an agreement that it then abrogated? To the United States, which nonetheless rescued the materials from certain oblivion and invested three million dollars in their preservation? Who "owns" the archive of the lost Iraqi Jewish past; who "owns" Iraqi Jewish memory? And what does the Iraqi Jewish memory contained in this archive mean to each of the parties claiming to be its rightful owner? Addressing these questions also necessitates open discussion of the relationship of the Iraqi Jewish past to the Iraqi national present and future—a question that, to my knowledge, has not been addressed in a public forum with representatives of contemporary Iraq.

In a similar sense, it is the need to grapple with questions of the Jewish past's relation to the national present and future—questions of ownership and patrimony, of complex and sometimes ambiguous relationships—that motivates much of the cultural production discussed in this book. The chapters' authors reveal the ways Amazigh, Arab, Iranian, and Turkish societies are now working through the open questions left by the departure of their Jewish citizens. The relationships in question are not always easy; sometimes they are even painful. There are as many perspectives on these questions as there are cultural producers. One might not agree with the perspectives expressed in each work discussed, or even with the way each chapter's author discusses them. But together, they open a critical conversation. As the last generation with personal memories of the Jewish-Muslim "lives in common" passes on, such cultural negotiations of the past will become the basis for collective memory of this historical experience, as well as the basis for a more capacious self-understanding: an understanding of what it means, in the broadest possible sense, to be an Iraqi, a Yemeni, an Algerian, in the knowledge that yes, "Jews once lived here."

—Lital Levy

Notes

1. Saʿdāwī was not the first non-Jewish Iraqi author to evoke Iraqi Jewish themes, questions, or characters in fiction. Khalid Kishtainy, Ali Bader, and others did so previously. See, for example, Bader's novels *Papa Sartre* (Arabic, 2001; English trans., 2009) and *Haris al-Tabagh* (The tobacco keeper; Arabic, 2008; English trans., 2011). See also Zeidel, "On the Last Jews of Iraq."

2. Saʿdāwī, *Frankenstein in Baghdad*, 135, 143.

3. Saʿdāwī, *Frankenstein in Baghdad*, 147.

4. Elayyan, "Monster Unleashed," 159.

5. Saʿdāwī, *Frankenstein in Baghdad*, 205.

6. Booker and Daraiseh, "*Frankenstein in Baghdad*," 398.

7. Saʿdāwī, *Frankenstein in Baghdad*, 207.

8. On the aforementioned Iraqi Jewish writers, see Levy, "Self and the City."

9. See Levy, "Arab Jew Debates."

10. See https://diarna.org.

11. Horn, "Inside the Incredible Effort."

12. Horn, "Inside the Incredible Effort."

13. See https://ijarchive.org/s/iraqi-jewish-archive/page/home.

14. "Iraqi Librarian Seeks."

Bibliography

Booker, M. Keith, and Isra Daraiseh. "*Frankenstein in Baghdad*, or the Postmodern Prometheus." *Journal of the Fantastic in the Arts* 32, no. 3 (2021): 388–403.

Elayyan, Hani. "The Monster Unleashed: Iraq's Horrors of Everyday Life in *Frankenstein in* Baghdad." *Arab World English Journal for Translation and Literary Studies* 1, no. 1 (2017): 158–70.

Horn, Dara. "Inside the Incredible Effort to Recreate Historic Jewish Sites Destroyed Years Ago." *Smithsonian Magazine*, June 2020. https://www.smithsonianmag.com/history/diarna-jewish-sites-not-seen-generations-visit-from-home-180974875/.

"Iraqi Librarian Seeks to Reclaim Jewish Artifacts." Associated Press, January 16, 2020. https://www.deseret.com/2010/1/17/20365080/iraqi-librarian-seeks-to-reclaim-jewish-artifacts.

Levy, Lital. "The Arab Jew Debates: Media, Culture, Politics, History." *Journal of Levantine Studies* 7, no. 1 (2017): 79–103.

———. "Self and the City: Literary Representations of Jewish Baghdad." *Prooftexts* 26, no. 1 (2006): 163–211.

Saʿdawi, Ahmed. *Frankenstein in Baghdad*. New York: Penguin, 2018.

———. *Frankinshtayn fi Baghdad*. Baghdad: Manshurat al-Jamal, 2013.

Zeidel, Ronen. "On the Last Jews in Iraq and Iraqi National Identity: A Look at Two Recent Iraqi Novels." *Journal of Modern Jewish Studies* 17, no. 2 (2018): 207–21.

ACKNOWLEDGMENTS

This book has benefited from the generosity of several colleagues and centers at Williams College. Brahim El Guabli would like to thank his colleagues Gail Newman, Katarzyna Pieprzak, Magnús Bernhardsson, Amal Eqeiq, Jeffrey Isarel, Saadia Yaqoob, and Zaid Adhami for taking the time to read and respond to the papers during the day-long workshop he organized at the Oakley Center for Humanities and Social Sciences under the theme "Refiguring Loss: Jews Remembered Through Amazigh/Arabic Cultural Memory." El Guabli's gratitude also extends to the Oakley Center for Humanities and Social Sciences, the W. Ford Schumann '50 Fund for Democratic Studies, the Gaudino Fund, the Jewish Studies Program, the Program in Comparative Literature, and the Davis Center, which all supported the workshop financially.

Mostafa Hussein would like to thank colleagues and staff in Frankel Center for Judaic Studies at the University of Michigan for demonstrating excitement about this project and for facilitating undertaking needed research and travels to be able to produce it.

Last, but not least, we would like to thank Professor Ella Shohat for her insightful comments, feedback, and lively discussion throughout the workshop and beyond.

Introduction

Scholarship on Jewish communities in the Maghreb and the Middle East has broken new ground through steering away from dominant narratives that approached Jews as a separate entity within Muslim societies. Specifically, Ella Shohat has drawn attention to the Orientalist modes of thinking that continue to underlie the myth of perpetual Jewish-Muslim enmity in art and language politics.[1] Shohat's work allows us to perceive narratives of separation as a production that contradicts both Jewish and Muslim values. By shifting course from two opposing historiographies that identify Jewish lives in Muslim lands in the modern times with the rise of anti-Semitism or with the era that brought about the demise of the Jewish communities in the Middle East, current scholarship on Jewish-Muslim relations examines Jews and Jewish topics as being part and parcel of their societies, be they Amazigh, Arab, Persian, or Turkish. Rather than treating Jews as aliens within largely Muslim societies, this new approach has shown the variegated geographies and uneven topographies of Jewish experiences within the extended area south of the Mediterranean and west of Asia, which was home to over six hundred thousand Jews until the end of the 1960s.[2] New historiographical approaches to the study of Jews in the modern Maghreb and the Middle East have rejected the arbitrary association between the identities of Sephardi and Mizrahi Jews and Zionism, thus challenging the conflation of Judaism with Zionism, and they have explored the way local reforms and the rise of nation-states have affected and shaped the lives of Jews in this expansive region. Spanning disciplines as far afield as sociology, legal studies, anthropology, and literary criticism, these scholars have examined the political, cultural, and social institutions and organizations that have facilitated the integration of Jews into their local societies. Further, they have considered the imperial influences and processes that fostered the Jews' separation from their communities of origin, leading to their uprooting in the middle of the twentieth century.

In this "Middle Eastern turn," as historian Orit Bashkin has identified it,[3] where the focus on Jewish themes in the region has drawn closer to the field of Middle East studies, we propose paying scholarly attention to the ways in which local communities in the Maghreb and the Middle East have interacted with, thought of, and written about the Jews who once lived in their midst. These groups have shared their challenging sociopolitical and economic realities, but, due to political and historical circumstances, they remain active and present primarily via memory, a source for generating national narratives despite no longer existing in proximity. Postcolonial in nature, this emergent historiography is critical of national elites, grand narratives, nationalist histories, and Zionist assumptions about Jews across languages and cultures. In the context of the decolonial moment in the middle of the twentieth century, Maghrebi and Middle Eastern Jews may have left their societies of origin for other horizons that seemed better economically, socially, culturally, or religiously, but their erstwhile existence in their predominantly Muslim societies has become a conspicuous marker of the deep transformation and mutilation these societies have experienced as a result of their Jews' emigration. We aspire in this volume to scrutinize the sequelae of separation and emigration in Maghrebi and Middle Eastern societies as they emerge in literature and film produced by non-Jewish, and mostly Muslim, citizens of these countries and by some of their Jewish counterparts, specifically from Iran. Although not Jewish, these writers and filmmakers have shown a genuine interest in reconnecting their own stories to Jewish lives through a cultural production that recuperates and centers Jewish histories, cultures, and lives that once were part of the societal fabric these creators inherited from their elders.

Remembering Jews is about the significance of the resurgence of Jewish memory as a main topic in Maghrebi and Middle Eastern cultural production in the last thirty years. The current volume emerged from a two-day workshop Brahim El Guabli convened at the Oakley Humanities Center at Williams College in May 2019 under the mentorship of Professor Ella Shohat. Spurred by the convener's observation that Jewish emigration to Israel and other parts of the world has had far-reaching consequences for these Jews' societies of origin, something that Maghrebi and Middle

Eastern literature and film are finally articulating openly and provocatively, this conference invited participants to engage with the "decades-old, albeit overlooked, question of Maghrebi and Middle Eastern societies' responses to the sudden and fast exodus of their Jewish communities."[4] This conversation at the Oakley Center was preceded by an equally stimulating conversation at a panel that Mostafa Hussein organized at the annual meeting of the Middle East Studies Association in Washington, DC, in 2017. Unlike most discussions that focus on historiography and other social scientific disciplines, these conversations drew mostly on literature and film produced by Muslims about Jews to probe how these media have become a locus for present engagements with the memory of departed Jews.

Up until 1948, Maghrebi and Middle Eastern cities and villages were inhabited by Muslims, Jews, and Christians alike. By 2012, some eight hundred and sixty-five thousand Jews had emigrated from their homelands in the Maghreb and the Middle East to the newly created State of Israel. Fewer than five thousand Jews live in the expansive area between Morocco and Iran today, highlighting the drastic attrition of populations that once were part of the societal and cultural fabric in these states and societies. Their relationship may not always have been ideal, but centuries of living alongside each other allowed Jews and Muslims to forge legal, social, and cultural practices that helped them navigate their relationships as well as negotiate the challenges that arose from the existence of a dominant majority and a dominated minority. Although historians have shown that the distinction was between Muslims and non-Muslims, questioning the relevance of the language of dominant and dominated, it is important to recognize that group power dynamics existed in these societies and expressed themselves in moments of conflict, moments we do not think were prevalent markers of the long history of Jewish-Muslim *covivance* ("shared living" in French). Rather than idealizing or "conflictualizing" Jewish-Muslim relations, *Remembering Jews* is a critical intervention that not only admits the asymmetrical power dynamics between given groups (namely Jews and Muslims included in predominantly Muslim societies) but also foregrounds the existence of long periods of millennial *covivance* that Jews and Muslims shared in their homelands. This is a situation that European colonial intervention in the region in the nineteenth century terminated gradually by undoing the social, linguistic, and cultural setups that allowed Jews and Muslims to converse with each other and negotiate their belonging to these societies.[5]

This imperialistic interference set in motion a transformative historical process that not only changed Jewish-Muslim relations but also widened the gap between these communities. Ella Shohat has demonstrated how a cultural and racial separation emanated from this intervention,[6] alienating the Jew from the Arab/Amazigh and paving the way for emigration and loss. As Norman Stillman has written, the "Muslim world and all of its people underwent a veritable metamorphosis during the course of the nineteenth century."[7] This "metamorphosis" has resulted from a multipronged Euro-American intervention that took on different manifestations in the Maghreb (primarily Algeria, Morocco, and Tunisia, and the Middle East under the rule of the Ottoman Empire), opening the way for the massive emigration of hundreds of thousands of Jews from their homelands in the Maghreb and the Middle East. Starting in the nineteenth century, European diplomats in the Ottoman Empire were already pushing for the separation of Muslims and other religious minorities, namely Christians and Jews.[8] The Damascus Affair of 1840, which is also known as the Damascus Blood Libel, intensified European pressure on the Ottomans to protect Jews from excesses of Christians and Muslims.[9] The legal exceptions that these European interventions allowed these minorities to have, while entirely justified by their inferior status in a predominantly Muslim state, were also part of a long-term design to use them as pawns in the imperialistic and expansionist project that was already emerging in Europe at the time. The famous *dhimmī* status of non-Muslims was ended thanks to the *Tanzimāt* (regulations) reforms, and the ʿAhd al-Amān (pledge of security) in Tunisia granted Jews and Christians equality before the law.[10] Jews in Egypt prospered economically under Khedive Ismaʿil's rule (1863–79), and Khedive Tawfiq in Egypt granted Jews "civil equality" in 1882 under the British Mandate.[11] Algeria was already under the French colonial system by 1830, and the status of its Jews became the object of different legal, educational, and cultural initiatives that culminated in their being granted French citizenship in 1870 thanks to the Decrée Crémieux.[12] Even Morocco, which was not under Ottoman control, was visited by Sir Montefiore, a Jewish political leader and philanthropist, in 1863 to urge Sultan Muhammad bin ʿAbd al-Raḥmān to "improve the legal and social position of Morocco's Jews."[13] The multipronged interventions to improve the status of Christian and Jewish minorities in these regions, whether genuine or simply subterfuge for European states to secure zones of influence within the Ottoman Empire and beyond, contributed to the cultural and social separation of Jews and Muslims, especially after the establishment of the Alliance Israélite Universelle (AIU) in Paris in 1860.

The AIU's school system played a pivotal role in the process that ultimately distanced Jews from Muslims culturally, socially, and legally. With its Talmudic motto "All Jews are responsible for each other"[14] and its founding principles articulated by the emancipated French Jewry, who felt responsible for their "persecuted" coreligionists elsewhere, the AIU had a comprehensive project that included cultural, social, and political advancement of Jews wherever they were.[15] In particular, AIU was part of a larger project to Gallicize Jews by offering Francophone education as part of the colonial civilizing mission. These schools, which were part of the larger response to the persecution of Jews in Europe, offered all sorts of support to Jewish communities in the Maghreb and the Middle East and as far as eastern Europe. The first AIU school was opened in the northern Moroccan city of Tetouan in 1862.[16] This educational mission de facto morphed into a diplomatic and assistance mission that went beyond the mere provision of education. The geographical and demographic reach of the AIU was such that its schools trained thousands of students in Morocco, Iran, Israel, Lebanon, Tunisia, and Syria, among others, throughout its existence.[17] Although the organization abided mostly by its secular approach to education so as to "westernize" Jewish communities, the establishment of the State of Israel and the pressure of Zionist organizations influenced it to reorient its mission to aid Jewish emigration. Laskier has documented the disagreements that took place between the AIU's officials and the Zionist organizations in Morocco in particular.[18] These disagreements aside, the AIU's schools played a major role in the secularizing project that created a rift between the now-secularized and westernized Jew and the still-traditional Muslim. Jews were learning French, which started to replace Arabic and Tamazight for the educated youth, and this modern education exposed them to new ideas and different ways of belonging beyond the local societies. Traditional nationalism or local belonging became obsolete for educated Jews, who looked toward Paris and London, as shown by Carlos de Nesry in his writings.[19]

The acquisition of French citizenship through the Decrée Crémieux further complicated the relationship between Jews and Muslims.[20] The latter had to contend with the fact that the indigenous Jews were now assimilable into Western culture, meaning that they abandoned the issue of independence. While Jews enjoyed their Frenchness, Muslims had to resist Gallicization and construct local nationalism, a concept founded on the rejection of French and Western culture that had now become part of Jewish identities in North Africa. This fact does not negate the existence of a sizable number of Jews who were not assimilated and who were supportive of the nationalist project. However, the particular polarization between Gallicized Jews and their Muslim counterparts in Algeria was very clear. Similarly, the French reinvention of North African Judaism through the intervention of Parisian Jewish authorities transformed the liturgy, furthering the cultural break between two formerly neighborly communities.[21] In the past, Jews and Muslims could understand each other because they spoke the same language, and they had a chance to comprehend each other's worshipping methods, as they were all rooted in local religious practices. However, European education, the civilizing mission, and citizenship politics further complicated the situation. The generations of Jews and Muslims who could understand each other were dying out, and the descendants were being pulled in oppositional directions. This was especially noticeable in the 1940s, a pivotal moment in the history of Jewish-Muslim relations. While Muslims were fighting colonialism both in their local countries and in Palestine (under the British Mandate at the time), most politicized Jewish leaders were incorporated into the anti-independence projects as well as the Israeli proestablishment politics in Palestine. These rifts and separations were the result of historical processes that local Jewish communities did not entirely control or assent, but the end result was a situation in which one had to choose between leaving and staying. In other cases, such as Morocco, Jewish emigration was negotiated between the monarchy and Israeli envoys,[22] pointing to the existence of internal interests that were served by the dislocation of Jews in some places.

This account of Jewish emigration and the factors that spurred it is not applicable to all Jewries in the Middle East. For instance, messianic and religious impetus for emigration to Palestine has always existed. However, the nineteenth century witnessed an increase in its traffic. Between 1881 and 1910, Yemenite Jews left for late Ottoman Palestine in response to political and economic volatility within Yemen. During this period they received no support from Zionist organizations, and they were even marginalized in Zionist historiography because their emigration was not rooted in European political ideology.[23] The story was different in the twentieth century, when the Zionist movement became active throughout the Arab world, advocating for emigration and working to convince Jewish communities to return to and redeem the land of their forefathers. For instance, from 1911 onward the Zionist labor movement played a crucial role in the encouragement and organization of Yemenite Jewish emigration. This process included plans to liquidate one segment of the Jewish communities in the Arab world, replace Palestinian Arab workers in Jewish settlements, and provide the Hebrew labor market in Palestine with cheap workers who would do difficult labor in the colonies.[24] While only a minority of Jews embraced the Zionist idea as salvation from their dire economic and social conditions, the founding of the State of Israel and the rifts it created almost universalized the Zionist appeal. Within Jewish communities themselves, there were deep clefts between those who tried to reconcile their Zionist convictions with their belonging to their immediate society.[25] In the Maghreb, many leftist Jews opposed Zionism and saw in it a negation of their Jewish identity, instead calling for its rejection.[26] Other Jews in the region sounded their critique of Zionism and rejected it completely.[27]

The transformations set in motion in the nineteenth century materialized in drastic ways. In addition to the creation of independent nation-states on the ruins of the Ottoman Empire, the ensuing conflict between Arab states and the nascent State of Israel, the displacement of Palestinians from their homes, and mass Jewish emigration to Israel and other parts of the world (including France and the United States), imperialist incursions in the region led to the biggest dislocation of any religious group. This created an impactful, albeit understudied, demographic impoverishment of entire societies and geographies in the Maghreb and the Middle East. Emigrations happen and populations move because of internal wars and conflicts, but for a vibrant and fully integrated religious community to move swiftly over the course of twenty years, leaving hearth and home without impending danger to the lives of the majority of its members, is an unprecedented phenomenon whose ramifications beg for more scholarly investigation. Granted, the Zionist appeal and roles have been elucidated in great part, but the roles of local elites and their cooperation with Zionism to facilitate and speed up Jewish emigration for various internal agendas have yet to be addressed.[28] Questions of benefit and loss for Arab political regimes, ones that paid lip service to Palestine while aiding Jewish emigration to the Holy

Land, have remained a taboo topic whose study could demonstrate the ways in which Jewish emigration served and benefited regimes internally. El Guabli's *Moroccan Other-Archives* has developed the argument that the construction of authoritarianism went hand in hand with the facilitation of Jewish immigration, leading to multilayered losses that Moroccan society has only recently been able to process through historicizing and archive creation.[29] Most importantly, considering the way educated and westernized Jewish community members threatened authoritarianism and its then-ongoing homogenizing endeavors, the idea is not far-fetched that the emigration of Jews—and also Christians—contributed to the construction of authoritarianism and to the disabling of pluralistic societies that could have emerged from continued Jewish-Muslim collaborations.[30] The most important case in point here is Abraham Serfaty, who was (and remains) one of the most popular political leaders among Moroccans. He cofounded the revolutionary organization Ilā al-Amām (Forward!) and expressed his commitment to the liberation of Palestine, refusing to leave his home country despite political persecution by Hassan II's regime.[31] This is to say that while the creation of the State of Israel in 1948 saw both the speedy departure of Jews and the officialization of Jewish-Muslim separation, as El Guabli shows, the causes that led to that point, including colonialism, Zionism, and internal factors motivated by the interests of local postcolonial regimes, need to be viewed in combination with each other to fully understand how the drastic rift between Jews and Muslims came to be.

Given this historical trajectory, Jews were a taboo topic in the Maghreb and the Middle East for almost seven decades. This rich history was relegated to oblivion, and important segments of society were deprived of the chance to mourn the loss of the world they grew up in and, from that, to accept the new situation of their homogenized societies and communities. Of course, the official and historical silencing of the existence of an erstwhile Jewish-Muslim life, especially among the younger generations, was contradicted by the existence of physical markers and ruins of this Jewish existence. From deserted cemeteries to old synagogues, both renovated and crumbling, Jews' ubiquitous presence is inscribed in the topographies of the Maghreb and the Middle East. Topography and toponymy continued telling a story that both state politics and the uncomfortable colonization of Palestine did not allow to be told. Despite bureaucratic, political, and procedural hurdles, Christian and Muslim individuals in Egypt frequent deserted Jewish spaces so as to bring to their historical consciousness a cosmopolitan and a tolerant society, as Mostafa Hussein has indicated.[32] More significant, however, are the stories told by older generations of Muslims who could remember a world they shared with their Jewish neighbors and friends. Aomar Boum has insightfully rendered the vibrancy of these memories, revealing how four generations of Muslims remember Jews.[33] Similarly, Emanuela Trevisan Semi and Hanane Sekkat Hatimi have demonstrated how Jews are remembered in the urban setting of Meknes,[34] illustrating how these memories share similarities and reveal differences between the different settings and contexts. The focus on ethnographic research in the Moroccan context has particularly overshadowed the writerly remembering and accounting for loss that has developed within literature and film.[35]

Part of a larger reemergence of Jews as a theme in Maghrebi, Middle Eastern, and diasporic literature and film, this cultural production has broken the silence over the absence of Jewish co-citizens from their societies. Morocco and Egypt seem to produce the lion's share of novels and films that revisit their Jewish histories.[36] Despite their small number, writers and producers in Egypt (about five in Cairo and fifteen in Alexandria) continue to pay special attention to Jews. The proliferation of Jewish literary representations that incorporate episodes from the long and rich Jewish history in Egypt, from ancient to modern times, can be read as a solidification of Egyptian national identity as it works to retrieve a pluralistic past where Jews were an integral part of the national and sociocultural fabric of the country.[37] In fact, the contemporaneous reemergence of Jews in cultural productions across different regions seems to announce the end of a period of silence and latency that prevented these societies from mourning their losses. Grappling with the loss of past Jewish communities is not merely vital for a healthier understanding of national identity, but also the sine qua non for the reorientation of these societies toward a new future. One could argue that until the 2000s Maghrebi and Middle Eastern societies never had an opportunity to mourn the richer and more diverse world they had lost. The emigration of Jews was costly not just in terms of the occupation of Palestine and its devastating effects for Jewish-Muslim relations, but also in terms of impoverishing Maghrebi and Middle Eastern societies' sense of being. Relationships, friendships, families, partnerships, and myriad forms of local collaborations and fraternities between Jews and Muslims were never grieved. Shohat's very productive reading of the implications of Said Sayegh's novel *L'Autre juive* as it "ruminates on deeply shared Moroccan cultural heritages and familial bonds" and depicts "a world without borders, whether geographical, biological, racial or linguistic" offers a segue into the loss of this borderless, familial, and shared world.[38] Loss, as such, has never been theorized and used as a framework to understand this bygone world and the consequences of its disappearance. Loss as a conceptual framework for the study of the literary and filmic Jewish return to a central role in Maghrebi and Middle Eastern public spheres accounts for all that was there but is no more, and that which older generations might remember and pass down, albeit through absence, to the younger generations.[39]

Although scholars of Jewish-Muslim relations have approached the topic through different disciplinary lenses, including enmity, cohabitation, remembrance, political participation, legal doctrine, and colonial and postcolonial educational politics, the generative potential of loss has escaped scholarly attention. In Freud's essay "Mourning and Melancholia," responses to loss take the form of either mourning, which helps over time to achieve closure, or "melancholia," which associates the object of loss with the loss of the ego, therefore making closure impossible. The Jewish populations' departure from Maghrebi and Middle Eastern societies could be seen as a cause for perpetual sadness, intertwined with the loss of Palestine and Andalus and other historical events. Indeed, loss does appear or is adumbrated in different academic works, but it is mainly linked to Jewish populations' loss of property or positions within their Arab states, rather than the more psychoanalytical and psychological meaning of loss as leading to mourning or melancholia in the Freudian sense.[40] In the Middle East, scholarship on Iranian and Iraqi Jews has articulated this Jewish loss. Shohat has analyzed how the works of Iraqi and Iranian Jewish authors engaged with the Iraq-Iran War (1980–88). The war, in Shohat's analysis, served as a vehicle for them to return to their lost homeland and become part of the events of a lost, distant, and intimate geography.[41] Writing in languages other than their native tongues, the Iranian and Iraqi Jewish authors use a linguistic medium, as Shohat observes, that reflects their diasporic status, midway between loss and the possibility of return. Lital Levy has alluded to loss in her analysis of Shimon Ballas's short story "Iyya," noting that Ballas depicts "the tragedy of the mass emigration of Baghdad's Jews not only from the point of view of those leaving, but also from the standpoint of those who are left behind."[42] Likewise, Orit Bashkin writes of the same story that "Jews and Muslims are presented as being part of the same family, and hence the departure of Jews from Iraq leaves a void that cannot be filled."[43] Boum and Oren Kosansky have underlined that the films they analyzed about Moroccan Jews are embedded in an "an aura of nostalgia, memory, and loss."[44]

The absence of a more engaged examination of how loss has served as the impetus for the prolific novelistic and filmic output about Maghrebi and Middle Eastern Jews can be attributed to two broad factors. The first is the continued occupation of Palestine, which has put ethical constraints on the possibility of casting the mostly voluntary Jewish emigration as a loss for Maghrebi and Middle Eastern societies. The assumption was that no loss could be equivalent to that of Palestine and the displacement of its people, creating a deadlock within which enacting rightful solidarity with Palestinians diminished the internal losses that other societies suffered via the loss of their Jewish populations and internal diversity. The second broad factor is disciplinary. There is no discipline of Jewish studies in the Maghreb and the Middle East, and the indigenous scholars who work on Jewish topics are rare and less vocal than their Jewish counterparts. Most of these indigenous scholars still focus on precolonial times, and they have to navigate political and archival constraints that limit their ability to write up-to-date histories. To overcome these constraints and maintain scholarly productivity, in some parts of the Middle East scholars of Jewish studies tend to focus primarily on the study of Hebrew and carrying out translation projects.[45] Other scholars are still confined to the old framework that conflates Judaism with Zionism, drawing on war-era literature to depict Jews negatively or sustain an image that is detrimental to Maghrebi and Middle Eastern societies' more nuanced and complicated perceptions of how central the colonial situation in Palestine is. This said, a new generation of US-based scholars in particular has taken on these issues in novel and doubly critical ways in order to chart a path for the birth of a Maghrebi / Middle Eastern–infused discipline of Jewish studies.

The other dimension of this disciplinary issue is related to the fact that Jewish studies is predominantly social-scientific, leaving literary studies outside the scope of the vibrant scholarship that is produced about the region. Ranging from musical to even legal issues, social scientists have delved into Jewish-Muslim *covivance* and shown the multidimensional aspects of Jewish-Muslim relations.[46] Nevertheless, literature written by

Maghrebi and Middle Eastern non-Jewish writers has mostly remained unclaimed by the discipline of Arabic studies and remains rarely treated by Jewish studies, the latter of which has mainly focused on literature by Jews or within bilingual contexts of Hebrew and Arabic.[47] This rich literary corpus offers an opportunity to reclaim Jewish topics for Arabic and Middle Eastern studies. In doing so, our aim is to create spaces and loci of intersection between Jewish studies and other fields focused on the Maghreb and the Middle East. Thus, we propose Maghrebi / Middle Eastern Jewish studies as a space of convergence and coalescence between these different disciplines. By doing so, we hope to open more space for an intersectional scholarship that draws on the different fields that examine Jewish topics in the region and to normalize the study of Jewish topics among scholars from the area. As such, loss offers both topical and disciplinary boundaries, ones that the current scholarship has yet to broach.

Taking these disciplinary considerations into account, loss (in this context) allows us to reflect on the internal dynamics within Arab societies themselves. Whether it leads to acting out or working through, loss has the capacity to pave the way for a new understanding of Jewish-Muslim relations, helping us theorize what it is that literature and films produced about Jews are saying. This is not necessarily about Jews themselves, but rather about the societies they left behind when they emigrated to Israel or other places. Moroccan novelists El Hassane Aït Moh and Muhammad Ezzedine Tazi, Egyptian novelists Kamal Ruḥayyim and Amru al-Jundi, Palestinian novelist Rabai al-Madhoun, Algerian novelist Amin Zaoui, and the Iraqi writers ʿAli Bader and Khdair al-Zaydi have all returned to different periods of the Jewish histories of their countries to remind their readers of the existence of a Jewish past that belongs to them.[48] In turn, this literature depicts social and political realities that may not be accessible to the majority of the populations today, but that were in fact part of a real existence until just a few decades ago. These novelists portray returns, identity conflicts, religious intolerance, and emigration as they affected these characters not only in their fictional worlds, but also in the real stories that might have inspired these novelists to produce their works. Brahim El Guabli has coined the phrase "al-kitāba al-dhākirātiyya" (mnemonic literature) to conceptualize this subfield that Moroccan and Arabic/Francophone Muslim litterateurs have dedicated to Jewish themes. As El Guabli defines it, mnemonic literature is a locus in which younger Muslim generations who were not old enough to live with Jewish people "remember their departed Jewish co-citizens and fill the voids of historical silences in a way that radically transforms the vacuum of amnesia into a locus for memory."[49] Rooted in an intergenerational transference of memory, mnemonic literature engages with loss and attempts to account for the void left by the departure of thousands of Jews from their countries of origin. Whether it takes the form of novels, short stories, or even films, this mnemonic cultural production is a primary site for the articulation of loss as a result of this Jewish emigration. By refilling Maghrebi and Middle Eastern cities and villages with Jews and Muslims, these works enrich an impoverished world with visions of a society that was once possible but is no longer, thus allowing loss to settle in as a consequence of this Jewish departure. Loss in mnemonic literature is located at the intersection between the reader's awareness of the current nonexistence of these Jewish populations and the history that literature recovers and brings back to life.

Maghrebi and Middle Eastern cinematic traditions have likewise returned to this Jewish-Muslim past in different ways. Both documentary and feature films as well as soap operas have depicted Jewish themes in recent years. Moroccan cinema once again accounts for the lion's share in the number of films, both documentary and fictional. Morocco is a very specific case in the Arab world due to the fact that some three thousand Jews still remain in the country. As such, it has been able to sustain its ties with its Jewish communities worldwide despite the vicissitudes of the situation in the Middle East. A precolonial-era agreement between Morocco and European powers set Moroccan citizenship in stone, in contrast to any other country in the region. A Moroccan can never lose his or her citizenship, and this fact alone has kept Moroccan Jews technically Moroccan despite their physical disappearance from the country. Whether they live in Israel or in other places, Moroccan Jews are still Moroccan under the law. Morocco's under-the-table relations with Israel are an open secret, and this fostered a different kind of relationship with Jewish communities compared to Iraq or Egypt, where Jews had to leave under very different circumstances. Kamal Hachkar's film *Tinghir-Jerusalem*, Kathy Wazana's film *They Were Promised the Sea*, and Youness Laghrari's film *Juifs marocains, destins contrariés* (Moroccan Jews: destinies undone) go in divergent directions in their search for Jews, but they all converge by depicting the fact that Morocco's Jews left under unclear circumstances as well as posing historical questions that address the void left by this departure. Beyond documentary films, *Where Are You Going Moshé?* and *Midnight Orchestra* were among the most successful feature films made about Jews in Morocco. It is important to note here that some of these films received taxpayer funding, indicating the existence of an official will to create space for the theme of Moroccan Jews in Moroccan cinema.

In Egypt, Jews are remembered for enriching Egyptian cultural heritage via their contributions to the theater and cinema industries. Recent works highlight the productions of Yaʿqūb Ṣannuʿ and his role in the making of Egyptian theatre. In some works, Ṣannuʿ is defined as "the father of the Modern Egyptian theatre."[50] Authors from the field of cinema have published monographs honoring the cinematic productions of Munir Murad and Laila Murad.[51] Togo Mizrahi, the Jewish director who discovered Laila Murad and introduced her to wider audiences, received the attention of contemporary Egyptian TV hosts, who introduced him as "the Egyptian" and "a pioneer" of Egyptian cinema.[52] Aside from drawing attention to such Jewish figures who participated in the enhancement of Egypt's cultural life and attempted to raise it to the same level as European countries, everyday Egyptian Jews are featured in a growing number of soap operas and films, both fictional and documentary. The objective of these television and film productions is to cast Egypt as a tolerant society that takes pride in its diverse social, cultural, and religious heritage, making the point that Egyptian Jews were always part and parcel of the fabric of Egyptian society. This view aims to push back against claims put forward either by diasporic Jews or by local Egyptians that Jews were never an integral part of the country and used to live as a community isolated from their surrounding society. Dismayed by the religious intolerance that one of her family members experienced in Egypt, Nadia Kamel wanted to retrieve glimpses of the multireligious society in Egypt from the past. In doing so, she produced the documentary *Salāṭah balādī* (An Egyptian salad), a principally Egyptian production filmed partly in Israel, containing interviews with the family members of her mother's cousin who emigrated to Palestine in 1946, retaining elements of Egyptian culture all the while. A few years later, Amir Ramses produced a historical documentary featuring several Egyptian Jews living in the diaspora. *ʿAn yahūd miṣr* (The Jews of Egypt) highlights the lives of Egyptian Jews during the first half of the twentieth century and covers the key historical and political events that influenced their lives up until their departure from their native country. The documentary was screened in 2012 in several movie theaters across Cairo. The television series *Ḥārat al-Yahūd* (The Jewish quarter) broke away from the prevalent narrative that excluded Jews from the sociocultural fabric of the Egyptian society by providing a historical account of the country during the 1948 War and its aftermath. In such a sensitive historical moment, Jews, Christians, and Muslims are portrayed as living together in a place that has been thought of as an exclusively Jewish space. In this volume, Jews are portrayed, as Iskandar Ahmad Abdalla shows in his chapter, in the series as a "metony[m] for a lost beautiful age, projected onto the present while also acting as its contrast, its role model, and the essence of the nation."[53]

By focusing on the ways in which the absence of Jews affected the lives of the societies in which they lived, and by putting an end to the assumption that Jews were segregated and lived in isolation from their immediate society, literature and film challenge assumptions of enmity and inherent separation between Jews and Muslims. Indeed, Jewish emigration from the Maghreb and the Middle East took place under traumatic conditions for both Muslims and Jews, leaving many unsutured mental wounds. Unfortunately, healing these wounds has never been a priority for political regimes. The need to recollect and reflect on what was lost or went missing with the emigration of Jews is probably what motivates older men and women to share stories from when they still lived with Jews. Likewise, literature has depicted how "something was missing from the neighborhood[s]" as Jews left their Alexandrian quarters.[54] In fact, Jewish emigration was experienced as a mutilation that ripped off an essential social and cultural element from the collective body. Nevertheless, the current state of scholarship about Jewish emigration does not account for emotions in this history. Recent historical research has brought the sensorial aspect to the fore,[55] but emotions remain elusive, thus allowing us to extend this history to literature and film and tap into its historical potential. The loss we are addressing in this book is both multidimensional and multiprocessual, spanning both public and private aspects of bygone Jewish-Muslim existence. This loss's multidimensional aspects can be noticed in the reduced cultural, social, and demographic diversity, something that has implications for democracy and pluralism in society.[56] Loss's multiprocessual dimensions can be noticed in the long-term projects that led to this moment of quasi-Jewless societies in the Maghreb and the Middle East. Through engagement with these unaddressed voids, mutilations, and traumas, *Remembering Jews* therefore aims to shift scholarly attention to the decades-old, but oft overlooked, question concerning the far-reaching consequences of Jewish emigration for the societies they left behind.

Maghrebi and Middle Eastern literature and film's articulations of loss do not merely address a topic that has been taboo for six decades. In fact, the articulation of Jewish loss is also one of the lost opportunities as well as a depiction of internal strife that was once explained away by being attributed to the situation in Palestine. The context of ongoing conflict with Israel, which became a justification for the internal repression of political pluralism and democratic reform within Arab states, comforted Arab regimes and allowed them to postpone all sorts of societal and cultural changes as long as the conflict continued to exist. Therefore, in addition to addressing the loss of Jewish communities who left the Maghreb and the Middle East, the literary and filmic resurgence of Jews in recent years indicates a social awareness of the different stakes that are involved in the history of such conflicts. Creative writers and filmmakers do not deny the Palestinian people's right to statehood and independence when they cast their erstwhile Jewish co-citizens in a positive light. Rather, they reclaim their agency as an able citizenry who has a right to knowledge and the dissemination of their history. In reclaiming this, the cultural producers we discuss in this book break taboos and raise new questions that pave the way for their societies to reckon with the impact of the absence of the Jews on their internal evolution. These aesthetic interventions open a wholly new scholarly avenue for a novel investigation of the place of Jews in contemporary Maghrebi and Middle Eastern cultural memories.

The topic of Jewish-Muslim relations lends itself easily to binaries of nostalgia and conflict. Aware of their dangers, *Remembering Jews* actively resists both. Both nostalgia and conflict have proven their limitations and even counterproductive natures. Nostalgia, on the one hand, idealizes a history that was rife with challenges, pain, and wounds, and it erases uncomfortable experiences that do not suit an idealizing narrative. Our goal is not to idealize the erstwhile Jewish-Muslim past, but rather to cast a new light on a silenced dimension of history whose ramifications are still felt in the present. Whether in cemeteries, empty synagogues, or other places marked as Jewish, Jewish pasts of Maghrebi and Middle Eastern societies defy silence and reemerge constantly in various forms. Conflict, on the other hand, exaggerates the inherence of Jewish-Muslim enmity, thus overriding the centuries of shared living between the two communities. Conflict may be the current response to the ongoing colonial situation in Palestine, but it blurs the picture of historical research and diminishes the potential that other sources offer to understand Jewish-Muslim relations in their depth and complexity. Neither nostalgic nor conflictual, *Remembering Jews* calls attention to a more productive theorization of what literature and film bring to the field of Jewish studies from the perspective of Maghrebi and Middle Eastern studies. The conceptual framework of loss places emphasis on the larger societal and mnemonic implications of the absence of Jews from the daily lives of communities in which they existed for millennia, allowing us to make a crucial intervention in rethinking the way in which Jewish themes have been traditionally studied in Arabic literature and film.

The need for critical studies like the ones we present here is even more pressing since the signing of the Abraham Accords in 2020. Bahrain, Morocco, and the United Arab Emirates have openly (and sometimes blatantly) displayed their craving for normalization with Israel, with little regard for Palestinian rights. These relationships have spurred interest in Jewish-Muslim relations, often taking the form of an unbridled filmic and novelistic output in the Gulf states. While the cultural works we discuss in this book emerged in their totality before 2020, therefore escaping the normalizing states' ideology, the mushrooming of novels, news stories, films, and songs about Jews in these areas before and since the Accords shows the role that culture serves in this project. The same states that created and nurtured the culture of conflict now foster a culture of nostalgia that could potentially delegitimize a richer and more compelling civil project that has emerged from the lower strata of society to address the loss of Jews. *Remembering Jews* is therefore not interested in cultural production that responds to normalization initiatives or is motivated by the political agendas of specific state parties. Rather, we focus on civil society's attendance to the historical void left by the departed Jews, something beyond statal intervention, orientation, and agendas.

These chapters speak to each other, creating a thematic and interdisciplinary conversation between the different regions and their Jewish experiences, which are linked through the topic of loss. In his chapter "Generative Absence," El Guabli offers a three-part analysis in which he presents an overview of the topic of Jewish loss in both literature and thought as well as film in the Maghreb and the Middle East. El Guabli expands his notion of generative loss into the realm of theorization in the work of Abdelkébir Khatibi, opening up more space for understanding loss's fundamental presence in Maghrebi and Middle Eastern ideation processes and concept creation. Morocco being the only Arabic-speaking Maghrebi and Middle Eastern country to have a museum for local Judaism, Nadia Sabri explores the history and space of the Museum of Moroccan Judaism in Casablanca. Entitled "Exile in a Contemporary Artistic Project in Morocco: Jewish Memories in Form and Concrete Territories," Sabri's chapter compares the place's invisible identity and the history it cocoons within its walls, arguing that that the museum contains "fragments of history in which places, dates, cultural histories, and objects of daily use from Morocco are evoked."

In his chapter, "On the Wrong Side of History: Jews in Algerian Literature," Abdelkader Aoudjit examines the ways in which Jewish-Muslim relations were marked by the context of the Algerian War of Independence between 1954 and 1962. Drawing on the history of Algerian nationalism, Aoudjit probes how Jewish citizens' failure to be part of the nation has placed them on the wrong side of Algerian history. Loss in Aoudjit's chapter foregrounds a historical process as well as a complicated present in which situated decisions in the past are used to adjudicate citizenship.

In his chapter, "Literary Representations of Jews in Twenty-First-Century Arabic Literature in Egypt," Mostafa Hussein reads against the grain to find erstwhile negative portrayals of Jews in Egyptian literature framed by the Israeli-Arab conflict. Hussein casts a new light on the current status of representations of Jews in Egyptian literature, whose aim is to portray Egypt as a multiethnic and multicultural society of which Jews were always an integral part. Directly in conversation with Hussein's chapter is Iskandar Ahmad Abdalla's chapter, entitled "*Al-Zaman al-Gamil* Refigured: Jews and Re-narration of the Nation on Egyptian TV." Abdalla draws upon the increasing interest in investigating the modern history of Egyptian Jews as *Ḥārat al-Yahūd* reimagines a pre-1948 Egypt, one that Abdalla argues insists on recovering "a cosmopolitan age." Jews in his analysis are objects of national nostalgia for an era in which all Egyptians shared a sense of belonging to a diverse society.

In "Death, Burial, and Loss in Ali al-Muqri's *Al-Yahūdī al-ḥālī* [The Handsome Jew]," Sarah Irving closely reads *Al-Yahūdī al-ḥālī*, a novel by the

Yemeni author Ali al-Muqri, which recounts the romance between a Muslim woman and a Jewish man in seventeenth-century Yemen. While the narrative asserts their rights to claim their specific identities and mutual love, actual relationships between Muslims and Jews are depicted as fatal. The fatality of Jewish-Muslim relations appears differently in Stephanie Kraver's chapter, "Bearing Witness and Resurrecting Kurdish-Arab-Jewish Memory in *Mādhā ʿan al-sayyida al-yahūdiyya rāḥīl?*," which explores the role of the Jewish woman in retelling the history of Jewish life and displacement in both Syrian and Lebanese Arabic novels.

Outside the Amazigh- and Arabic-speaking areas in the Maghreb and the Middle East, Iran and Turkey have also experienced, albeit in different circumstances and variable degrees, the attrition of their Jewish populations. İlker Hepkaner's chapter, "Documenting and Debating Turkey's Loss," analyzes two documentary features from the mid-2010s that broke new ground in representations of the history, memory, and contemporary lives of Jews in Turkey. Hepkaner argues that these documentaries are part of a larger debate about the losses that Jewish culture endured in Turkey, one that exists within the even larger discussion about the status of minorities in the country. Departing from the premise of this book as being about Muslim cultural producers and the loss of their Jewish co-citizens, Lior B. Sternfeld's chapter, "Narrating the Homeland from Exile: Iranian Jewish Writers Writing on Their Departure, Identity, and Longing," examines Iranian Jewish writers' memoirs, fiction, and autobiographies in different diasporic communities in Israel and the United States. Using a historical approach, Sternfeld's chapter oscillates between past existence, present concerns, and future anxieties of these writers. Iran emerges as a lost home and an object of loss in their works. For Sternfeld, loss carries both physical and metaphysical meanings.

Due to factors beyond our control, Iraq is absent from the book. However, we also would like to stress the fact that the scholarship of Lital Levy, Orit Bashkin, and Ronen Zeidel, among others, has already charted the path for the study of cultural and literary histories of this important country's Jews.[57]

All in all, the loss of Jewish populations permeates cultural production in the area extending from Morocco to Iran. As these chapters reveal, it is not just the loss of relationships that figures in these works, but also, and probably even most importantly, the sense of it no longer being possible to live in multiethnic, multireligious, and multicultural societies that is being processed in many of these works; the departed "Jew" serves as a most fitting excuse to delve into the realms that were, for a long time, impossible to discuss openly. As El Guabli asserts in his chapter, similar to post–World War II Europe, which entered an "era of the witness," the Maghreb and the Middle East have been living the "age of loss," which is grounded in an endeavor to understand the self in relation to what could have been achieved had the Jews and other minorities stayed.

The questions we and our coauthors raise in this book have acquired an even greater significance after Hamas's sudden attack on Israel on October 7, 2023, and the ensuing devastating war Israel unleashed on Gaza. With thousands of Palestinians killed and hundreds of thousands displaced, there is no doubt that the memory of this unprecedented, televised war will have a deep impact on the way younger generations of Muslims view Jews. Therefore, it remains to be seen how much of the conclusions we present in this book can withstand the test of the new mnemonic, literary, political, and cultural landscape that will emerge in the aftermath of this extremely transformative war.

Notes

1. Shohat, "On Orientalist Genealogies," 118, 143, 145. Shohat makes a powerful case against the use of Judeo-Arabic as another manifestation of this "separationist" ideology, which seeks to isolate the Arab from the Jew. See Shohat, "Question of Judeo-Arabic," 19.
2. Bashkin, "Middle Eastern Shift."
3. Bashkin, "Middle Eastern Shift."
4. This quote is from Brahim El Guabli's introduction to the conference held at Williams College in 2019.
5. Hayoun, *When We Were Arabs*, 94–154.
6. Shohat, "On Orientalist Genealogies," 92, 104.
7. Stillman, *Jews of Arab Lands*, 95.
8. Stillman, *Jews of Arab Lands*, 95–103.
9. Stillman, *Jews of Arab Lands*, 105.
10. Stillman, *Jews of Arab Lands*, 98.
11. Stillman, *Jews of Arab Lands*, 99. See also Laskier, *Jews of Egypt*, 9–10.
12. Shohat, "On Orientalist Genealogies," 11; Roberts, *Citizenship and Antisemitism*, 5–13.
13. Stillman, *Jews of Arab Lands*, 99.
14. Rodrigue, *Jews and Muslims*, 8.
15. Rodrigue, *Jews and Muslims*, 7.
16. Laskier, *Alliance*, 147–71.
17. Winter, "René Cassin," 208.
18. Laskier, *Alliance Israélite Universelle*, 194–225.
19. See de Nesry's books *Juif de Tanger* and *Israélites marocains*.
20. Roberts, *Citizenship and Antisemitism*, 143–200.
21. Zytnicki, "'Oriental Jews' of the Maghreb," 35.
22. Bin Nun, "Quête d'un compromis."
23. Parfitt, *Road to Redemption*, 51–55.
24. Parfitt, *Road to Redemption*, 55; Ariel, *Jewish-Muslim Relations*, 45.
25. Campos, *Ottoman Brothers*, 211–12; Starr, *Togo Mizrahi*, 8; Beinin, *Dispersion of Egyptian Jewry*, 34.
26. Serfaty and Elbaz, *Insoumis*.
27. Behar and Zvi Ben-Dor, *Modern Middle Eastern Jewish Thought*, 141–98.

28. El Guabli, *Moroccan Other-Archives.*

29. El Guabli, *Moroccan Other-Archives.*

30. El Guabli, *Moroccan Other-Archives.*

31. El Guabli, *Moroccan Other-Archives.*

32. Hussein, "Jewish Spaces in Egypt."

33. Boum, *Memories of Absence.*

34. Trevisan Semi and Sekkat Hatimi, *Mémoire et représentations.*

35. See El Guabli, "Breaking Ranks"; El Guabli, *Moroccan Other-Archives.*

36. In "Dissenting Narratives," Najat Abdulhaq draws attention to the politics of this film and literature from a very different position. However, we disagree with her focus on the expulsion of Jews from the regions under study. We believe that a more nuanced analysis is needed to reflect the different situations of Jews in different parts of Tamazgha and the Middle East.

37. Hussein, "Hasan, Marcus, and Cohen."

38. Shohat, "Orientalist Genealogies," 145.

39. El Guabli, "Breaking Ranks"; El Guabli, *Moroccan Other-Archives.*

40. For a survey of the losses of Jews and Jewish properties across the Arab world from North Africa to Iraq, see Fischbach, *Jewish Property Claims.* As Joel Benin has noted, the author's ability to explore and conduct research on such a politically explosive topic was possible thanks to previously conducting intensive research on the dispossession of Palestinian properties, an equally explosive topic for Israelis and Jews and non-Jews in the West. See Fischbach, *Records of Dispossession.* Aside from approaching the issue of Jewish personal and property loss in the context of the Palestinian-Israeli context, Shayna Zamkanei offers a new perspective on the ways in which Jews from Maghrebi and Middle Eastern societies understood the issue of their lost assets and argues that "the nature of property claims are multidimensional and cannot be reduced to the question of whether they serve Israeli state interests" ("Property Claims of Jews," 79).

41. Shohat, "Lost Homelands, Imaginary Returns."

42. Levy, "Self and the City," 187.

43. Bashkin, *New Babylonians,* 225.

44. Kosansky and Boum, "'Jewish Question,'" 438.

45. On the case of Egypt, see Hussein, "Hebrew on the Nile."

46. Silver, *Recording History*; Starr, *Remembering Cosmopolitan Egypt*; Marglin, *Across Legal Lines.*

47. Levy, *Poetic Trespass.*

48. Aït Moh, *Captif*; Tazi, *Anā al-mansī*; Ruḥyymm, *Diary*; Al-Jundi, *Missiyyā*; Al-Madhoun, *Al-Sayyida*; Zaoui, *Dernier juif.* Bader's *Ḥāris al-Tabagh* (The guardian of the tobacco shop) from 2008 and Zaydi's *Atlas ʿAzrān al-Baghdādi* (ʿAzrān al-Baghdadi's atlas) from 2015 are noteworthy examples here. On Iraqi novelists' return to Jews, see Zeidel, "On the Last Jews."

49. El Guabli, *Moroccan Other-Archives.*

50. Badawi, "Father of the Modern Egyptian Theatre."

51. Starr, *Togo Mizrahi*; Hammad, *Unknown Past.*

52. 'Isa, "Togo Mizrahi al-Mukhreg al-Yahudi."

53. See "*Al-Zaman al-Gamīl* Refigured: Jews and Re-Narration of the Nation on Egyptian TV," in this volume.

54. See Hussein, "Jewish Representations," in this volume.

55. Fahmy, *Street Sounds.*

56. El Guabli, "Other-Archives."

57. Levy, "Self and the City"; Bashkin, *New Babylonians*; Zeidel, "On the Last Jews."

Bibliography

Abdulhaq, Najat. "Dissenting Narratives—The Figure of the 'Arab Jew' in Contemporary Arabic Literature and Film." In *Disseminating Jewish Literatures: Knowledge, Research, Curricula,* edited by Susanne Zepp, Ruth Fine, Natasha Gordinsky, Kader Konuk, Claudia Olkand, and Galili Shahar, 53–67. Berlin: De Gruyter, 2020.

Aït Moh, El Hassane. *Le Captif de Mabrouka.* Paris: L'Harmattan, 2009.

ʿAdl, Muhammad al-, dir. *Ḥārat al-Yahūd.* Aired beginning March 20, 2015, on CBC Drama. 30 episodes.

Ariel, Ari. *Jewish-Muslim Relations and Migration from Yemen to Palestine in the Late Nineteenth and Twentieth Centuries.* Leiden: Brill, 2013.

Badawi, Muhammad Mustafa. "The Father of the Modern Egyptian Theatre: Yaʿqub Sannuʿ." In *Early Arabic Drama*, edited by Muhammad Mustafa Badawi, 31–42. Cambridge: Cambridge University Press, 1988.

Ballas, Shimon. "Iyya." Translated by Susan Einbinder. In *Keys to the Garden: New Israeli Writing*, edited by Ammiel Alcalay, 69–99. San Francisco: City Lights Books, 1996.

Bashkin, Orit. "The Middle Eastern Shift and Provincializing Zionism." *International Journal of Middle East Studies* 46, no. 3 (2014): 577–80.

———. *New Babylonians: A History of Jews in Modern Iraq*. Stanford: Stanford University Press, 2012.

Behar, Moshe, and Zvi Ben-Dor Benite. *Modern Middle Eastern Jewish Thought: Writings on Identity, Politics, and Culture, 1893–1958*. Waltham: Brandeis University Press, 2013.

Beinin, Joel. *The Dispersion of Egyptian Jewry: Culture, Politics and the Formation of Modern Diaspora*. Berkeley: University of California Press 1998.

Benjelloun, Hassan, dir. *Where Are You Going Moshé?* 2007. Morocco: Bentaqueria Productions (as Bentaqerla Productions); Canada: Productions Jeux d'Ombres, 2007. DVD.

Bin Nun, Yigal. "La Quête d'un compromis pour l'évacuation des Juifs du Maroc." *Pardès* 1 (2003): 75–98.

Boum, Aomar. *Memories of Absence: How Muslims Remember Jews in Morocco.* Stanford: Stanford University Press, 2013.

Campos, Michelle. *Ottoman Brothers: Muslims, Christians, and Jews in Early Twentieth-Century Palestine*. Stanford: Stanford University Press, 2010.

Cohen-Olivar, Jérôme, dir. *L'Orchestre de minuit*. Morocco: Dark Island Pictures and Les Films du Desert, 2016. DVD.

De Nesry, Carlos. *Les Israélites marocains à l'heure du choix*. Tangiers: Éditions Internationales, 1958.

———. *Le Juif de Tanger et le Maroc*. Tangiers: Éditions Internationales, 1956.

El Guabli, Brahim. "Breaking Ranks with National Unanimity: Novelistic and Cinematic Returns of Jewish-Muslim Intimacy in Morocco." In *Generations of Dissent: Intellectuals, Cultural Production, and the State in the Middle East and North Africa*, edited by Alexa Firat and Shareah Taleghani, 159–87. Syracuse: Syracuse University Press, 2020.

———. *Moroccan Other-Archives: History and Citizenship After State Violence*. New York: Fordham University Press, 2023.

———. "Other-Archives: Literature Rewrites the Nation in Post-1956 Morocco." PhD diss., Princeton University, 2018.

Fahmy, Ziad. *Street Sounds: Listening to Everyday Life in Modern Egypt*. Stanford: Stanford University Press, 2020.

Fischbach, Michael R. *Jewish Property Claims Against Arab Countries*. New York: Columbia University Press, 2008.

———. *Records of Dispossession: Palestinian Refugee Property and the Arab-Israeli Conflict*. New York: Columbia University Press, 2003.

Freud, Sigmund. "Mourning and Melancholia." In *The Standard Edition of the Complete Psychological Works of Sigmund Freud*, edited by James Strachey and Anna Freud, 14:243–58. London: Hogarth Press and Institute of Psycho-Analysis, 1917.

Hachkar, Kamal, dir. *Tinghir-Jerusalem: Echoes from the Mellah*. Paris: Les Films d'un Jour, 2013. DVD.

Hammad, Hanan. *Unknown Past: Layla Murad, the Jewish-Muslim Star of Egypt*. Stanford: Stanford University Press, 2022.

Hayoun, Massoud. *When We Were Arabs: A Jewish Family's Forgotten History*. New York: New Press, 2019.

Hussein, Mostafa. "Hasan, Marcus, and Cohen Redefining Literary Representations of Jews in Contemporary Egypt."

Paper presented to MESA, Washington, DC, 2017.
———. "Hebrew on the Nile: The Rise of Jewish Studies in Egypt." *Haaretz*, August 3, 2020. https://www.haaretz.com/middle-east-news/egypt/.premium-jewish-studies-on-the-nile-the-rise-of-hebrew-and-jewish-degrees-in-egypt-1.9042817.
———. "Jewish Spaces in Egypt." Paper presented to Middle East and North Africa Jews, Pennsylvania State University, 2021.
'Isa, Ibrahim. "Togo Mizrahi al-Mukhreg al-Yahudi." YouTube video, 4:52. May 7, 2021. https://youtu.be/PlJLgnTKOLA.
Jundi, ʿAmrū al-. *Missiyyā*. Cairo: al-Dār al-Miṣriyya al-Lubnāniyya, 2014.
Kamel, Nadia, dir. *Salāṭah baladī*. 2007. Egypt, Switzerland, France, 2007.
Kosansky, Oren, and Aomar Boum. "The 'Jewish Question' in Postcolonial Moroccan Cinema." *International Journal of Middle East Studies* 44, no. 3 (2012): 421–42.
Laghrari, Youness, dir. *Moroccan Jews: Destinies Undone; Juifs marocains, destins contrariés*. 2014. Paris: Younslag Films, 2014. DVD.
Laskier, Michael. *The Alliance Israélite Universelle and the Jewish Communities of Morocco, 1862–1962*. Albany: SUNY Press, 1983.
———. *The Jews of Egypt, 1920–1970: In the Midst of Zionism, Anti-Semitism, and the Middle East Conflict*. New York: New York University Press, 1992.
Levy, Lital. *Poetic Trespass: Writing Between Hebrew and Arabic in Israel/Palestine*. Princeton: Princeton University Press, 2014.
———. "Self and the City: Literary Representations of Jewish Baghdad." *Prooftexts* 26, no. 1 (2006): 163–211.
Marglin, Jessica. *Across Legal Lines: Jews and Muslims in Modern Morocco*. New Haven: Yale University Press, 2016.
Madhoun, Rabai al-. *Al-Sayyida min tal-abīb*. Beirut: al-Muʾassassa al-ʿArabiyya li-al-Dirāsāt wa-al-Nashr, 2014.
Parfitt, Tudor. *The Road to Redemption: The Jews of the Yemen, 1900–1950*. Leiden: Brill, 1996.
Ramses, Amir, dir. *ʿAn yahūd miṣr*. Cairo, 2012.
Roberts, Sophie B. *Citizenship and Antisemitism in French Colonial Algeria, 1870–1962*. Cambridge: Cambridge University Press, 2017.
Rodrigue, Aron. *Jews and Muslims: Images of Sephardi and Eastern Jewries in Modern Times*. Seattle: University of Washington Press, 2003.
Ruḥayyim, Kamal. *Diary of a Jewish Muslim*. Translated by Sarah Enamy. Cairo: American University in Cairo Press, 2014.
Serfaty, Abraham, and Mikhaël Elbaz. *L'Insoumis: Juifs, Marocains et rebelles*. Paris: Desclée de Brouwer, 2001.
Shohat, Ella. "Lost Homelands, Imaginary Returns: The Exilic Literature of Iranian and Iraqi Jews." In *Moments of Silence: Authenticity in the Cultural Expressions of the Iran-Iraq War, 1980–1988*, edited by Arta Khakpour, Shouleh Vatanabadi, and Mohammad Mehdi Khorrami, 20–58. New York: New York University Press, 2016. https://doi.org/10.18574/nyu/9781479883844.003.0006.
———."On Orientalist Genealogies: The Split Arab/Jew Figure Revisited." In *The Arab and Jewish Questions: Geographies of Engagement in Palestine and Beyond*, edited by Bashir Bashir and Leila Farsakh, 89–121. New York: Columbia University Press, 2020.
———. "The Question of Judeo-Arabic." *Arab Studies Journal* 23, no. 1 (2015): 14–76. http://www.jstor.org/stable/44744899.
Silver, Christopher. *Recording History: Jews, Muslims, and Music Across Twentieth-Century North Africa*. Stanford: Stanford University Press, 2022.
Starr, Deborah. *Remembering Cosmopolitan Egypt: Literature, Culture, and Empire*. New York: Routledge, 2009.
———. *Togo Mizrahi and the Making of Egyptian Cinema*. Berkeley: University of California Press, 2020.

Stillman, Norman. *The Jews of Arab Lands: A History and Source Book*. Philadelphia: Jewish Publication Society of America: 1979.

Tazi, Mohammad Ezzeddine. *Anā al-mansī*. Casablanca: al-Markaz al-Thaqāfī al-ʿArabī, 2015.

Trevisan Semi, Emanuela, and Hanane Sekkat Hatimi. *Mémoire et représentations des Juifs au Maroc: Les voisins absents de Meknès*. Paris: Publisud, 2011.

Wazana, Kathy, dir. *They Were Promised the Sea*. Canada: BiCom Productions, 2013. DVD.

Winter, Jay. "René Cassin and the Alliance Israélite Universelle: A Republican in Post-Holocaust France." In *Post-Holocaust France and the Jews, 1945–1955*, edited by Seán Hand and Steven T. Katz, 203–26. New York: New York University Press, 2015.

Zamkanei, Shayna. "Property Claims of Jews from Arab Countries: Political, Monetary, or Cultural?" *Jewish Culture and History* 18, no. 1 (2017): 79–95.

Zaoui, Amin. *Le Dernier juif de Tamentit: Roman*. Algiers: Barzakh, 2012.

Zeidel, Ronen. "On the Last Jews in Iraq and Iraqi National Identity: A Look at Two Recent Iraqi Novels." *Journal of Modern Jewish Studies* 17, no. 2 (2018): 207–21.

Zytnicki, Colette. "The 'Oriental Jews' of the Maghreb: Reinventing the North African Jewish Past in the Colonial Era." In *Colonialism and the Jews*, edited by Ethan B. Katz, Lisa Moses Leff, and Maud S. Mandel, 29–53. Bloomington: Indiana University Press, 2017.

CHAPTER 1

Generative Absence

Jewish Loss as a Catalyst for Literature, Film, and Thought

BRAHIM EL GUABLI

Jews have resurfaced in Tamazghan (broader North African) and Middle Eastern cultural production in very transformative ways. The unprecedented cinematographic and literary output dedicated to Jews from these areas, decades after their mass emigration, demonstrates the realization of the deep loss inflicted on these societies by the departure of about eight hundred thousand of their Jewish citizens between 1948 and 1980.[1] Entire villages and neighborhoods were emptied of their Jewish inhabitants, and many Muslims never recovered from witnessing the havoc that Jewish emigration wrought on their Jewish-Muslim homelands. In addition to losing an important element of their ethnic and social fabric, Tamazghan and Middle Eastern societies lost languages, economic opportunities, culture, and social frameworks through which Jewish-Muslim relations were negotiated. The emigration of Jews also marked the end of an era and the beginning of another due to the impactful demographic transformations that the absence of Jews spurred in formerly interreligious societies. For a very long time, the shifting geopolitics of struggle in Israel/Palestine had foreclosed the possibility of accounting for and working through the multidimensional losses that arose from the traumatic separation of Jews and Muslims.

This chapter seeks to articulate the larger ramifications of loss in catalyzing literary, cinematographic, and theoretical works that center on Jewish topics. Surveying some of the Arabic and French-language works produced in the region since the 1980s, this chapter furthers the questions I have discussed in my book *Moroccan Other-Archives: History and Citizenship After State Violence* to probe the stakes of loss as a paradigm for the study of Jewish-Muslim relations. Further, the chapter argues that cultural producers build on the powerful faculty of memory and its transnationally exportable tools to articulate loss as a generative force. This analysis serves to record the different ways in which Jewish loss has been generative on many levels, including the emergence of a body of literature and film in which the Jewish-Muslim past is treated with respect, curiosity, and critical reminiscence, beyond any facile nostalgia or idealization. Moreover, this chapter draws on what I have called "al-kitāba al-istidhkāriyya" (mnemonic literature), which I have situated at the intersection of memory, archives, and history, to demonstrate how creative writing has recuperated the Jewish-Muslim past to reflect loss in Morocco.[2] I define "mnemonic literature" as the literary portrayal of Jewish-Muslim relations and histories through the lens of intergenerational memory (all to account for the former existence of Jews among Muslims), and I argue that it has been at work in Amazigh, Arabic, and Francophone texts for some time now. Finally, the chapter reveals how the unprocessed loss of Moroccan Jews has been central to Abdelkébir Khatibi's process in theorizing some of his seminal concepts. Together, the three sections of this chapter unveil how the emigration of Jews has underpinned transformative literary, cinematographic, and theoretical projects that have had internal and transregional ramifications for culture and thought in Tamazgha and the Middle East.

TRANSNATIONAL LOSS: MAGHREBI AND MIDDLE EASTERN LOSSES IN NOVELS AND FILMS

Cultural producers in the Maghreb and the Middle East have broken a multidecade silence concerning their vanished Jewish co-citizens, and in turn have privileged seeking closure for the loss wrought upon their societies as a result of the attrition of their Jewish populations. Documentary film has been particularly prolific in this regard. Kamal Hachkar's *Tinghir-Jerusalem: Echoes from the Mellah* recovers stories of Amazigh Jews and their Muslim counterparts from the village of Tinghir, in southeast Morocco. Born in Morocco and raised in France, Hachkar travels between southeast Morocco and different cities in Israel/Palestine (where Tinghiri Jews moved) in order to interview his characters about their shared life in the village of Tinghir, and he also interrogates the causes of their separation and distancing. Majid Shokor's *On the Banks of the Tigris*, similarly to Hachkar's film, uses music as a lens through which one can search for the lost Jewish-Muslim homeland that bound Jews and Muslims in Iraq. Shokor, an actor and refugee who lives in Australia, travels to Iraq, Israel/Palestine, Holland, and the United Kingdom to find Jewish-Iraqi musicians as well as many other Iraqi Muslims who knew their work, recording their stories along the way. His documentary shows how this generation of Iraqi Jews has recreated and sustained a musical Iraq in Israel despite the absence of the Muslim milieu of their youth. Also using music as a backbone of its storyline, Safinez Bousbia's documentary *El Gusto* (Taste) delves into the history of an Algerian band that used to have both Jewish and Muslim players. Thanks to the filmmaker's efforts, they are reunited after fifty years of disbandment, in the aftermath of Algeria's independence in 1962. The surviving members of the band finally perform together again, recreating a musical scene long thought lost.

The intergenerational nature of these documentaries is clear. Hachkar, Shokor, and Bousbia were not yet born when Jews left Morocco, Iraq, and Algeria. Their cinematographic endeavors are undergirded by a desire to know a history that was not available to them, albeit to different degrees and and in different circumstances. Despite living in separate countries, the three filmmakers shared a lack of historical knowledge, and this worked as an impetus for their desire to make sense of the erstwhile existence of Jews in their societies. This context is what helped these films challenge the ordinary silence about Jewish-Muslim relations. By adopting an inquisitive position to fill in the blanks of history through interviews (the locus of memory par excellence), these filmmakers stumbled into spaces that would have been kept outside the purview of cameras and recording devices forever. Not only do they articulate loss, but they also show the emotional and somatic toll that separation has taken on both Jews and Muslims.[3] Beyond the tears that the characters shed and the corporeal pain they express, their narratives transmit the burden of their legacy to the Muslim filmmakers. It is particularly significant to observe that it is a young generation of Muslim filmmakers who are looking for these Jews, marking the advent of the "era of loss" in Tamazghan and Middle Eastern cultural production. While Europe saw an "era of the witness" in the aftermath of World War II,[4] this contrasting era in Tamazgha and the Middle East is a period in which younger Muslim generations are now coming to terms with a sort of "historical silence," a process that deeply impacted the religious and cultural makeup of their societies.

Despite the production of many feature films about Jews, only documentary films and soap operas elicited significant media attention during the 2000s.[5] The attempts to ban *Tinghir-Jerusalem* and *El Gusto* in Morocco and Algeria respectively brought their directors a degree of exposure. This, in turn, increased their viewership and opened venues of international film festivals for their screening. In terms of soap operas, *Ḥārat al-Yahūd* (The Jewish quarter) and *Um Hārūn* (Harun's mother) also elicited unprecedented attention to the topic of Jewish-Muslim relations. Much ink has been spilled about *Ḥārat al-Yahūd* since it first aired on Egyptian national television in 2013. As Iskandar Ahmad Abdalla shows in his essay for this collection, *Ḥārat al-Yahūd* laments the "good and beautiful time" of cosmopolitan Egypt, casting the Muslim Brotherhood as the evil that caused the departure of Egyptian Jews. Although this depiction of the Muslim Brotherhood is ahistorical, *Ḥārat al-Yahūd* marked a significant shift in Egyptian discourse about Jews. Most recently, Dubai-based Saudi channel MBC produced *Um Hārūn*, a very provocative series about Jews in the Gulf, particularly Kuwait. The show was filmed in the United Arab Emirates and Kuwait and was fully funded by Gulf money. Critiques have mainly taken issue with its many historical and factual errors. The journalist Alā' al-Lāmī wrote in the Lebanese daily *al-Akhbar* that *Um Hārūn* is "an artificial soap opera that is also empty in terms of its story and topic," underlining that it is part of the endeavor to normalize with Israel.[6] States, particularly in Morocco and the Gulf, have used the media as a means to shore up support for the Abraham Accords,[7] and official media have often followed suit. In this regard, state-sponsored normalization projects undermine civil society's endeavors to reconcile Tamazghan and Middle Eastern societies with their Jewish heritage by focusing attention on normalization with Israel.

Alongside documentary film, novelistic output exhibits a transformation in the way that Arabic literature depicts Jews. Replacing long-standing clichés and anti-Semitic portrayals of Jews as sexually impotent, usurers, and untrustworthy traitors, recent literature published in the region has humanized Jews by depicting them as friends and partners, complicating the history of their indigeneity to their former homelands and disrupting the distinction between diaspora and homeland. Egyptian novelist Kamal Ruḥayyim represents the existence of a category of Arabs who hail from Jewish and Muslim parents in his novel *Yawmiyyāt muslim yahūdī* (Diary of a Jewish Muslim),[8] challenging the myth of religious homogeneity through the character of Galal, who is both Jewish and Muslim. Tunisian novelist Khawla Hamdi's novel *Fī qalbī unthā 'ibriyya* (There is a Hebrew woman in my heart) introduces the reader to the complicated world of Jewish-Muslim childhoods and shared families. This is principally done through the fictionalized true story of a young girl named Rima who gets adopted by a Jewish family after the death of her mother.[9] Saudi novelist Ḥamad Ḥamīd al-Rāshīdī's novel *Majnūn laylā al-yahūdiyya* (The madman of Layla the Jewish woman) takes place in Egypt and tells the love story of Ibrahim, a Muslim man, and Layla, a Jewish woman, all through the eyes of a Saudi student who befriends them both in Cairo. Although questions of the Arab-Israeli conflict in Palestine exist in the background of these novels, the characters navigate them productively, and this sheds a new light on how positive depictions of Jews neither diminish the Palestinian cause nor whitewash colonization.

Al-Yāhūdī al-'akhīr (The last Jew), published by Australia-based Iraqi novelist Abdul-Jabbār Nāṣir, narrates the story of Nājī Na'ūm, an Iraqi Jewish doctor who refuses to leave Iraq at the height of Jewish emigration from the country. In an extremely telling exchange between Nājī and the Mijbil, one the leaders of the coup against General Qāsim's progressive regime in Iraq, the stakes of the novel are clarified:

> "What perplexes me is the secret of your staying in the city. Why didn't you emigrate like the rest of the Jews? Did the Zionist gangs ask you to remain so that you are their eye, watching what happens here?"
>
> Nājī didn't respond and contented himself with a nonchalant look that provoked Comrade Mijbil, and his face darkened, screaming impatiently: "Answer me . . . Are you challenging me, you Jew?"
>
> A feeling of pride invaded Nājī because he shook the freak's self-confidence: "Why should I emigrate? I am staying because this land

> is my homeland, and the people in this country are my people. They are pleasant, and they are not like you."[10]

This conversation depicts a surreal situation in which Nājī, an Iraqi citizen, must prove why he will not emigrate as his coreligionists did in the 1950s. In the rife context of the Arab-Israeli conflict, leaving was the expected act for Jews, while staying, as this novel depicts it, was an extraordinary decision. Rather than bringing them heroic accolades, it was one that turned them into suspects.

Literature has served as a locus for the emergence of a generative approach to Jewish-Muslim relations, one contextualized through the lens of loss. Throughout Tamazgha and the Middle East, literary works depict dynamic and complicated lives, extending from intertwined family histories to shared homelands and citizenship. Framed through the logic of conflict, past Arabic literature represented Jews in demeaning or explicitly anti-Semitic ways.[11] Current literary depictions of Jews are subtle, less confrontational, and more attuned to the broader structural issues that left their imprint on both Jews and Muslims. Literature is and remains a product of its time, and it is not surprising that writings about Jews possess a significant archival potential.[12] The art form also helps us to contextualize literary production in terms of specific authors themselves as well as the general atmosphere that they were navigating while in the process of crafting their works. After the June 1967 War and the ensuing *Naksa* (setback), the term used to describe the Arab defeat and its aftermath, the entire Arabic literary field was reshaped on account of growing resentment toward *iltizām* (commitment), the "keyword" for Arab writers for a long time.[13] The Arab defeat catalyzed a soul-searching period among the Arab intelligentsia, and their responses ranged from disillusionment with Nasserism in many parts of the Arabic-speaking countries to the rise of Marxist-Leninist secret organizations, as was the case in Morocco.[14]

Jīl al-naksa (the "generation of the setback") revolutionized Arabic literature and thought, predominantly in response to Arab military losses in the successive wars with Israel. M. M. Badawi has written that "the initial response to the disaster was one of shock and loss of balance. When authors were not stunned and dumbfounded, they often expressed themselves in nightmarish visions."[15] Arab writers discovered that commitment did not prevent defeat, and so they sought to find more space to process the setback in anxiety-laden works. In his turn, literary critic Sabry Hafiz listed the different ways in which Arab writers tried to cope with the defeat, ranging from "feeling[s] of humiliation and self-abasement, the occasional rhetorical tone in an attempt to dissociate oneself from the shame of defeat to the extent of denying responsibility for it, and the obvious veneration for deeds of heroism, resistance and self-sacrifice."[16] From theater to poetry to philosophy, Arab creative writers of the commitment generation reconceived their world in order to overcome the existential questions that they faced, ones that shaped their cultural and social reality. The current generation of Muslim littérateurs in the Maghreb and the Middle East is also currently attempting to process the legacies of these histories. They are doing so by principally turning more toward history and memory to center local realities, delving into the diverse manifestations of loss in their own specific countries. Unlike the older generation, which attempted to theorize what was then known as the Arab world, contemporary writers hold more nuanced views of their societies' situations, and they acknowledge the diversity of experiences within them. Novelists throughout the region have challenged the social and historical taboos that once prevented them from confronting their Jewish past, shedding light on the urgent and general need to revisit the erased histories of Jewish-Muslim relations.[17]

Loss cannot be divorced from daily life. Psychoanalysis has demonstrated that responses to loss take the form of either mourning or melancholia, the former allowing healing and the latter trapping a person who experiences loss in an incessant acting out, taking its toll on them over time. In clearer, albeit less complex, terms, Dominick LaCapra has drawn on Freudian mourning and melancholia to distinguish between working through and acting out in the way that subjects respond to loss.[18] Working through, like mourning, leads to the realization that the object of loss is separate from the self, while acting out (which is another way to say compulsive repetition in the Freudian sense) entraps the subject in a vicious circle in which the separation between the past and the present is absent for the subject.[19] More significant, however, is LaCapra's assertion that the study of trauma does not only have ramifications for research and scholarship but also has a "bear[ing] on social and political issues."[20] For a long time, Arabic intellectual production was embroiled in a melancholic state when processing defeat in the aftermath of the 1948, 1967, and 1973 wars in the Middle East. This melancholic state was fed by a culture of blind *iltizām* and unreflective hypernationalism, both of which played out in ways that benefitted the very reactionary forces that the proponents of "commitment culture" wanted to battle. Instead of a self-perpetuating commitment, contemporary creative writers in the region are aware that self-reflexivity is fundamental for a transformative reconfiguration of their position in the world.

The fundamental concern that underlies the novelistic and cinematographic output about Jews is the need to recognize that Maghrebi and Middle Eastern societies have lost on many fronts in either forcing their Jews out or negotiating their departure. The old approach, which arose in the context of defeat, has fed from feelings of dejection and "abjecthood" that went hand in hand with the violent loss of Palestine. As LaCapra has compellingly affirmed, the disorientation and hurt experienced by individuals and groups as a result of crises and catastrophes lead to the emergence of myths of crisis or catastrophe that "serve an ideological function in authorizing acts or policies that appeal to [them/myths] for justification."[21] The period between the June 1967 War and the 2000s witnessed the construction of many myths that attempted to explain why the "Arab world" was defeated, giving rise to various answers, which, it turned out later, regimes in the region used to further consolidate authoritarianism and breed historical amnesia. In response to these erstwhile tendencies, the new trend, in literary and intellectual terms, recognizes the internal and external significance of loss and attempts to build on it to activate local agency and give a new meaning to Palestine itself.

MOROCCAN "MNEMONIC LITERATURE": THE JEW AS THE ABSENT MEMBER OF THE NATION

Like many Maghrebi and Middle Eastern countries, Morocco is a land in which Judaism is etched into both the country's topography and its peoples' memories. A sizable portion of the country's citizens were Jewish until the massive migration diminished the community's numbers tremendously between 1948 and 1967. Moroccan languages continue to evoke this Jewishness. Amazigh names such as *lmllāḥ* (the mellah), *lmdint n udāyn* and *lqbūr n udāyn* (the Jewish cemetery), *aggrrām n udāyn* (the Jewish saint), and *ljamā n udāyn* (the Jewish mosque/synagogue) retain the word *udāyn* (Jews), attributing places to a past Jewish existence.[22] Everyone visiting parts of Morocco where Jews used to live has to contend with this heritage, which continues to pervade all aspects of life. I first encountered these words in my village on the outskirts of Ouarzazate, where the oldest parts of the village were called *lmallāḥ*, but none of the elders I interviewed had any memories of Jews being there during their youth. Later, assigned as a teacher in the Atlas Mountains between 1999 and 2009, I encountered more examples of places that retained signs of Jewishness inscribed in the topographies of remote villages. In Tizgui N'Barda, a village in the rural commune of Telouet, the ruins of a former synagogue are still called *ljamā n udāyn*. Likewise, in Agouim, which was one of the centers of Jewish life on the road between Ouarzazate and Marrakesh, shops that have been closed for decades are called *tiḥuna n udāyn* (Jewish shops). These small and still-locked shops could serve as a starting point for a microhistory of financial success, familial hardships, and transnational dealings, as well as the way that they played out in a small village in the Moroccan High Atlas Mountains.

Jews may have left physically, but their imprint is still present in the spaces they used to inhabit. Almost every village has a Muslim guard who watches over the ruins and serves as a contact point for Jewish visitors, many of whom come from time to time to visit the vestiges of their ancestors. Guards such as Adda Boullah in my village and El Maleh in Tizgui N'Barda, to mention just these two, occupy an ambiguous position between Judaism and Islam and, most importantly, between local society and the Jewish diaspora, thus extending their horizons beyond the community in which they physically live. Although neither Adda Boullah nor El Maleh, who had no elementary education, could put their thoughts about Jewish-Muslim relations in theoretical terms, their daily care for places that are no longer occupied by living people is in and of itself a theoretical position in that the act embodies a form of rational thinking that imbricates Jewish places into the Muslim community.[23] In fact, when looking at the broader significance, it is less that the guards care for and attend to the ruins themselves and more the memory of the people who once breathed life into these places that matters.

The parallels between these guards and the littérateurs who recover Jewish lives in their writings are striking. After a long silence over Jewish topics in Moroccan literature, novelists, mostly belonging to a younger generation, have made Jewish characters central to their literary works. The rediscovery of this topic, which was paradoxically highly present in Moroccan daily life but largely absent from discursive and literary practices at the time, has now seeped deeply into cultural memory. Ḥasan Riyāḍ's *Awrāq ʿibrīyya* (Hebrew papers), which won the Moroccan Writers' Union book prize in 1996, was the first novel to depict an entirely Jewish theme. *Awrāq ʿibrīyya* could be said to have paved the way for other, more significant literary projects that started to appear in the 2000s. This literary subgenre, which I have called mnemonic literature, is mainly driven by young writers who did not experience the Jewish-Muslim life that they describe, or if they did, they were too young to grasp its significance. Taking advantage of memory's potential to unsettle historical narratives and foreground new concerns, writers of mnemonic literature have made Jews a real topic of discussion among Moroccan readers, doubling down on the controversies and praise elicited in equal measure by cinematographic works.

Thanks to this younger generation of Moroccan authors, Morocco finds itself confronted by unresolved questions about its Jewish history and the effects of the Jewish community's leaving the country. El Hassane Aït Moh's *Le Captif de Mabrouka* (The captive of Mabrouka) raises the issue of the departure and return of Moroccan Jews through the character of Walter Barukh Kinston, who returns to recover his parents' house in the city of Ouarzazate.[24] Mohammed Ezzeddine Tazi's novel *Anā al-mansī* (I am the forgotten) depicts the local and transnational transformations that led to the emigration of the Jews of Fez between the Protectorate period and 1967.[25] Adopting a microhistorical approach, the novel depicts the internal disagreements within the Jewish families with regard to emigration, complicating the story of their departure. Hassan Aourid's *Cintra* uses the colonial-era Cintra bar in Casablanca to address historical silence via the story of a Moroccan nationalist named Binmanṣūr who was married to a Jewish woman before her departure to Israel in 1947.[26] The novel reveals how two competing nationalisms pulled Jews and Muslims apart at this particular point in time, namely when Israel was declared a state and King Mohammed V gave his Tangier speech, which asserted Moroccan independence.[27] Driss Miliani's novel *Casanfa* re-Judaizes the city of Casablanca by having the Jewish main character frame his observations about this city by the Hebrew calendar.[28] Casablanca is then experienced and perceived through the eyes of a Jewish man as he hops from one bar to another before his disappearance under mysterious circumstances. Ibrahim Hariri's

Shamma aw Shtrit (Shamma or Shtrit) delves into the familial ties that unite Jews and Muslims by creating the story of a Casablanca family whose Jewish mother and Muslim husband were separated by the June 1967 War, resulting in the separation of their two children. The daughter moves with her mother to Israel while the brother stays back with his father in Morocco.[29] One can imagine how socialization in a context of conflict drives their ideologies apart, setting them up to argue about Palestine and Zionism at international gatherings.

This familial dimension of Jewish-Muslim relations is further developed in Mohamed Ouissaden's latest novel, *ISRAE, Elle . . .* (ISRAE, she . . .). Unfolding mainly in Marrakesh and Casablanca, the novel follows the story of Israe, an atheist of Muslim descent, who marries Kamal, a bisexual Jewish man, and together they work on making a film about Jewish emigration from Morocco. Because the photographer Mohamed, who owns a crucial photo they need for their film to be shown in the United States, is reluctant to deliver it to them, Kamal and Israe resort to deceit by luring Mohamed to fall in love with her. Deceit turns into marriage between Israe and Mohamed. Later, her father, who appears on a program for missing people, reveals that he is looking for a missing brother, named Mohamed, who lives in Marrakesh. The father adds that he and Mohamed were born to the same mother, but Mohamed's father is Jewish. Thus Israe discovers that she married a Muslim man whose father is Jewish (meaning that, according to religious law, he occupies an ambiguous space between Judaism and Islam) but also that this man is her paternal uncle. The tragic ending of the novel insinuates the idea that the erasure of history could lead to devastating biological consequences.

Thanks to the pioneering work that these novelists have done to memorialize and inscribe heretofore invisible life stories, their literature has brought attention to history as a space for both Jewish-Muslim citizenship and the lost dimension of the Moroccan nation. As the stories of these novels unfold, the reader is overtaken by the sense of impoverishment brought upon Moroccans as a result of the lack of interfaith spaces of encounter, something that Jewish-Muslim intimacy had previously allowed to exist. As Jews emigrate, the story of their existence as integral members of the Moroccan nation raises deeper questions, ones that leave the reader wondering about the possibility of ever reviving this extinct world. Like the guards Adda Boullah and El Maleh who watched over Jewish vestiges in their respective villages, creators of mnemonic literature have given themselves a crucial memorial and historical function, and it will undoubtedly have consequences for the ways in which Jewish Morocco is conjured in the local and national imagination.

Interpersonal relationships aside, this mnemonic literature interrogates the very possibility of a different Morocco. Indeed, Jews stand in for the lost nation. Morocco had the largest Jewish community in the Maghreb and the Middle East until 1967, but the majority left the country after the coronation of King Hassan II in 1961. In reality, the facilitation of the emigration of Moroccan Jews coincided with the tightening of political repression in the country during what came to be known as the "years of lead." While Hassan II's regime was shutting down all possible avenues for the emergence of a democratic state in Morocco, the parallel negotiation of the departure of Moroccan Jews retrospectively reveals that expediting Jewish emigration was part of the authoritarian project.[30] Moroccan historian Abdallah Laroui has articulated the importance of minorities for democracy:

> The existence of a Christian minority, in addition to the Jewish minority or other, in a Muslim society is a guarantee for the success of the democratic project in the country. . . . Diversity is the guarantee of democracy, and we cannot demand that Western countries grant their full rights to Muslim minorities and in the meantime do not undertake granting [our] minorities the same rights.
>
> Democracy cannot be produced in a racially, religiously, culturally, and linguistically homogeneous country. Japan does, however, represent a counterexample to this conception, but democracy was imposed on Japan and if it were not militarily defeated, there would not be democracy.[31]

Laroui goes on to stress that the "biggest fear is the homogenization of the source."[32] Laroui is right to identify the nefarious effects of religiously and culturally homogenous societies on the establishment of a democracy, and the departure of Jews from Tamazgha and the Middle East has inflicted a major loss on these societies. Of broader significance is that Jewish loss indicates that authoritarian regimes benefited from their use of Israel/Palestine as subterfuge, principally through homogenizing their societies by letting their Jews emigrate, to further entrench their rule.

Following this line of analysis, I propose that the reemergence of Moroccan Jews in film and mnemonic literature cannot be divorced from a wish to relive the experience of multireligious and diverse societies. Social, cultural, and economic losses are real and palpable, but the sneakier and even more dangerous homogenization of societies has limited the potential for change and restricted the room available for experimentation with new models for politics and society. The novel, and specifically the mnemonic novel, has been the result of this will to experiment with new ways of historicizing the makeup of Tamazghan and Middle Eastern societies and cultures.

LOSS AS A VECTOR FOR IDEATION: JEWS AS A FUNDAMENTAL INSPIRATION OF THEORIZATION

The multilayered loss of Tamazghan and Middle Eastern Jews did not just inspire literary and cinematographic works. It also catalyzed intellectual projects that left their imprint on the humanities as a whole.[33] Abdelkébir Khatibi's theoretical work is particularly informed by his relationship to the void left by the departure of Moroccan (or even Tamazghan) Jews. Loss permeates the process of Khatibi's ideation and creation of critical knowledge. A native of the coastal city of El Jadida, Khatibi studied sociology at the Sorbonne before returning to Morocco in 1964 to join the Institute for Scientific Research, a center for advanced study. In 1966, he became the director of the Institut de Sociologie (Institute of Sociology), where, alongside anthropologist Paul Pascon, he undertook the challenging task of decolonizing and de-Orientalizing sociology.[34] However, the Moroccan state's wariness of the outcome of the events of May 1968, in which leftist youth rebelled against the French state, led it to shut down the Institut de Sociologie in 1970, thus diminishing the possibility of empirical sociological research.[35] As a result, Khatibi distanced himself from this academic discipline, but he continued to use its theoretical tools to "capture signs visualized in [social changes] in dress, behavior, acculturation, [and] mixing of languages."[36]

The Jew, or rather the figure of the Jew, in Khatibi's work responded to various temporally situated needs, and it reflected (albeit very subtly) the way that loss undergirded his intellectual project. Similarly to German sociologist Georg Simmel and Martiniquais author Édouard Glissant,[37] Khatibi utilized the idea of "the Jew" to engineer his conceptualizations of *bi-langue* (bilanguage), *pensée-autre* (other-thought), *identité fluide* (fluid identity), and *étranger professionnel* (professional stranger). Delineating these three different portrayals in Khatibi's literary and theoretical output shows that despite the physical absence of Jews from Morocco, their erstwhile presence in the country shaped his theoretical and literary project.

The Jew as a Professional Stranger

The Jew is pivotal to Khatibi's earliest conceptualization of professional strangeness, as articulated in several of his books.[38] In his theorization, the Jew is a professional stranger, a person who develops a capability of inhabiting multiple languages and cultures rather than being apprehensive toward "foreignness." Perhaps a result of the Alliance Israélite Universelle's network of schools in tandem with colonial modernity in the Tamazgha (both of which were at the core of separation between Muslims and Jews and the latter's eventual emigration), the Jew for Khatibi is bilingual and adopts foreign names.[39] This sets up the figure of the Jew as one who is receptive to inhabiting other cultures and embarking on other processes of becoming. However, it was not until 1987 that Khatibi fleshed out his definition of the professional stranger as someone who is always in a state of "wandering . . . through the boundaries of countries, territories, cultures, and dissidences."[40] Twenty years later, he returned to the same issue in his last book, *Le Scribe et son ombre* (The scribe and his shadow), writing that "it happens that I introduce myself as a Moroccan as well as a professional stranger."[41] To those who wonder what this "job" was, he says that he would reply that being a professional stranger "is not a job [but] a mobile position in the world [in which] we are able to cross borders between languages, civilizations, and markets."[42] Interestingly, only the Jew who left Moroccan society to inhabit other languages and cultures answers to this definition.

Professional strangeness is not, however, merely limited to mobility or linguistic and cultural adaptability. It is also a critical disposition in the world vis-à-vis sacred texts in particular. In this sense, Khatibi presents the Jew as someone who is "endowed with reason and freedom of the mind."[43] Considering Freud as a professional stranger whose work revolutionized the reading of sacred texts, Khatibi affirms that to desacralize is to "rationalize in a very rigorous, even intractable, manner."[44] In *Le Scribe et son ombre*, he writes that "the Muslim is invited to share [the] line of thinking" of the Jewish professional stranger. This Jew that Muslims are called upon to emulate "carries within [himself] the weight of an ex-centered alterity and of a truly lived ethics."[45] To further explain the significance of the professional stranger, he quotes the Prophet Muhammad's famous *ḥadīth* stating that "Islam began as something strange, and it shall return to being something strange, so give glad tidings to the strangers." While this obvious invitation to Muslims to take this constructed Jew as a role model for their attitude concerning their world is quite clear, the specific connection between the professional stranger and the *ḥadīth* that Khatibi wishes to underline remains opaque. Instead of fleshing out the meaning he gives to these connections, he only stresses Islam's enigmatic celebration of strangeness!

Khatibi further emphasizes how the figure of the Jew reminds us that both Islam and Judaism have had an ambiguous historical relationship with foreignness. In this, a space opens up for an encounter between the two religions. One way to reflect on this is to underline that, for Khatibi, the figure of the Jew provides the model of an open, generative, and conflictual reading of the sacred text that he calls upon Muslims to embrace. Pushing this even further, Khatibi asserts that "we are all Jews in so far as we have become readers of a book, a prophetic book."[46] Jewishness is neither a "particularity" nor a "singularity," since the Jew exists in everyone who believes in the sacred.[47] A further hint can be found in a letter he sent Jacques Hassoun in 1983: "What does it mean to be Jewish today, if not the end of a horizon of the Book, of a certain horizon which is, in itself, undefinable? To be Jewish is even in the text beyond the book. That's why there are as many exact, performative and external readings of the book itself as there are Jews."[48] The contradiction that Khatibi was trying to resolve lay in the way that the sacred texts had taken over Muslim lives. Khatibi affirms in a 1985 letter to Hassoun that "the Islamic body was donated, sacrificed for the Text."[49] Around the same period he was corresponding with Hassoun, he published *Maghreb pluriel* (Plural Maghreb), in which he revisits this question of the body sacrificed to God, namely through the hypostatized universal triumvirate of "body," "text," and "love."[50] Instead of the "Text" surrendering itself to Muslim will, as was probably the case when Muslims praised foreignness so as to shatter the accepted norms of pre-Islamic Arabia, Khatibi seems to say that Muslims subjugated themselves to the book.

The Jew as a "Frientimate"

Le Même livre (The same book) is a collection of about fifty letters that Khatibi and Hassoun exchanged between 1980 and 1985. In the original introduction, Khatibi highlights that "this book is an encounter or rather the effect of an encounter. One of us, who was born in Alexandria, lives in Paris, and the other, who was born on the shore of the Atlantic in El Jadida, lives in Morocco."[51] Revising the meaning of this correspondence in 2009, Khatibi wonders: "When a psychoanalyst and a writer publish an exchange of letters and co-sign it, what is the significance of this public confidence? Who is it addressed to?"[52] He goes on to add that "this is a quite atypical correspondence between two intellectuals, one from an Alexandrine Jewish family, and the other, from a Moroccan Muslim family."[53] In foregrounding the atypical nature of his lengthy correspondence with Hassoun, Khatibi alludes to its subversive potential, especially given that the letters were destined to leave the private sphere and enter the public domain upon publication.

The pioneering nature of Khatibi and Hassoun's epistolary book reflects the mood of a growing mutual interest in Jewish-Muslim relations. By 1985, Identité et Dialogue (Identity and dialogue), an association of Moroccan Jews living in France, had already published the proceedings of a groundbreaking conference held in Paris between December 18 and December 21, 1978, under the title *La Communauté juive marocaine: Vie Culturelle, histoire sociale et évolution* (Moroccan Jewish community: Cultural life, social history, and evolution). Combining autobiographical presentations with academic papers, this conference was, according to the organizers, the first time that Moroccan academics of Muslim and Jewish origins, including the ones who moved to Israel, came together for "a frank and direct dialogue, to tell each other not only how they perceive each other, but also the sort of grievances they can communicate to each other."[54] Taking into account this context, Khatibi and Hassoun were corresponding with each other at a moment when Morocco was reconnecting with its Jewish communities globally.

However, the uniqueness of *Le Même livre* comes from its focus on a public and intellectual friendship that is situated in a determined historical context. I propose to call this correspondence an indulgence in "frientimacy"—an uncensored, playful journey in which Khatibi and Hassoun draw from their intellectual and personal lives in order to nourish a writing project with deep intellectual and political implications. Khatibi's and Hassoun's frientimacy blurs the boundaries between the private and the public. It started as *une amitié intellectuelle* (intellectual friendship), but it surpassed its original intellectual focus over time and developed into frientimacy. For instance, Hassoun announces the birth of his first granddaughter, while Khatibi informs him of his marriage. Both Khatibi and Hassoun share with each other their exhilaration and happiness about things that were happening in their lives, as well as complaints of fatigue as the result of intense writing and intellectual work. As time passes, Khatibi and Hassoun shift from using the formal *vous* (plural you) to the less formal *tu* (singular you). Khatibi remarks, "I have realized that our correspondence is becoming more personal. We probably have nothing to lose, speaking freely in a language that is foreign to both Hebrew and Arabic."[55] This frientimacy overcomes the guardedness of their early correspondence and instigates a kind of serious playfulness that does not, however, disengage from the world as shown. For instance, one can see this in the shift of their conversations in 1982 to focus on the Israeli invasion of Lebanon.

Frientimacy requires understanding the psychology of one's interlocutor. This understanding manifests in the way that Khatibi and Hassoun broached sensitive topics either openly or in convoluted terms depending on the context. In a letter dated July 14, 1984, Hassoun asks Khatibi a pivotal question that had been latent in their correspondence for a long time, but one that both maneuvered to avoid asking until then: "At this point, I wish to ask you: And you, do you feel touched by the departure of Moroccan Jews with whom you cohabitated? This absented part of the Moroccan people, how did it touch you? I wish that you will respond to me about this."[56] Khatibi responds to Hassoun from Tangier on July 22, 1984, excitedly writing, "I don't wish to wait too long before responding to your question about my feelings about the departure of Moroccan Jews."[57] In a good mood, he underlines how "the movements of departure, travel, and exodus pique [his] imagination,"[58] thus pushing him to answer Hassoun's letter more quickly than normal.

Hassoun's once silent question about the emigration of Moroccan Jews offers Khatibi the opportunity to insert himself into their history, furthering his engagement in frientimacy. In his response, Khatibi presents one of the first articulations of loss that Moroccan society experienced as a result of the departure of Jews:

> Now, when I remember the Jews of my childhood, here, it's words such as *zim* or *mā ʾ al-ḥayā* that I remember in my mouth in a certain way. It's this unsalted and crusty bread that has always intrigued me. Thanks to a Jewish friend (and a communist), it was only later that I was able to know and truly savor sweets, wines, and the heavenly delicacies of Moroccan Jewish cuisine, which we are currently losing to exile toward other mouths. . . . It's generally after Mimouna. I want to recount [this] because these little details take me back in time to my own "Jewishness," which, whether I want it or not, is a tattoo on my pure childhood.[59]

The mass emigration of Moroccan Jews transformed them into an object of loss for Khatibi. As Israeli historian Michael Laskier has demonstrated, Morocco had the largest Jewish community in the lands of Islam, but the country lost two hundred and twenty thousand of its citizens to emigration between 1948 and 1964.[60] The authors of *Histoire du Maroc: Réactualisation et synthèse* (History of Morocco: reactualization and synthesis) have noted the demographic transformation of villages and the areas whose Jews left.[61] With only a few thousand Jews left in the country, the Jewish emigration irrevocably transformed Morocco's religious and cultural landscape as well as the possibility of Muslim-Jewish intimacy therein.

In their absence, Jews had become part of Khatibi's culinary and olfactory memory. The Jew recovered here is not the professional stranger, like Hassoun, but rather someone who left behind an image enmeshed in memories of food, including *pain azim* (matzah) and *mā ʾ al-ḥayāt* (*mahia* / water of life / eau de vie), a Jewish alcoholic beverage distilled from figs or dates. Moroccans continue to mythologize *mahia* even today. However, instead of locating the act of remembering in the mind, Khatibi's embodied approach attributes memory to the mouth, the nose, and the ears. The mouth remembers the delicious Jewish foods and the nostrils are filled with the smells of this displaced cuisine. The ears remember Moroccan Jews through the specific Andalusian dialect, which did not adhere to the standard Arabic pronunciation of the sound qaf (ق), instead pronouncing it as a short alif (أ). Remembering Jews in this Khatibian approach is an operation that requires the mobilization of all senses. Because of its malleability, memory allows loss to be narrativized and incorporated into newer forms of knowledge, conjuring situations that were not available to those who did not experience them at the time.

If culinary, olfactory, and acoustic memories evoke loss for Khatibi, memories of cemeteries and old Jewish men evoke guilt. Revisiting his childhood, he tells Hassoun with much remorse that it was the children who attacked the Jewish quarter.[62] Reflecting on his childhood memories, he confesses that they "stole kippahs of old Jews so that we could resell them."[63] Khatibi attributes this behavior to childhood naughtiness before asserting that "I only did it once, once."[64] Similarly, cemeteries are prominent in his childhood memories of Moroccan Jews. He admits to having stolen "talismans," but this time he also did the same thing in "Muslim marabouts."[65] Simmel has underlined that one of the privileges of being a stranger is an openness to sharing things that have a confessional nature, experiences one would "carefully withhold from a closely related person."[66] It is specifically this productive space between "nearness and distance" where frientimacy resides, and it allows Khatibi to share memories of a childhood laden with guilt vis-à-vis his Jewish co-citizens.

Instead of dwelling on guilt, Khatibi draws on these memories to appreciate the formative childhood he had in El Jadida. He underlines how the Jewish dimension is a part of his plural identity: "Now, I think that my childhood was more complex in its emotional formation. Biographically, I lived my youth in . . . a weft of cultural elements, simultaneously Arab, Muslim, Berber, French, Jewish, [infused with] a Portuguese mythology."[67]

The Jewish communities to which Khatibi refers here without much detail have escaped the radar of scholarship. Mustapha Jmahri, a social historian of El Jadida, has authored a unique local history of the Jews of the city. Of note in Jmarhi's book is the fact that Mazagan was home to "Muslim, Jewish, and Protestant populations" as early as 1820.[68] He also emphasizes the role of the Portuguese colonizers of Mazagan in shaping Jewish and Muslim identities, revealing how, similarly to Essaouira, the Jews of El Jadida occupied and discharged important commercial, linguistic, and ambassadorial functions for Moroccan monarchs.[69] Jmahri also attributes the decline of the Jewish population of El Jadida to a famine that struck Morocco in 1856–57. This famine is depicted by the aforementioned novel *Awrāq ʿibrīyya*, which literary critic Aḥmad al-Madīnī has highlighted as telling a "story whose people were not of much concern to Moroccan literature."[70]

The "Jew" in Khatibi's construction is not one but multiple. He is an absence whose culinary, sensorial, or olfactory traces are left to bear witness to his former existence among Muslims. His evocation stirs up feelings of guilt and evokes the flaws of the self in its connection to the minority Other. Oddly, however, at the time of Khatibi's writing, some ten thousand Moroccan Jews still lived in the country, and yet he had nothing to say about them. To him, they seem to have already left and have become an object of memory, lamentation, and indignation. The question that stems from this is whether he refuses to be a guard of memory, especially when considering his description of the Muslim guards of physical remnants of the Jews' presence. Contrasting still-present empty homes with the departure of Jewish people, he writes to Hassoun in 1984 that the Muslim guard is a "witness, often old, forsaken, a last trace, a corpse that persists in this myth. But the tragedy of these witnesses is pitiful; it's more of a decomposition than a testimony; a watchman over death rather than a vestige that hopes."[71] Perhaps the finality of this Jewish world in Khatibi's understanding is what explains his representation of local Jews as absences, all in contrast to Hassoun's reminiscences about Egyptian Muslims, who are full of vivid life.

Throughout this chapter, I have described how literature and film in Tamazgha and the Middle East have captured and portrayed the departure of Jews from these regions as loss. The first two sections of the chapter probed loss as an object of literary works and documentary films both regionally and locally. Regionally, I have shown that loss has been at the center of novels and films produced in these two areas. Locally, I investigated the case of Morocco in order to give a more concrete example of the stakes involved in representations of the absence of Jews as loss. Further, I take loss to be a conceptual approach to works that have drawn on the topic of Jewish emigration, claiming that it has had dire effects on the internal evolution of these societies. Finally, I draw on Khatibi's deployment of the figure of the Jew to demonstrate how the loss of Moroccan Jews to emigration has been central to his conceptual work.

These three moves show the generative nature of loss as a paradigm for the study of Jewish-Muslim relations and opens up a direly needed space for fresh perspectives on this history. In approaching these works through the lens of loss, the goal is to go beyond prevalent readings that have mainly focused on conflict, as these tend to come at the expense of critical thinking concerning the significance of literature and film for societies that are far from the site of the Arab/Israeli conflict. An awareness that the colonial conflict in Israel/Palestine has engendered many losses, including the loss of local Jews and the diverse societies that could have been, should mark a paradigm shift in the way that Jewish-Muslim relations are studied and discussed.

Notes

A portion of this chapter was previously published as Brahim El Guabli, "Textual Traces: Khatibi and His Jews," *PMLA / Publications of the Modern Language Association of America* 137, no. 2 (2022): 347–54, reproduced with permission.

1. Sociologist Yves Chevalier has written that until 1954, scholars estimated the number of North African Jews to be close to 500,000, including "240,000 in Morocco, 150,000 in Algeria, and 100,000 in Tunisia. By the end of 1967, only 30,000 remained in Morocco, 10,000 in Tunisia, and 2,000 in Algeria." In a matter of thirteen years, the Maghreb lost 448,000 to different migrations. See Chevalier, "Juifs d'Afrique du Nord," 271.

2. El Guabli, *Moroccan Other-Archives*. Unless otherwise indicated, all the translations from Amazigh, Arabic, and French are mine.

3. The viewer cannot emerge unaffected from watching these films. The Jewish interviewees are old, and most of them have never recovered from their own loss of their former homelands in the Maghreb and the Middle East. The Muslim interviewees, likewise, still express a lack of understanding of why their Jewish friends and neighbors left.

4. Wieviorka, *Ère du témoin*.

5. Online newspapers are particularly interested in these topics because they increase their readership, and anything that might stir controversy is published to generate more revenue, thus posing some serious ethical questions about the practice of journalism in this area.

6. Al-Lāmī, "Um Hārūn."

7. The Abraham Accords included normalization between Israel and Bahrain and the United Arab Emirates first. Morocco and Sudan joined a later stage. The Accords initiated a period of open deals between the United States and these countries so as to accrue benefits from American patronage of their local issues as well as their diplomatic relations with Israel.

8. Ruḥyymm, *Diary*.

9. Hamdī, *Fī qalbī*.

10. Nāṣir, *Al-Yahūdī*, 148–49.

11. Egyptian scholar Muhammad Sayyid Ahmad Mitwallī locates this change in 2003 and attributes it to a shift in the parameters of the way that Arab-Israeli conflict is perceived. See Mitwallī, "Ṣūrat al-yahūd."

12. El Guabli, *Moroccan Other-Archives*.

13. Pierre Cachia has noticed that in second half of the twentieth century "commitment was now the keyword" ("Critics," 437).

14. Serfaty and Daure-Serfaty, *Mémoire de l'autre*, 73–103.

15. Badawi, "Commitment," 876.

16. Quoted in Badawi, "Commitment," 877.

17. The archetypical plots of these novels usually depict Jews and Muslims as occupying the same neighborhood or national space together before the situation in Palestine causes a rift in their relationships. Sometimes these novels depict Jewish-Muslim couples or love stories, while others depict Jewish-Muslim encounters abroad in neutral spaces. With a few exceptions, novels rarely make any forays into depicting the larger structures that reshaped Jewish-Muslim relations, since most of them focus on local politics and daily interactions, which are the loci in which loss is experienced and confronted.

18. Golbderg, "Interview with Professor Dominick LaCapra."

19. LaCapra, *Writing History*, 70.

20. LaCapra, *Writing History*, ix.

21. LaCapra, *Writing History*, xii.

22. For a longer reflection on my personal experience with Jewish toponymies in Morocco, see El Guabli, "Voies," 107–11.

23. El Guabli, "Voies," 109–10.

24. Aït Moh, *Captif*.

25. Tazi, *Anā al-mansī*.

26. Aourid, *Cintra*.

27. For an analysis for this speech, see Ḍarīf, *Al-aḥzāb*, 40–45.

28. Al-Miliani, *Casanfa*.

29. Hariri, *Shamma*.

30. El Guabli, *Moroccan Other-Archives*.

31. Al-ʿArwī, "ʿAbd Allāh al-ʿArwī muḥ āwiran," 184.

32. Al-ʿArwī, "ʿAbd Allāh al-ʿArwī muḥ āwiran," 185.

33. Khatibi, *Scribe*.

34. Khatibi, *Scribe*, 31.

35. Khatibi, *Scribe*, 34–35.

36. Khatibi, *Scribe*, 36.

37. Simmel and Glissant respectively used the figure of the Jew to theorize both the status of the stranger and rhizomatic identity in their works. See Simmel, *Sociology of Georg Simmel*, 402–8, esp. 404; Glissant, *Poetics of Relation*, 20.

38. The concept comes up in different degrees of detail in Khatibi and Hassoun's *Même livre*; Khatibi, *Figures de l'étranger*; Khatibi, *Féerie*; Khatibi, *Scribe*.

39. Khatibi stressed the fact that "the Jew is always bilingual," adding that he knew many Arab Jews who were named Jacques. See Khatibi and Hassoun, *Même livre*, 140.

40. Khatibi, *Figures de l'étranger*, 141.

41. Khatibi, *Scribe*, 15.

42. Khatibi, *Scribe*, 15

43. Khatibi, *Scribe*, 106.

44. Khatibi, *Maghreb pluriel*, 38.

45. Khatibi, *Scribe*, 106.

46. Khatibi and Hassoun, *Même livre*, 92.

47. Khatibi and Hassoun, *Même livre*, 92.

48. Khatibi and Hassoun, *Même livre*, 79.

49. Khatibi and Hassoun, *Même livre*, 162.

50. Khatibi, *Maghreb pluriel*, 23.

51. Khatibi and Hassoun, *Même livre*, 7.

52. Khatibi, *Scribe*, 103.

53. Khatibi, *Scribe*, 103.

54. Ifrah, *Juifs du Maroc*, n.p.

55. Khatibi and Hassoun, *Même livre*, 123.

56. Khatibi and Hassoun, *Même livre*, 103.

57. Khatibi and Hassoun, *Même livre*, 106.

58. Khatibi and Hassoun, *Même livre*, 106.

59. Khatibi and Hassoun, *Même livre*, 106–7.

60. Laskier, "Jewish Emigration," 323.

61. Kably, *Histoire du Maroc*, 712.

62. Khatibi and Hassoun, *Même livre*, 107.

63. Khatibi and Hassoun, *Même livre*, 107.

64. Khatibi and Hassoun, *Même livre*, 107.

65. Khatibi and Hassoun, *Même livre*, 107.

66. Simmel, *Sociology of Georg Simmel*, 404.

67. Khatibi and Hassoun, *Même livre*, 108.

68. Jmahri, *Communauté juive*, 27.

69. Jmahri, *Communauté juive*, 27.

70. Al-Madīnī, "Al-Yahūdī ʿal-mansī."

71. Khatibi and Hassoun, *Même livre*, 94.

Bibliography

Aït Moh, El Hassane. *Le Captif de Mabrouka*. Paris: L'Harmattan, 2009.

Aourid, Hassan. *Cintra*. Rabat: Tūsnā, 2016.

ʿArwī, ʿAbd Allāh al-. "ʿAbd Allāh al-ʿArwī muḥāwiran." In *ʿAbd Allāh al-ʿArwī: Al-ḥadātha wa-asʾilat al-tārīkh*, edited by Abdelmajid Kaddouri et al., 181–87. Casablanca: Jamiʿat al-Ḥasan al-Thānī al-Muḥammadiyya Kulliyyat al-Ādāb wa-al-ʿUlūm al-Insāniyya Benmsīk, 2007.

Badawi, Muhammad Mustafa. "Commitment in Contemporary Arabic Literature." *Cahiers d'Histoire Mondiale* 14, no. 1 (1972): 858–78.

Bousbia, Safinez, dir. *El Gusto*. 2012. Paris: Zylo, 2012. DVD.

Cachia, Pierre. "The Critics." In *Modern Arabic Literature*, edited by Muhammad Mustafa Badawi et al., 3:417–42. Cambridge: Cambridge University Press, 1992.

Chevalier, Yves. "Les Juifs d'Afrique du Nord Émigration et intégration: À propos de deux ouvrages de Doris Bensimon-Donath." *Revue Française de Sociologie* 14, no. 2 (1973): 271–76.

Ḍarīf, Muḥammad. *Al-aḥzāb al-siyyāsiyya al-maghribiyya*. Casablanca: Ifriqiyya al-Sharq, 1988.

El Guabli, Brahim. *Moroccan Other-Archives: History and Citizenship after State Violence*. New York: Fordham University Press, 2023.

———. "Les Voies et les voix du Maroc Juif." In *Vues du Maroc juif: Formes, lieux, récits*, edited by Nadia Sbari, 107–11. Rabat: Le Fennec, 2021.

Emerman, Marsha, dir. *On the Banks of the Tigris*. 2015. Australia: Ronin Films, 2015. DVD.

Glissant, Édouard. *Poetics of Relation*. Translated by Betsy Wing. Ann Arbor: University of Michigan Press, 1997.

Goblberg, Amos. Interview with Professor Dominick LaCapra, Cornell University. Yad Vashem, June 8, 1998. https://www.yadvashem.org/odot_pdf/Microsoft%20Word%20-%203648.pdf.

Hachkar, Kamal, dir. *Tinghir-Jerusalem: Echoes from the Mellah*. 2013. Paris: Les Films d'un Jour, 2013. DVD.

Hamdi, Khawla. *Fī qalbī unthā ʿibrīyya*. Gizah: Dar Kiyan li-al-Nashr wa-al-Tawzīʿ, 2013.

Hariri, Ibrahim. *Shamma aw Shtrit*. Casablanca: Afrīqia al-Sharq, 2013.

Ifrah, Albert, ed. *Juifs du Maroc: Actes du colloque international sur la communauté juive marocaine: Vie culturelle, histoire sociale et évolution (Paris, 18–21 décembre 1978)*. Paris: Pensée Sauvage, 1980.

Jmahri, Mustapha. *La Communauté juive de la ville d'El Jadida*. El Jadida: Cahiers d'El Jadida, 2013.

Kably, Mohamed, ed. *Histoire du Maroc: Réactualisation et synthèse*. Rabat: Publications de l'Institut Royal pour la Recherche sur l'Histoire du Maroc, 2012.

Khatibi, Abdelkébir. *Féerie d'un mutant*. Monaco: Rocher—serpent à plumes, 2005.

———. *Figures de l'étranger dans la littérature française*. Paris: Éditions Denoël, 1987.

———. *Maghreb pluriel*. Paris: Denoël, 1970.

———. *Le Scribe et son ombre*. Paris: Éditions de la Différence, 2008.

Khatibi, Abdelkébir, and Jacques Hassoun. *Le Même livre*. Paris: Éditions de l'Éclat, 1985.

LaCapra, Dominick. *Writing History, Writing Trauma*. Baltimore: Johns Hopkins University Press, 2014.

Lāmī, Alāʾ al-. "ʿUm Hārūnʾ al-ḥaqīqiyya laysat yahūdiyya . . . wa lam tʿish fī al-kuwayt in ʿAlāʾ." *Al-Akhbar*, May 1, 2020. https://al-akhbar.com/Media_Tv/287999.

Madīnī, Aḥmad al-. "Al-Yahūdī ʿal-mansī' fī mirʾāt al-riwāya al-maghribiyya." *Raseen*, January 25, 2016. http://www.rasseen.com/art.php?id=7aecbf71adfbabbb197caf436b0eb197487858c4.

Miliani, Driss al-. *Casanfa*. Al-Iskandarīyya: Dār al-ʿAyn li-al-Nashr, 2016.

Laskier, Michael M. "Jewish Emigration from Morocco to Israel: Government Policies and the Position of International Jewish Organizations, 1949–56." *Middle Eastern Studies* 25, no. 3 (1989): 323–62.

Mitwallī, Muhammad Sayyid Ahmad. "Ṣūrat al-yahūd fī al-riwāya al-ʿarabiyya al-muʿāṣira ruʾya sardiyya mughāyira." *Risālat al-Mashriq* 34, no. 2 (2019): 63–107.

Nāṣir, Abdul-Jabbār. *Al-Yahūdī al-akhīr*. Cairo: al-Dār al-Miṣriyya al-Lubnāniyya, 2015.

Ouissaden, Mohamed. *ISRAE, Elle* . . . Casablanca: Marsam, 2021.

Riyāḍ, Ḥasan. *Awrāq ʿibrīyya*. Rabat: Maṭbaʿat al-Maʿārif al-Jadīda, 1996.

Ruḥyymm, Kamāl. *Diary of a Jewish Muslim*. Translated by Sarah Enamy. Cairo: American University in Cairo Press, 2014.

Serfaty, Abraham, and Christine Daure-Serfaty. *La Mémoire de l'autre*. Paris: Au Vif, 1992.

Simmel, Georg. *The Sociology of Georg Simmel*. Translated by Kurt Wolff. New York: Free Press, 1950.

Tazi, Mohammad Ezzeddine. *Anā al-mansī*. Casablanca: Al-Markaz al-Thaqāfī al-ʿArabī, 2015.

Wieviorka, Annette. *L'Ère du témoin*. Paris: Plon, 1998.

CHAPTER 2

On the Wrong Side of History

The Jews in Algerian Literature

ABDELKADER AOUDJIT

Given the animosity that exists between the Algerian and Israeli governments, one might expect Algerian writers to portray Jews in the same negative, stereotypical terms as those of their European counterparts. Such is not the case. The "villain Jew" stereotype that pervaded European literature until the middle of the twentieth century is virtually nonexistent in Algerian novels and plays. Overall, Algerian writers' attitude toward Jews is one of benign neglect. Even though there are references to Jews in several Algerian novels, most are peripheral. Jews play important roles only in Rachid Boudjedra's *La Dépossession* (The dispossession; 2017), Waciny Laredj's *Al-Bayt al-andalusī* (The Andalusian house; 2011), Mouloud Mammeri's play *Le Foehn, ou, La Preuve par neuf* (The Foen, or Casting out nines; 1957), Tahar Ouettar's *Al-Zilzāl* (The earthquake; 1974), and Amin Zaoui's *Le Dernier juif de Tamentit* (The last Jew of Tamentit; 2012). Algerian authors depict Jews as native to the country and an indissociable part of Algerian society. They describe the centuries-long harmonious coexistence between them and Muslims and point out that the two communities spoke the same languages and shared many customs and traditions. They also recount the suffering that Muslims and Jews endured and the prejudices and hostility they both faced during the Spanish Inquisition and the French occupation.

An important theme in Algerian literature complicating the relationship between Muslims and Jews is the decision of the Jewish community to side with the French during the War of Independence and of some Jews to take up arms—with the help of the Israeli government—against those who thought of them as their brethren. Those actions, which Algerians perceived and continue to perceive as a betrayal, had a devastating effect on individuals and on Algerian Jews' collective psyche and caused a rift between the two communities so deep that its effects are still being felt today in Algeria. Still, several Algerian novels include feelings of loss and affectionate nostalgia for what many Algerians and Jews perceive as a golden age of Muslim and Jewish peaceful coexistence, when the two communities were supportive of one another. Feelings of loss and lingering nostalgia are especially noticeable in *La Dépossession* and *Le Dernier juif de Tamentit*. A more powerful engagement with loss, however, is to be found in *Al-Zilzāl*, an intriguing and sometimes Kafkaesque novel full of resentment, despair, and many regrets.

At the political level, there are some timid calls for, if not rapprochement with the Jews, opening up a debate on the issue. Indeed, recently the Algerian government invited some prominent Jewish entertainers of Algerian descent such as Robert Castel, Alexandre Arcady, and Roger Hanin to visit the country and rolled out the red carpet for them, and in 2013 it renovated Constantine's synagogue and Jewish cemetery. Furthermore, in 2018 Echourouk TV produced a documentary on Algerian Jews and broadcast it on March 31.[1] Algerians now widely acknowledge the presence of Jews in the country, albeit hiding "behind Arabic names."[2]

The purpose of this essay is to explore how Algerian authors depict the Jews—who have since become either French or Israeli; to highlight the historical events that directly influenced their writings; and to show that what Algerians think of as Jewish betrayal subsumes and ties together all the other themes and makes any attempt at reconciliation between Algerians and their Jews in the near future difficult.

Except for Mammeri's *Le Foehn*, written at the height of the War of Independence, and Ouettar's *Al-Zilzāl*, published in 1974, all the works that mention the Jews in one way or another were written during the past forty years. They belong to a new trend in Algerian literature that seeks to draw attention to previously neglected people and events in history and to transcend the simplistic and hegemonic readings of Algerian history that emphasize one dimension of Algerian identity—Arabic language and culture or Amazigh ancestry, for example—at the expense of others.[3] Previously, Algerian authors were concerned with questions of assimilation and nonassimilation (1893–1945), decolonization and the War of Independence (1945–65), and modernization and its discontents (1965–85). The new Algerian authors are particularly interested in the deconstruction of the colonialist distinction between Arabic speakers and Tamazight speakers as if they were two separate ethnic groups each endowed with simple, unchanging, and constraining identities. Instead of looking at Algerian identity in terms of rigid boundaries, origin, authenticity, and closure, the new Algerian authors propose that national identity be reconceived as a complex and ongoing creative activity in which Amazigh, Muslim, Arab, and other cultural elements meet, change as a result of the encounter, and merge to create a distinct Algerian nation.

Rather than focus on one work in particular, this chapter more usefully brings together information from all of the novels and the play that refer to the Jews to substantiate its thesis. Indeed, even though all the works shed some light on important facets of Algerian-Jewish relations, some, such as Kateb Yacine's *Nedjma* (1956) and Zaoui's *Al-hub qabla qalil* (Love a little while ago; 2015), mention the Jews only in passing. Furthermore, different works concentrate on different historical periods of Algerian history or present specific aspects of the relationship between Algerians and Jews: Boudjedra's *La Dépossession* focuses on World War II and Muslim-Jewish solidarity during that period, Zaoui's *Le Dernier juif de Tamentit* mainly on the Saharan Jews, and Laredj's *Al-Bayt al-anadalusī* on the plight of Muslims and Jews during the Spanish Inquisition. Obviously, therefore, each of these novels and other works alone would not be sufficient, but together they offer a comprehensive view of the issue: they capture the dimensions, subtleties, and contradictions of Algerian-Jewish relations and clarify what the relations were, what they have become and why, and what their prospects for the future are.

Among the Algerian works of literature that talk about the Jews, two in particular stand out: Mammeri's play *Le Foehn* and Ouettar's novel *Al-Zilzāl*. Focusing on the war and its aftermath, they bring to a tragic finale the long and tumultuous history of the Jews in Algeria and highlight their anguished fight against themselves and the world. The former blends humor and bitter truth to describe the difficulty the Jews had piecing together their loyalty to France and the French's prejudices against them; the latter, fusing personal and ethnic destinies, dramatizes the emotional and spiritual cost of the Jews' decision to turn their backs on their history and tradition in order to become French. A section of the chapter is devoted to these two works.

Throughout the chapter the two communities are referred to as "the Muslims" and "the Jews" until the outbreak of the War of Independence in November 1954, when the Jews unequivocally took sides with the partisans of French Algeria and the nationalist leaders lost all hope of rallying them to their cause; from then on "the Algerians" and "the Jews" are used. An Algerian is someone who, in the words of poet Jean Sénac, "has opted for the Algerian nation."[4] The Jews did not; they ceased being Algerian.

THE JEWS ARE INDIGENOUS TO THE MAGHREB

Several Algerian novels address the problem of identity, ethnicity, and origins and make the Jews native to the land and an integral part of Algerian society. One of the more probing examples of this is Kateb's *Nedjma*, where Nedjma, who represents Algeria and with whom the four friends Rachid, Mourad, Lakhdar, and Mustapha are in love, is described as the daughter of a "Jewess from Marseille."[5] A similar idea is found in Yamina Mechakra's novel *La Grotte éclatée* (The exploded cave; 1979), which describes the experience of women during the War of Independence, civilians as well as those who served alongside men in the mountains. The narrator says that she was brought up successively by a Catholic, a Jewish, and then a Muslim family; she was equally at home in Islam, Judaism, and Christianity; and she moved effortlessly from one to another: "I prayed in some houses to our lord Mohamed, in others to Moses or Jesus. . . . On Saturdays, I gave up the dress and the crown of Islam for the dress and the crown of Jews. For me, the sky included three great worlds where I had no borders: that of Moses, that of Jesus, and that of Our Lord Mohamed."[6]

The idea that the Jews are native to the land and were an integral part of Algerian society also plays a significant role in Boudjedra's *La Dépossession*, where he says that the Algerian Jews are "Judaized Berbers,"[7] as well as in Zaoui's *Le Dernier juif de Tamentit*, where he rejects approaches to identity that are based on simplistic and essentialist binary oppositions such as Amazigh/Arab and Muslim/Jewish by showing that the search for authentic identity is futile[8] and by presenting hybrid characters such as Hadj Mimoun and his family members. Laredj, likewise, insists on the complex character of Algerian society and history and the futility of the search for authentic origins. In *Al-Bayt al-andalusī*, the main character, Mourad Basta, whose ancestor, Sidi Ahmed Ben Khalil (Galileo el Rojo), was expelled from Spain during the Inquisition, asks, "Was my grandfather a Christian or a Muslim? Was Soltana [his ancestor's wife] Jewish or Muslim, or neither? Did Marina and Celina [his ancestor's daughter and granddaughter] practice a religion other than that of the love of others? To this day, I do not know and I have not asked anyone to enlighten me on this point. I'll be buried here, no matter who my neighbor is."[9]

Nedjma, La Grotte éclatée, Al-Bayt al-andalusī, La Dépossession, and *Le Dernier juif de Tamentit* are mostly fictional, but they also refer to historical characters and events. Indeed, Jews started migrating from the Middle East to the Maghreb since as far back as the tenth century BCE, when some left the Nile Valley, where Egyptian King Shishak I kept them captive after he sacked Jerusalem in 930 BCE.[10] According to the Romano-Jewish historian Titus Flavius Josephus, another group of Jews sought refuge in the Maghreb to escape from Egypt, where Ptolemy I Soter (366–282 BCE) banished one hundred thousand of them after he invaded Palestine in 301 BCE.[11] A third great wave of Jewish migration to the Maghreb took place after the Romans, under Emperor Titus (30–80 CE), pillaged Jerusalem and destroyed its Great Temple in 70 CE.[12] Another wave of Jewish emigrants made its way to the Maghreb during Emperor Trajan's reign (53–117) in 115 CE, this time in the wake of the violent repression that followed their rebellion in Cyrenaica and Egypt.[13] More Jews moved to the Maghreb in 132 CE after they rebelled a second time in Palestine and Emperor Hadrian, in retaliation, massacred thousands of people and razed Jerusalem to the ground to build a new city. According to Saint Jerome (347–420 CE), there was in his time a chain of Jewish colonies that extended from the Atlantic Coast to the Middle East.[14] The Jews assimilated gradually into the local population, adopting the language and customs of the Imazighen (Amazigh people) while remaining faithful to their religion. Many Imazighen, on the other hand, adopted Judaism, integrating it into their own culture and forging a unique synthesis of tradition and a new religion.[15] According to Arabic-speaking historians Abou Obaid al-Bakri (1014–1094 CE), Mohamed al-Idrissi (1100–1165 CE), Ali ibn Ibizar (d.

1310–1320 CE), and Abderrahamane ibn Khaldoun (1332–1406 CE), many Amazigh tribes were practicing Judaism when the Muslims arrived in the Maghreb.[16] A final set of Jewish migrations took place as a result of their persecution in 1391 CE and their final expulsion from Spain in 1492 CE. The Jews who emigrated to what is now the Maghreb in ancient times are called *Toshavim* (natives), while those who were displaced by the Christian reconquest of Spain are called *Megorashim* (expelled). Many Algerian Jews, especially those who were expelled from Spain, settled in the coastal cities: Algiers, Tlemcen, Bejaia, and Constantine. Others settled in the south of the country: the Touat Valley, Ghardaia, and Laghouat. The Algerian Jews who lived in the south are commonly known as "Saharan Jews."

In addition to depicting the Jews as an important part of Algerian history, Algerian authors point out that Muslims and Jews lived in harmony for many centuries: both groups spoke Arabic and Tamazight, shared the same customs, enjoyed the same music,[17] visited each other's places of pilgrimage, and celebrated births and mourned deaths together.[18] Abraham's family in *Le Dernier juif de Tamentit* even observes Ramadan.[19] To a schoolboy who asks, "So the house was owned by Jews? What brought them to a land of Muslims?" Mourad Basta of *Al-Bayt al-andalusī* replies that Algeria used to be a place where different religious groups—Muslims, Christians, and Jews—mixed and lived together in peace: "This country now belongs to the Muslims, but in the past the same thing that happened to our ancestors happened to the Jews, the fanatic Spaniards burned them or forced them to flee to our country, where they found a certain peace; they lived here like all of us. They worked as craftsmen in the Casbah, Bab Azoun, Bab Djedid, in the Friday souk."[20] In fact, the Algerian Jews distinguished themselves not only by their commercial activities and their diligence as craftsmen, as Laredj rightly notes, but also by their excellence in music as singers of the Andalusian Malouf style of Constantine (Cheikh Raymond Leyris, 1912–1961; Simone Tamar, 1932–1982; Lili Boniche, 1922–2008) as well as of the popular Raï style of western Algeria (Reinette l'Oranaise, 1915–1998; Maurice El Médioni, 1928–).[21]

Besides pointing out that Muslims and Jews lived in harmony, Zaoui, Ouettar, and Boudjedra also make known that Muslims and Jews were involved in romantic and marital relationships across the religious divide. Thus, in *Le Dernier juif de Tamentit*, which focuses on the Saharan Jews, Abraham's Aunt Thamira falls in love with and marries the imam and muezzin of the neighboring town, Tidikelt;[22] in *Al-Zilzāl,* Abdelmadjid Boularouah, the main character, marries Sara, who is Jewish; and in *La Dépossession,* the narrator's father marries, with the blessing of his grandmother, Henriette Gozlan, a Jewish woman "brought back from the Constantine ghetto and who never converted to Islam."[23]

At stake in Algerian literature's treatment of Jews is not merely a description of how Muslims and Jews lived, by and large, peacefully, but the fact that they were joined by suffering and sacrifice that went beyond religion during the Spanish Inquisition and then the French occupation of Algeria. Thus, Zaoui paints a vivid and disturbing portrait of the brutal treatment and exclusion of Muslims and Jews by Christian Spain in *Le Dernier juif de Tamentit.* For example, he explains that Hadj Mimoun's ancestors left Spain after Inquisitors burned Ephraim al-n'Kaoua alive in a street of Seville—or Toledo—in 1391 on the suspicion that he practiced Judaism secretly, and following a hasty trial.[24] Laredj likewise dramatically documents the harrowing lives of Muslims and Jews and their resilience during the Inquisition in *Al-Bayt al-andalusī.* Effectively, during the fourteenth and fifteenth centuries, Spain went through a period of social turmoil and extreme violence directed against Muslims and Jews, including those who converted to Catholicism, known as *Moriscos* and *Marranos,* respectively. Although they identified with Christianity and many pledged allegiance to the Spanish king, the *Moriscos* and *Marranos* were, in the eyes of the Spanish religious authorities, still Muslims and Jews and were subjected to a steady process of dehumanization. They were kept in check through fear and intimidation, forbidden to speak Arabic and Tamazight, thrown into dungeons, and tortured in the most horrendous fashion. Those who were lucky enough to escape torture and murder were expelled to countries around the Mediterranean and faced starvation, disease, and pirates.[25]

Except for the tragic events of 1490 involving Saharan Jews—described by Zaoui in *Le Dernier juif de Tamentit*—when Mohamed ibn Abdelkarim al-Maghili, known for his fanaticism and harsh treatment of Jews, incited a mob to attack the Jews and their Muslim sympathizers and to burn the synagogue of Tamentit,[26] the two communities lived peacefully for centuries. *Le Dernier juif de Tamentit* captures all of this. It is more than a biography of al-Maghili. It is, first, a tale of an intense love affair between two young people, a Jew, Abraham, and a Muslim, Barkahoum, who meet every day at 12:23 at a pizzeria in a trendy neighborhood of Algiers. It is also a semifictional history of a Saharan Jewish family, the Al n'Kaoua. As the novel progresses and the two lovers act out their erotic obsessions, they tell each other stories about their childhoods and adolescences, their families, and their ancestors, mixing fact and fiction, myth and reality. Thus, the novel moves back and forth in time across several generations of Abraham's family, chronicling its successes and failures in search of a place to call home. It starts with the wise man Ephraim Al n'Kaoua, who is murdered during the Inquisition. The saga of the family continues with the adventures of physician and philosopher Ephraim Jr., who rides a lion from Marrakech to Tlemcen in 1391 using a snake as a bridle. He heals the ailing daughter of the sultan, Abou Tashfin, endears himself to him, and, as a reward, the sultan allows the family to settle in the city and build a synagogue. The family's odyssey ends in Tamentit, its final destination.

THE FIRST RUPTURE BETWEEN THE MUSLIMS AND THE JEWS: THE DÉCREE CRÉMIEUX OF 1870

The relationship between Muslims and Jews started to become complicated after the French occupation of Algeria in 1830, and especially after the Décree Crémieux of October 24, 1870, which granted the thirty-seven thousand northern, but not Saharan, Algerian Jews French citizenship with most, but not all, its associated privileges and legal protections. The decree was intended to make the Jews who benefited from it loyal to France and to divide the native population. While the European settlers and many mainland French rejected the Decree,[27] as did the Algerian rabbis,[28] most Jews welcomed it enthusiastically. The Muslims, on the other hand, met it with indifference; they did not think that granting French citizenship to the Jews would change their own conditions in any way.[29]

Citizenship, however, only partly mitigated the discrimination and prejudices that the Jews were subjected to during the French occupation of the country. It did not put an end to the visceral anti-Semitism of the European settlers; to the contrary, it exacerbated it. As the narrator's father puts it in Boudjedra's *La Dépossession,* "That's when the anti-Semitic wave hit our Jewish brethren. Already in 1870! Yes that's it . . . The Pieds-Noirs [European settlers] didn't want the Jews and they . . . They didn't wait until 1940! Oh no! This was already the case in 1870."[30] In reality, even though the Jews were no longer classified as natives, abandoned their Algerian names, and imitated French dress and habits, they did not become, in practice, the equals of the Europeans.[31] They continued to face legal discrimination—city halls many times refused to register Jewish births and marriages on fabricated legal grounds[32]—and to endure attacks in everyday life because the Europeans, who controlled the politics and economy of the country, refused to give up their position of dominance.[33] Soon after the promulgation of the Decree, anti-Semitic organizations led by Edouard Drumond demanded its abrogation, and anti-Semitic newspapers such as *L'Antijuif algérien* (The Algerian anti-Jew), *La Silhouette* (The silhouette), and *Petit Africain* (Little African) began a campaign of propaganda and intimidation against the Jews.[34] Fanaticized, the Europeans waited eagerly for an opportunity to strike. The 1894 Dreyfus affair, about an Alsatian Jewish captain who was court-martialed for allegedly passing military secrets to Germany and sentenced to life imprisonment, gave them the excuse they needed to launch terrorist attacks against the Jews. In 1897, radical anti-Semites won local elections in Constantine and in several other towns after they had already won in Oran in 1886.[35] The Europeans' hatred of Jews erupted into violence soon after. On May 17, armed gangs of Europeans looted the Jewish quarter of Mostaganem; and from May 20 to 22 they vandalized Jewish businesses in Oran. The publication of novelist Émile Zola's open letter *J'accuse*, in which he accused the French authorities of anti-Semitism, triggered even more violent actions in Algiers between January 20 and 25, 1898. Mobs of Europeans assaulted Jews, looted their shops, and burned their synagogue, under the indifferent eyes of the police and army—staffed by many anti-Dreyfusards, and with the complicity of the Catholic Church. Similar attacks took place in Blida, Boufarik, and Sétif. No Muslim participated in any of those acts of aggression and vandalism.[36]

MUSLIMS AND JEWS UNITED IN MISERY: WORLD WAR II

In 1940, the Vichy government, which participated in the deportation of seventy-six thousand Jews from France to death camps in Germany, revoked the Décree Crémieux, stripping Algerian Jews of their citizenship. The Jews again became the targets of open official discrimination and persecution. The government banned them from the civil service, limited their access to schools, universities, and certain businesses and professions, and allowed their property to be seized.[37] A *numerus clausus* (law) by the Vichy government reduced the quota of Jews in medical professions to 2 percent. Another law forbade medical professionals from practicing in Muslim neighborhoods, but they defied the order in a show of solidarity with the Muslims.[38] Yet another law banned the Jews from European markets.[39] As if these harsh measures were not enough, the government sent thousands of Jews to forced labor camps throughout Algeria.[40] In the beginning of 1941, hordes of overexcited Europeans carried out pogroms against Jews in all the major cities of Algeria. In Algiers, they burned Jewish houses and businesses and assaulted, humiliated, killed, and raped dozens of Jews. The Muslims "were appalled and hid Jewish families as they could."[41]

This widespread persecution of the Jews that swept the country under Vichy and their deportation to labor camps, where they "performed the most arduous work,"[42] are other major themes of Boudjedra's *La Dépossession*. The novel examines the effects of a complex and turbulent history on Muslims and Jews, focusing on the narrator, his father, his uncle, and their Jewish friends and business partners Jacob Timsit and his father-in-law, Abraham Serfati. Boudjedra calls attention to the fact that the Muslims suffered the same kind of indignities as the Jews under the Vichy regime by pointing out that the narrator's uncle, Ismaël, and Jacob Timsit "were locked up between 1940 and 1942."[43] He further makes clear that both Muslims and Jews were victims of hatred and prejudice on the part of the relatively poor European immigrants from France, Italy, Spain, and Malta throughout the duration of the French presence in Algeria: "[Those] who starved to death in France, Italy, Spain and elsewhere came in the vans of the French army in 1830. They had quickly become the most ferocious scoundrels of colonization and the worst tyrants. They hated the indigenous population, abused it, despised it, and hated the Jews, especially the Jews . . . forgetful that they were of their recent past when they scratched the ground for food in Sicily, Sardinia, and Malta, or when they vegetated in the big cities, burdened by unemployment, disease, and the humiliations of their bosses."[44]

THE SECOND AND FINAL RUPTURE BETWEEN THE MUSLIMS AND THE JEWS: THE WAR OF INDEPENDENCE

The history of Algerian Jews took yet another turn with the War of Independence (1954–62). At the beginning of the war, the Front de Libération Nationale (National Liberation Front, FLN) leaders called on the Algerian

Jews to join them in their fight against colonialism, calling them "compatriots" and "Algerian brothers."[45] They reminded them of the centuries-long peaceful coexistence between the Muslims and the Jews, their many common customs, and the help and protection that the Muslims provided them in World War II. They also reminded them of the segregation, indignities, and pogroms they suffered at the hands of the Europeans and the latter's visceral anti-Semitism.[46] Despite repeated appeals, however, only a handful of Jews, among them William Sportisse, Pierre Ghenaïssia, Daniel Timsit, Maurice Laban, and Henri Alleg, joined the Armée de Libération Nationale (National Liberation Army, ALN). It is to these Jewish militants that Boudjedra alludes by means of Jacob Timsit and his family in *La Dépossession*[47] and Zaoui by means of Abraham's parents, who took to the mountains,[48] and his uncle Rislane, who sewed uniforms for the combatants in *Le Dernier juif de Tamentit.*[49] For their part, the leaders of the Jewish community adamantly refused to join the fight against the colonialists, arguing that while "interesting," the FLN initiative was "inadmissible in the actual state of affairs."[50] They proclaimed loud and clear: "We are French, we are republican, we are liberal, and we are Jewish."[51] Even though they sided with the French, most Jews did not openly oppose the FLN and did not engage in acts of violence against the Muslims. Many, however, eager to prove their loyalty to France, became vehemently hostile toward them. In fact, some became among the most antagonistic to the independence of Algeria and, paradoxically, joined the right-wing and rabidly anti-Semitic terrorist group Organisation Armée Secrète (Secret Armed Organization, OAS), which for two years murdered thousands of people—mainly Muslims—set off bombs, and burned public buildings, including the library of the University of Algiers.[52]

To further complicate the matter, as early as 1955, Mossad, the Israeli spy agency, had formed and armed, with the connivance of the French authorities, several Jewish militias that engaged in violent terror campaigns against Muslims in Algiers, Oran, and Constantine.[53] It is likely that either Mossad or right-wing Europeans were behind the assassination of the famous Jewish musician Raymond Leiris on July 22, 1956. The Muslim population and the FLN had nothing to gain from it, but the French needed a scapegoat, so they broadcast that Muslims killed Leiris, hoping to set the two native communities against each other. They succeeded, as the news ignited an explosion of anger and attacks and counterattacks raged between

Muslims and Jews in Constantine for several days, much to the delight of the Europeans. To stir up discord was a constant tactic of the right-wing Europeans and Mossad.

The French military authorities in Algiers, who were no friends of the Muslims and the FLN, concluded after an investigation that the burning of the Algiers synagogue in 1960, which some blamed on Muslims, was the work of right-wing settlers,[54] as was the murder of Henri Chakroun on September 1961, according to Jewish ex-OAS militant Henri Chemouilli.[55] The real danger to the Jews in Algeria in those turbulent years came, as Émile Touati explains, from "what we call down there the 'colons,' French people, and more often 'neo-French,' and not some proclaimed natural sentiment of the [Muslim] masses."[56]

STORIES OF BETRAYAL: MOULOUD MAMMERI'S *LE FOEHN* AND TAHAR OUETTAR'S *AL-ZILZĀL*

That the Jews wanted to become French was no surprise. In the decades following the Décree Crémieux and until the independence of Algeria, many Jews were obsessed with integrating into French society, believing that the only way they could do so was to reject their heritage and sacrifice all aspects of their identity that distinguished them from Europeans. They adopted French habits and customs with an evangelical zeal: they dressed like the French,[57] took up their lifestyle, changed or Gallicized their names,[58] and started calling bar mitzvahs "communions" and synagogues "temples." To their great resentment and disappointment, however, the French would not accept them as fully their own and considered them, at best, parasites. What did not make sense to the Muslims was that the Jews would ignore French anti-Semitic acts of discrimination and brutality and, more importantly, would turn against the Muslims. Because the Jews experienced oppression, one would expect them to empathize with and understand the Algerians' struggle for freedom, but that was not the case.

It is the attitude of those Jews who were caught in the uncomfortable position of not really belonging to either Algeria or France but who stopped at nothing to please the French that Mouloud Mammeri satirizes in *Le Foehn*. He is not entirely unsympathetic to his anonymous Jewish character's plight, however. After watching or reading the play, one feels that the Jewish character is more to be pitied than blamed. The satire is also directed at the Europeans, who claim patriotism, godliness, and respectability while harassing and demeaning Muslims and Jews.

Le Foehn is a powerful and moving dramatization of real events that happened during the Battle of Algiers in 1957. However, the play is more than a polemic against the injustices of colonialism; it is also an absorbing and provocative story involving real people: Tarik, his mother, Zohra, and his sister, Aïni, on the one hand, and on the other hand, Brudieu, who is both mayor and military commander, his daughter, Brigitte, his mistress, Giovanna, and his hatchet man, Baldacci, who is of Italian descent. They all have complex inner lives but at the same time exemplify particular attitudes toward the revolution. The struggles between the two families and between father and daughter are microcosms of the larger political conflicts. Tarik's family represents Algerians united against the colonialists, Brudieu represents right-wing European settlers, and Brigitte represents the liberal intellectuals and professionals who preach cohabitation in a system where the 10 percent European minority has more rights and fewer duties than the 90 percent Algerian majority—casting out nines. Events quickly move the characters toward an inevitable confrontation. In the second act, Brudieu learns of a plot against him and decides to turn the tables on the FLN militant who is behind it and who is later executed. To lay the blame on the Algerian laborers and also to collect insurance money, Brudieu sets his own vineyards on fire. He also gathers his farmhands in a farcical show of allegiance to him and to France.

At the meeting, Brudieu proclaims, "Gentlemen, it is good to see you again. We are here among Frenchmen, among good Frenchmen, Catholics and Muslims mixed together." Baldacci whispers into Brudieu's ears, "Sir, there is a Jew in the crowd." Brudieu's answer is quick and unequivocal; without even lifting his eyes to the face of the Jew, he tells Baldacci, "What's he doing here? Get him out." Baldacci replies that they should not be too direct: "We need a pretext." Brudieu keeps suggesting excuses to get rid of the unwanted guest, but none of them is satisfactory. First he advises Baldacci to tell the Jew that "there is a charge to attend the meeting." Baldacci replies, "He is rich." Brudieu then instructs his lieutenant to tell the Jew that the meeting "is reserved for war veterans." Baldacci answers that he saw the Jew's card: "Military medal, and two citations." Still, Brudieu refuses to acknowledge the Jew and downplays his contribution to the French military. He says, "He earned them in the service corps." Baldacci retorts,

"Campaigns of Tunisia, Italy, France, Germany." Weary, Baldacci sighs, "Poor France!" Changing tactics, Brudieu proclaims, "Regardless of race or religion, Catholics, Israelites, and Muslims mingled, as there may be several beliefs among the French, but there is only one France." Oblivious to the hostility around him, the Jew shouts, "Long live France!" Brudieu sternly rebukes him: "But we are not here to wax lyrical. Literature we leave to the Frankaouis [mainland French]."[59]

At one point Baldacci launches a vitriolic rant against communists, socialists, and Jews, openly advocating the extermination of the last: "There are too many rotten things in France. . . . One cannot build on what's rotten. Before taking a trowel, one must first wield the sword, the machine gun and the flame. . . . One must sweep, clean, start fresh, kill, cut, slash, burn, up, down, everywhere. . . . The communists executed! The Jews in the oven, the socialists in jail."[60] Still unmoved, the Jew continues to turn a deaf ear to the assembly's hostility and threats; he yells, "What about the motion?"[61] After Baldacci tells him that it is the Jew again, Brudieu answers, without looking at the unwelcome intruder, "No wonder. I told you: you should have sent him to the chief rabbi."[62]

Throughout the duration of the meeting, the Jew is ridiculed and humiliated by the very people he wants to please, but will not give up; he constantly interrupts the speaker, looking for signs of approval. He believes that showing hostility toward the FLN will endear him to the assembly, but to no avail, despite his best efforts. He is painfully unable to understand what is going on or to find the moral energy to react because, first, he may be a victim of self-hatred and have a tendency to self-destruct; second, he has a prescient feeling that the collapse of the colonialist regime is near and is panicked by the possibility of losing whatever privileges he has; or third, he has been totally co-opted by the colonialist rhetoric. Most likely he thinks and behaves the way he does for all the above reasons. He is a disconnected and alienated person.

The Jews' betrayal of Algerians, with its accompanying issues such as the tension between the drive toward becoming French and loyalty to one's ethnic group, and its devastating effects on the Jewish soul are also an important theme of Tahar Ouettar's *Al-Zilzāl*. This novel tells the story of the return to Constantine from Algiers of landowner Abdelmadjid Boularouah, who is in search of relatives among whom to divide his estate to avoid it being nationalized in the context of the agrarian reform of 1971.

He walks, rambles, and staggers through the streets of the city, railing against everything and everyone. His thoughts go back and forth between past and present as what he sees triggers flashbacks to his childhood. Amid his rage and hallucinations is a great sense of loss. He yearns for the quaint Constantine that he thinks has disappeared and been invaded by debauched hordes from the countryside and given way to crowds, industry, and sheer commercialism. He weeps for Sara, his Jewish ex-wife, and for himself, and wishes he had been nicer to her (140);[63] he laments the disappearance of the Jewish neighborhood and wonders if Constantine would have remained the beautiful city it used to be if the Jews had stayed (148). Yet, deep in himself, he knows that the world will never be the same again.

Boularouah recounts that there were sometimes clashes, often instigated by Europeans, between Muslims and Jews during the War of Independence. He contrasts the nobility of spirit of his father, who prevented his workers from killing his Jewish prisoner during one of their confrontations, to the total lack of sympathy of the latter, who he feels would not have hesitated to execute his adversary if the roles had been reversed (175–76).

More importantly, Boularouah claims that the Jews made two grave mistakes. The first was when, obsessed with moving up to a position of power and status, they went against the Jewish commercial tradition by becoming civil servants and landowners. This "conversion," he believes, put an end to their hegemony over all aspects of commercial activity in the country, especially the east: "They were the kings of Constantine, dictating to the inhabitants of the city their line of conduct: all the east of the country was devoted to them. They decided how many gold teeth were suitable, and people acquiesced. They fixed the amount of gold the bride should carry with her, and their decision was carried out. They specified the kind of material to wear according to the seasons and circumstances. They asserted their dominance in all branches of commerce and, despite all this, they chose to submit to the supreme interest of colonialism" (193).

According to Boularouah, the Jews made an even graver mistake when they aligned themselves with the colonialists and espoused their political vision. In fact, most refused to help in the war effort and cared little for the plight of the Muslims even though they faced prejudice enough on their own. Instead they became aggressive, at times even more aggressive than the French: "As for the Jews, they cut the bridges behind them. Unfaithful to a long practice, they made a mistake. They misunderstood the unfolding of history, their intelligence betrayed them. While in France they retained their personality, here in Algeria they abandoned it to assimilate to the French, to present themselves as proud and haughty colonialists" (192–93).

In both cases the Jews went against their past, their traditions, and their very Jewishness. First, because it is not only religion but also commerce that constitutes the collective heritage of the Jews in *Al-Zilzāl*. Jewishness and commerce, according to Boularouah, have always gone hand in hand: "The thesis according to which Judaism is a mindset born from the practice of commerce envisaged as the only means of making a living; according to which any person or collectivity can be Judaized, to one degree or another, if it adopts trade as the only livelihood. . . . This thesis is not so far from the truth" (193–94). Second, according to Boularouah, by failing to acknowledge the Algerians' commitment to their culture and history and their persistence in their struggle for national independence, the Jews forgot that it was this same kind of attachment to cultural and spiritual heritage that enabled them to survive prejudice, discrimination, and pogroms with resilience and fortitude throughout their history. In Boularouah's words, the Jews "have not been able to forge a personal vision of the future of this people [Algerians]. And yet, for millennia, have they not safeguarded the qualities which made of them a people and a nation?" (193). In sum, the Jews let down both the Muslims and themselves.

Just like the pathetic Jewish character of *Le Foehn*, many, if not most, Algerian Jews would not admit that "assimilation" was an illusion, a psychological genocide that robbed them of their personality while preventing them from being fully accepted by the French. "One fine day," Boularouah says, "they saw themselves packing their suitcases and leaving more or less loaded with luggage, desperate, they fled, sharing the fate of the French," but "they were pushed back" (193) and had no idea of the hostility that awaited them on the other side of the Mediterranean.

The Jews' irrepressible urge to move up to a position of power led to a disaster. As a result of being rejected by the people to whom they thought they belonged, turning their backs on Algeria, and cutting themselves off from their ethnic tradition, they were left without a sense of identity or direction. As Boularouah puts it, "When, wounded and bruised, the

French were forced to leave, the Jews had to follow them, taking away in the rout the debris of their Judaism" (194). He concludes, "The Jews of Algeria lacked insight. Of all the Jews in the world, they were the least intelligent. They were not real Jews" (194).

The Jewish community's decision to side with the French not only had a devastating effect on the Jewish collective psyche but was perceived and continues to be perceived by Algerians as a betrayal. The Jews' attitude and actions were all the more disconcerting considering that Algerians not only did not take part in anti-Jewish pogroms but defended the Jews in World War II. In fact, shortly after the abrogation of the Décree Crémieux, the German and Vichy governments asked the inhabitants of Algeria to help them liquidate Jewish businesses in the context of what they called "the economic Aryanization" of the country.[64] The Europeans needed no urging; thousands of them submitted applications.[65] The Muslims, on the other hand, behaved in an exemplary manner throughout the war. No Muslim took part in the liquidation of Jewish companies and none bid to buy them.[66] According to Pierre-Jean Le Foll-Luciani, a spy who talked to the Oulémas (Muslim religious scholars) reported in July 1940 that the Muslims refused adamantly to be used by some Frenchmen to stir up tensions and conflict between them and the Jews.[67] Furthermore, the rector of the Paris mosque, Kaddour Benghabrit, hid adult Jews in the basement of the mosque and gathered them in women's prayer rooms—forbidden to men—during police and German military raids. Benghabrit also sent Jewish children to stay with the Muslim families who lived on the mosque's campus, and gave many people counterfeit birth certificates asserting their identity as Muslims, to enable them to escape deportation to Nazi death camps.[68] In addition, all the Muslim nationalist organizations and parties condemned the new anti-Jewish laws and objected vehemently to the way the Jews were treated.[69] Algiers councilman Ben Brimath openly dissociated himself from what he called "the fanatical politics" of Mayor Regis.[70] Finally, the Muslims did not see any objection to Jews recovering their citizenship after the war ended. As nationalist leader Ferhat Abbas put it, "We are not opposed to the Jews' efforts to recuperate their rights as French citizens.... We do not want equality by lowering their status to meet ours."[71] Cheikh al-Okbi of the Association des Oulémas Algériens (Algerian Association of Religious Scholars, AOMA) and Messali Hadj, the leader of the Parti du

Peuple Algérien (Algerian People's Party, PPA), likewise rejected "equality from below."[72]

The Algerians' refusal to obey Vichy's edicts and to join in the anti-Semitic hysteria that took over Algeria in World War II is depicted by Boudjedra in *La Dépossession*, where the narrator describes his father and other members of his family as staunch defenders of Jews. He says that his father was an admirable man who endangered his own life and future to help them; "He opposed the wave of anti-Semitism that ravaged the country's Jewish community" and "was sent to prison very often and for the slightest offense."[73] The narrator further explains that "during the first two years of Vichy," his father "went to visit his Jewish friends scattered in camps across the country (124 camps where almost all Algerian Jews were jammed opened)."[74] He adds that his family never hesitated to help their Jewish friends in times of dire need: "Mr. Timsit and his father-in-law Mr. Serfati hid for a moment in Bougie in the superb Turkish villa of the family of Lalla Khadija (Uncle Ismaël's wife). They remained there for two months and it was there that they were arrested by the police."[75] Finally, he points out that his uncle Ismaël befriended "the two men of Jewish faith,"[76] Timsit and Serfati, when he was a supervisor of the camp where they were detained, and made them his business partners after they were released: "One was to join his accounting firm and the other to become his banker in charge of the financial monitoring of the consulting firm, in association with Mr. Kader."[77] During World War II the Jews reciprocated in kind Muslims' solidarity with them: many Jewish doctors and nurses continued caring for Muslim patients, defying the ban on practicing in Muslim neighborhoods imposed by the Vichy government,[78] and Jewish notables made donations to Muslim charities despite their own financial difficulties.[79]

La Dépossession is not just a tale of war and suffering, it is also a powerful testimony to Muslim and Jewish solidarity as they struggled together against Nazism and colonialism. It is a deep, nostalgic, and emotional look at a heroic period of Algerian history.

PROSPECTS FOR RECONCILIATION BETWEEN ALGERIANS AND JEWS

Sixty years after the war, the memory of many Jews' unfortunate decision to side with the French remains alive in Algerians' collective consciousness.

In Laredj's *Al-Bayt al-andalusī*, whenever someone suggests inviting Jewish entertainers who were born and grew up in Algeria to sing in the new cabaret, the authorities reply that the request is unacceptable because the Jews were complicit with the colonialists and still hold a grudge against Algeria: "No . . . no . . . no! It's not appropriate. . . . He ate from the same dish as the murderers of our children, and he toasted to their health. When he proposed another, with a rich record as a musician, the same officials jumped in their seats: 'Where do you come from, Mr. Mohamed? The man is forbidden to stay here. A Jew! As soon as he is on the other side of the sea, he insults Algeria and dirties it in front of its enemies at home and abroad.'"[80]

The officials' firm and unequivocal answer to the cabaret's owner sums up precisely how Algerians feel about the Jews and how complicated their relationship with them still is despite the initiatives undertaken recently by the Algerian government, such as the renovation of Constantine's synagogue and Jewish cemetery.

The Algerians' feelings toward Jews are reinforced by the Israeli government's hostility toward Algeria throughout the duration of the War of Independence: it supported, strangely enough, the anti-Semitic European terrorist organization OAS, which murdered thousands of people, mainly Muslims;[81] it established an armed organization known as the Misgeret (Framework) that terrorized Muslims all over the country for years;[82] and it consistently voted against Algerian independence at the UN.[83] Israeli prime minister David Ben-Gurion suggested to French president Charles de Gaulle that he divide Algeria into European and Muslim areas, giving the Europeans the fertile and rich coastal regions and confining the Muslims to the arid mountains and highlands of the interior.[84] The Algerians have not forgotten Israel's alliance with their worst enemies.

The memory of the Jews' position during the War of Independence remains fresh, making their rehabilitation in the eyes of Algerians unlikely in the near future. The novels and play analyzed in this chapter capture all the layers of the breakup and all the complexity of emotions the situation has generated: anger and disappointment, but also yearning for past times. They show that by siding with the French who mistreated and rejected them and turning their back on their fellow Algerians, the Algerian Jews not only caused a deep rift between the two communities but also betrayed their Jewishness. They were on the wrong side of history.

Notes

1. Soltane, "Echourouk News."
2. Zaoui, *Al-hub*, 209.
3. Aoudjit, *Algerian Historical Novel.*
4. Sénac, *Le Soleil*, 20.
5. Kateb, *Nedjma*, 111–12.
6. Mechakra, *Grotte éclatée*, 33.
7. Boudjedra, *Dépossession*, 145.
8. For example, Abraham, one of the narrators, is not certain what his "real" name is (Abraham, Ibrahim, or Salim) and does not want to know the origin of "Abraham"; Zaoui, *Dernier juif*, 11, 121–22, 124.
9. Laredj, *al-Bayt*, 10.
10. Chenouf, *Juifs d'Algérie*, 143; Meynier, *Algérie des origines*, 46–47.
11. Chenouf, *Juifs d'Algérie*, 18; Meynier, *Algérie des origines*, 47.
12. Meynier, *Algérie des origines*, 74.
13. Chenouf, *Juifs d'Algérie*, 18; Meynier, *Algérie des origines*, 74.
14. Chenouf, *Juifs d'Algérie*, 20; Meynier, *Algérie des origines*, 74.
15. Meynier, *Algérie des origines*, 47.
16. Chenouf, *Juifs d'Algérie*, 20.
17. Zaoui, *Al-hub*, 93.
18. Zaoui, *Dernier juif*, 29, 33, 37, 97, 122.
19. Zaoui, *Dernier juif*, 23.
20. Laredj, *Al-Bayt*, 140.
21. Aous, *Musiques d'Algérie*, 127–28.
22. Zaoui, *Dernier juif*, 52.
23. Boudjedra, *Dépossession*, 74.
24. Zaoui, *Dernier juif*, 42.
25. Laredj, *Al-Bayt*, 57–58.
26. Gwarzo, "Life and Teachings," 51; Zaoui, *Dernier juif*, 60, 130–31.
27. Chenouf, *Juifs d'Algérie*, 97.
28. Chenouf, *Juifs d'Algérie*, 76.
29. Kaddache, *Algérie des Algériens*, 476–77.
30. Boudjedra, *Dépossession*, 170.
31. Le Foll-Luciani, *Juifs algériens*, 35.
32. Chenouf, *Juifs d'Algérie*, 97.
33. Le Foll-Luciani, *Juifs algériens*, 40–41.
34. Chenouf, *Juifs d'Algérie*, 80.
35. Chenouf, *Juifs d'Algérie*, 80.
36. Chenouf, *Juifs d'Algérie*, 80.
37. Chenouf, *Juifs d'Algérie*, 86; Le Foll-Luciani, *Juifs algériens*, 162.
38. Le Foll-Luciani, *Juifs algériens*, 84–85.
39. Le Foll-Luciani, *Juifs algériens*, 85.
40. Le Foll-Luciani, *Juifs algériens*, 91.
41. Boudjedra, *Dépossession*, 160.
42. Chenouf, *Juifs d'Algérie*, 86.
43. Chenouf, *Juifs d'Algérie*, 36.
44. Chenouf, *Juifs d'Algérie*, 56–57.
45. Chenouf, *Juifs d'Algérie*, 141, 159.
46. Chenouf, *Juifs d'Algérie*, 159.
47. Boudjedra, *Dépossession*, 15, 45, 106–7.
48. Zaoui, *Dernier juif*, 111–12.
49. Zaoui, *Dernier juif*, 86.
50. Chenouf, *Juifs d'Algérie*, 141.
51. Soltane, "Echourouk News."
52. Chenouf, *Juifs d'Algérie*, 142; Le Foll-Luciani, *Juifs algériens*, 197–98.
53. Laskier, "Israel and Algeria," 11–12.
54. Chenouf, *Juifs d'Algérie*, 141.
55. Chenouf, *Juifs d'Algérie*, 143; Le Foll-Luciani, *Juifs algériens*, 198.
56. Touati, "Perspectives," 12.
57. Le Foll-Luciani, *Juifs algériens*, 49.
58. Chenouf, *Juifs d'Algérie*, 193–94.
59. All quotations in this paragraph are from Mammeri, *Foehn*, 47.
60. Mammeri, *Foehn*, 50.
61. Mammeri, *Foehn*, 51.
62. Mammeri, *Foehn*, 51.
63. Subsequent parenthetical page references in this section are to Ouettar, *Al-Zilzāl*.
64. Le Foll-Luciani, *Juifs algériens*, 84.
65. Le Foll-Luciani, *Juifs algériens*, 84.
66. Chenouf, *Juifs d'Algérie*, 87.
67. Le Foll-Luciani, *Juifs algériens*, 82.
68. Monnier, "Résistance," 43.
69. Le Foll-Luciani, *Juifs algériens*, 83.
70. Chenouf, *Juifs d'Algérie*, 103.
71. Stora, *Trois exils*, 97.
72. Le Foll-Luciani, *Juifs algériens*, 101.
73. Boudjedra, *Dépossession*, 169–70.
74. Boudjedra, *Dépossession*, 170.
75. Boudjedra, *Dépossession*, 135.
76. Boudjedra, *Dépossession*, 113.
77. Boudjedra, *Dépossession*, 113.
78. Le Foll-Luciani, *Juifs algériens*, 85.
79. Le Foll-Luciani, *Juifs algériens*, 85.
80. Laredj, *Al-Bayt*, 345–46.
81. Laskier, "Israel and Algeria," 7.
82. Laskier, "Israel and Algeria," 2.
83. Laskier, "Israel and Algeria," 2.
84. Laskier, "Israel and Algeria," 2.

Bibliography

Aoudjit, Abdelkader. *The Algerian Historical Novel: Linking the Past to the Present and Future*. New York: Peter Lang, 2020.

Aous, Rachid. *Musiques d'Algérie*. Toulouse: Presses Universitaires du Mirail, 2002.

Boudjedra, Rachid. *La Dépossession*. Tizi Ouzou: El-Ikhtilef, 2017.

Chenouf, Aissa. *Les Juifs d'Algérie: 2000 ans d'existence*. Algiers: El-Maarifa, 2004.

Gwarzo, Hassan I. "The Life and Teachings of al-Maghili, with Particular References to the Saharan Jewish Community." PhD diss., University of London, 1972.

Kaddache, Mahfoud. *L'Algérie des Algériens: De la préhistoire à 1954*. Paris: Paris-Méditerranée, 2003.

Kateb, Yacine. *Nedjma*. Paris: Seuil, 1956.

Laredj, Waciny. *Al-Bayt al-andalusī*. Beirut: Dar al-jamal, 2011.

Laskier, Michael M. "Israel and Algeria amid French Colonialism and the Arab-Israeli Conflict, 1954–1978." *Israel Studies* 6, no. 2 (2001): 1–32.

Le Foll-Luciani, Pierre-Jean. *Les Juifs algériens dans la lutte anticoloniale: Trajectoires dissidentes (1934–1965)*. Rennes: Presses Universitaires de Rennes, 2015.

Mammeri, Mouloud. *Le Foehn, ou La Preuve par neuf*. Paris: Publisud, 1957.

Mechakra, Yamina. *La Grotte éclatée*. Algiers: SNED, 1979.

Meynier, Gilbert. *L'Algérie des origines: De la préhistoire à l'avènement de l'Islam*. Paris: La Découverte, 2007.

Monnier, Vincent. "La Résistance de l'esprit." *Le Nouvel Observateur*, October 18, 2007.

Ouettar, Tahar. *Al-Zilzāl*. Algiers: SNED, 1974.

Sénac, Jean. *Le Soleil sous les armes: Eléments d'une poésie de la résistance algérienne*. Rodez: Subervie, 1957.

Soltane, Amira. "Echourouk News produit un documentaire sur les juifs d'Algérie." *L'Expression*, March 19, 2018.

Stora, Benjamin. *Les Trois exils: Juifs d'Algérie*. Paris: Hachette, 2006.

Touati, Émile. "Perspectives Nord-Africaines." *Évidences: Revue Publique sous l'égide de l'American Jewish Committee* 6, no. 42 (1954): 12.

Zaoui, Amin. *Le Dernier juif de Tamentit*. Algiers: Barzakh, 2012.

———. *Al-hub qabla qalil*. Algiers: El-Ikhtilef, 2015.

CHAPTER 3

Literary Representations of Jews in Twenty-First-Century Arabic Literature in Egypt

MOSTAFA HUSSEIN

In June 2018, the Egyptian parliament approved the revised law of antiquities proposed by Minister of Antiquities Khāled Al-ʿAnānī. Among the major revisions was redefining the missions carried out by "the authorized committee" of the Supreme Council of Antiquities, whose task was to preserve and maintain artifacts in the entire country. In the newly revised law, the authorized committee is defined as "a committee that relates to Egyptian, Greek, and Romanian artifacts, or that relates to Islamic, Coptic, or Jewish artifacts." The revisions, compared to the 1983 version of the law, integrate "Jewish artifacts," whereas previously the committee's mission was limited to Islamic and Coptic archaeological sites and artifacts in addition to those dated from the Greek and Romanian historical periods in Egypt. The conservation of and the supervising over Jewish sites previously was administered within the division of Islamic archaeology. This was an affirmative step toward the inclusion of Jewish artifacts in the country's cultural heritage. A few months later, the minister of antiquities announced the allocation of a special budget for the restoration and renovation of Jewish synagogues in Egypt. In February 2020, the Egyptian government celebrated the grand reopening of Eliyahu Hanavi synagogue, one of Egypt's oldest synagogues, located on Nabi Daniel Street in downtown Alexandria, after two years of renovation and restoration work.[1] This new direction taken by the government aimed at protecting and promoting the Egyptian national ethos and pushing back against demands from international Jewish organizations to fund renovating the Jewish monuments in the country.[2] About the motivations behind the renewed Egyptian interest in the country's Jewish heritage, Al-ʿAnānī publicly stated, "We do not want anyone to offer us money to renovate our past."[3] This statement indicates the patriotic nature of this kind of project. It denounces interventions from international organizations that have criticized the country for neglecting the history and the culture of Jews in Egypt, guided by a genuine interest in the Jewish past in Egypt as far as it buttresses the Egyptian ethos by displaying the country as pluralistic and cosmopolitan and, as popularly known, *um el-dunya* (the mother of the world).[4]

The government's plans to restore Jewish monuments triggered multiple responses from local Egyptians on social media. The Israeli embassy in Cairo and its Facebook group, Israel in Egypt, welcomed the announcement of additional funds in support of Jewish cultural sites. Commenters' responses to Egypt's decision reflected a variety of views on Egypt's Jewish past and the ways contemporary Egyptians should relate to it. Whereas rejectionists found this announcement to be striking evidence of the close collaboration between Egypt and Israel and the promotion of Israel's acceptance in the Middle East (normalization) despite its separatist policy toward Palestinians, optimists cheered the policy, urging Israel to treat Islamic sites and places in Israel/Palestine with reciprocal respect and reverence. Between the two camps, skeptics voiced their reservations, questioning the significance of restoring these places as houses of worship when the number of Egyptian Jews living in the country had dwindled since the 1950s, going so far as to deem such a project worthless and pointless. The plans were prompted by calls from international Jewish organizations and internal Jewish voices but, no less significantly, were superseded and paralleled by a growing literary movement that has reshaped and disseminated Jewish imaginaries in twenty-first-century Egypt.

LITERARY REPRESENTATIONS OF JEWS

Today there are only about twenty Jews living in contemporary Egypt, making social interaction between them and the Muslim majority extremely limited.[5] Nevertheless, the representation of Jews in contemporary Arabic literary works published in Egypt is substantial and deserves scholarly attention.[6] As in Benedict Anderson's suggestion that the novel and the newspaper should be seen as playing a central role in the construction of "imagined communities,"[7] the proliferation of Jewish imaginaries in Arabic works can be read as a solidification of the Egyptian national identity by reviving its pluralistic past, when Jews were an integral part of the national fabric.

The first decade of the twenty-first century in Egypt witnessed the appearance of several literary works featuring Jewish characters. In *Ḥadd al-ghawāyah* (The edge of error; 2004), ʿAmr ʿAfia relates the complex relationship between a Muslim man and a Jewish woman who was born in Egypt, immigrated to Israel, and then returned to Egypt after she became disappointed with the continuous state of war in Israel. In *Ṭuyūr al-'anbar* (Birds of ambergris; 2000), Ibrāhīm ʿAbdelmegīd introduces Alexandria as a cosmopolitan city where Jews lived side by side with other religious communities until their unexpected departure in the wake of the triple invasion of 1956, when Israel partnered with Britain and France in a joint military operation against Gamal ʿAbd el-Nasser's regime. Mostafa Nasr's *Yahūd al-iskandariyyah* (Jews of Alexandria; 2016) vividly explores the social, political, and economic conditions of Jews in Alexandria by bringing together historical and fictional accounts covering the late nineteenth to the late twentieth century. These are not the first Egyptian authors to depict Jewish figures; 2003 saw the publication of Ṣunʿ Allāh Ibrāhīm's novel *Amrīkānlī: Amrī kān lī* (The matter was mine), about a professor who goes on sabbatical to Chicago for a semester and meets a Jewish woman. Similarly, in *Chicago* (2007), ʿAlāʾ al-Aswānī relates the story of Nagī, who, during his studies at the University of Illinois, gets to know a Jewish girl.[8] These novels are not included in the present analysis, however, since they provide a perspective on Jews in another space, America, which merits its own separate study. The Jewish characters in the selected novels play a more active, central role in the narrative in comparison with the short story collections, composed not long after the signing of the Egyptian-Israeli peace treaty, by Alexandrian Naʿīm Taklā. In *Qafazat al-ṭa'ir al-'asmar al-naḥīl* (Jumps of the skinny brown bird; 1982) and *Madinah fawqa qishrah wāhiyyah* (A city on a brittle shell; 1984), Jewish figures function as triggers for nostalgia, invoking sweet memories without playing an active role in the narratives.[9]

The three novels examined here, *Ḥadd al-ghawāyah, Ṭuyūr al-'anbar,* and *Yahūd al-iskandariyyah,* belong to the new-consciousness novel genre. This genre, according to Mary Youssef, depicted Egyptian society from antiquity to the present as a heterogenous society consisting of "several groups based on imagined and lived differences in race, ethnicity, religion, culture, language, and gender."[10] It characteristically responds to "the resurgent, distinctive imaginings of what Egypt is, and who its inhabitants are, by foregrounding their racial, ethno-religious, cultural, linguistic, and class differences, and at the same time postulating a creative vision for resistance against discourses and practices of differentiation."[11]

This genre, as Mary Youssef has argued, does not completely disassociate itself from preceding novelistic productions from the last four decades of the twentieth century. Perhaps a continued feature is the emphasis on the urban setting rather than agrarian society. In cities like Cairo and Alexandria literary works underscore "the popular spirit of uncertainty" among city dwellers emanating from regional wars, increasing class differences, ruthless socioeconomic circumstances, and the absence of political and social reforms.[12] The urban setting, as seen in the novels studied, "epitomize[s] the spatial flux of modernity, in which tension between traditional life and values, embodied in the constant influx of immigrants from Egypt's peripheries to its metropolises, and the increasing transforming urban life, embodied in city dwellers' restless lifestyle, are highlighted."[13] An urban setting is at the center of these three novels, specifically Alexandria, a city situated on the southern shore of the Mediterranean across from Europe. If the deployment of space resonates with reflections on and of identity, as Muḥammad Siddīq has indicated, Alexandria serves as a territorial manifestation of a multiethnic and multireligious Egyptian identity.[14] Through this lens, the current analysis explores and identifies the ways in which Jews in Egypt, whether immigrant or native city dwellers, are represented as an integral part of the social and cultural fabric of Egypt. I argue that these Egyptian novels exhibit a particular sensitivity toward the multiplicity of identities that constitute the complex Egyptian population, imagining their society as a multiethnic one in a way that expresses their rejection of the monolithic identity of the nation-state model.

The linkage between Egyptian Jewry and Alexandria imbues the city with a positive connotation by transforming it into a pluralistic space and a cosmopolitan asylum. Yet the depictions of Jews in these texts are not confined to wealthy, multilingual, and Western-oriented Jews; they include poor, monolingual, and illiterate Jews as a way to challenge the dominant stereotypical treatment of Jews in television and cinema. Most significantly, the juxtaposition in the novels between cosmopolitan Jews, immigrants whose presence in the country coincided with an imperial and colonial Egypt where they had no particular investment in Egyptian culture, and Levantine Jews, local inhabitants who spoke Egyptian Arabic and were part of the country's social fabric, provides a poignant assessment of the complicated and multiethnic nature of Egyptian society, which was made up of different social groups.[15]

These novels were published during the first decade and a half of the twenty-first century, yet they engage with the Egypt that preceded the Free Officers Revolution of 1952 and the tripartite invasion of 1956. While they embody the Jewish presence in Egypt in various historical times ranging from the late nineteenth to late twentieth centuries, relying on texts, oral narratives, and even imagination to write about Jews, the events concerning the main Jewish characters take place in Alexandria, which is represented as cosmopolitan in nature.[16] To some extent the novels are free from the influence of Israel's emergence on Arabic literary texts published in Egypt between 1948 and 1879, which failed to distinguish between Zionists and Jews, yet the issue of Zionism reverberates throughout them.[17] They are also largely void of the stereotyping of Jewish characters that loomed large in the works of twentieth-century Egyptian authors. The connection between Jews and Alexandria leads us to question the ways in which space and identity interact with each other.

The following analysis provides a nuanced understanding of the use of Jewish characters in novels to explore Jewish people's roles in twenty-first-century Egyptian society and culture. In my view, the preoccupation with investigating the degree to which their portrayal is aimed at either inflaming antagonism against Jews or promoting rapprochement with them fails to appreciate the function of the "imagined Jew" within the collective memory of a given society, especially Arab societies in the Middle East.[18] Jews are almost absent from modern Egyptian space, yet they have never left Egypt's collective memory. The invocation of Jews in contemporary literary works contributes to the reconstruction of a multiethnic society where minorities are integrated into a complex social fabric. The use of Jewish characters in the construction of a cosmopolitan contemporary

Egypt aims to promote tolerance between various social groups in the country and to bring attention to the contributions minorities can bring to society. Yet the depiction of this cosmopolitan society in these novels is far from ideal, as some writers also highlight points of tension in the relations between Jews and Muslims in Egypt.[19] Since the novels use Alexandria as the setting for exploring their Jewish figures and their interactions with non-Jewish communities in the city, it is useful to investigate the connection between place and identity.

SPACE IN A COSMOPOLITAN SOCIETY

The ways that spaces are produced and interact with identity offer a window onto the social relations of various segments of Egyptian society. "Space," according to Michel de Certeau, "is a practiced place. Thus, the street geometrically defined by urban planning is transformed into a space by walkers. In the same way, an act of reading is the space produced by the practice of a particular place: a written text, i.e., a place constituted by a system of signs."[20] Building on Certeau's view, Lital Levy notices in her study of the literature of Jewish Baghdad that, "if space is created through practice, then in narratives set in this richly multiethnic . . . city, identity is recreated anew each day through one's relation to space and its boundaries."[21]

Such is the case in the representation of space in *Ḥadd al-ghawāyah*, *Ṭuyūr al-'anbar*, and *Yahūd al-iskandariyyah*, where the Jewish quarter is represented as an integral part of the pluralistic Egyptian society within which Jews and Arabs interact. As it emerges in the novels, the Jewish quarter, by virtue of the presence of non-Jews who reside and work there, is not a purely Jewish space. For instance, the narrator in *Ṭuyūr al-ʿAnbar* relates that a handful of non-Jewish residents live and work in the Jewish quarter.[22] In such a mixed space, social interactions are part of daily life. In *Yahūd al-iskandariyyah*, 'Um Maḥmūd prepares a phyllo-type pastry pancake, *faṭīr*, for Naẓīra, her Jewish friend, who eats it without expressing concerns about whether the butter her Muslim friend uses is kosher.[23] While eating the food, Naẓīra and 'Um Maḥmoūd exchange jokes and share exciting details about the Jewish, Christian, and Muslim residents of the neighborhood.[24]

By the same token, Jews are not restricted to the Jewish quarter as their sole space, and their presence beyond the quarter integrates their Jewishness into the city, turning it into a pluralistic place. Jews' place of residence was not confined to a certain type of house inhabited only by lower-class residents. Some Jews owned palaces, such as 'Āmīr bey, who was known to be the head of the Alexandrian Jewish community. In the novel, 'Āmīr lives in his own house and visits *sūq al-samak* (the fish market), where substantial numbers of Jews reside, to hire people to do jobs for him.[25] Al-Hādiya, the wife of John, the central Jewish figure in the first chapter of *Yahūd al-iskandariyya*, works as a nurse at the public hospital, where she treats without discrimination patients from different religious backgrounds.[26] Benyāmīn the barber frequently visits the rich neighborhood Ḥay al-Qanāsil (the consuls' neighborhood) to get higher compensation for his services. Jews also are not excluded from working within the government. Dov, the head of the accountants in Egypt, is the financial adviser of the khedive, Sa'īd.[27]

A SHARED RELIGIOUS-CULTURAL SPHERE

Cross-religious veneration of holy sites is a highly significant cultural phenomenon that is considered to be the result of centuries of coexistence between Jews and Muslims in Egypt.[28] Historically, Jews would visit Muslim sanctuaries seeking blessing and miracles, and Muslims would visit Jewish sacred sites with similar hopes and wishes. In the quasi-historical nineteenth-century Egypt of *Ḥadd al-ghawāyah*, for example, Sara, a Jewish woman, has given birth to three children, but none of them survived. When she becomes pregnant for the fourth time, she seeks a miracle far and wide, whether in a synagogue or a mosque, hoping to give birth to a healthy child.[29]

Her search reveals the depths of intercultural knowledge that once existed in Egypt. For instance, ʿAliyyah, Sara's Muslim neighbor, advises her to visit "Maimonides' synagogue where there is a blessed room."[30] ʿAliyyah is surprised that Sara, despite being Jewish, did not know about it. Such knowledge and religious boundary-crossing existed among Jews as well. Upon the advice of Rachel Farag, a Jewish woman, Sara went to the imam of Sīdī al-Shaʿrānī's mosque. Rachel told her that many years ago a mother-to-be sought the blessing of the sheikh there and her fourth child, Yaʿqūb Ṣannūʿ—an allusion to the famous Jewish journalist and playwright Yaʿqūb Ṣannūʿ, who was actively involved in late nineteenth-century Egypt's domestic politics by resisting colonialism and advocating Egyptian nationalism—survived.[31] When Sara tells her husband Jacob about her plan, he does not oppose it.[32] In such a traditional society, the husband's assent was crucial, and his giving it indicates the extent to which Jewish families were integrated into the wider Islamic culture, while, of course, preserving their Jewish particularity. When she presents herself before the imam in her veil, he asks for her name before giving his blessing, and she tells him, "Rachel Yaccov [*sic*] Abdelwāhed." Disclosing her true name would not necessarily have revealed her true religious identity, for Sara/Sarah was a common name among Jews and Muslims. Rather, she appears more confident and comfortable taking on an unmistakably Jewish name in introducing herself. The imam is not surprised to find out that she is Jewish, as apparently, her religious identity is a matter of only marginal concern. In his eyes, ultimately, Jews and Muslims are monotheists worshipping the same God. While reading prayers and blessing her, the imam says, "Name your son Ibrāhīm and devote him to Islam even if he would remain Jewish."[33] Rachel and Jacob obey, raising their child as a Muslim and sending him to learn "the principles of Islam and Qur'ān at Ibn Maymūn's school in Dārb al-Barābra" while the child remains Jewish.[34]

The choice of names, as in the case of the imam's advice to name their son Ibrāhīm, is a crucial element in ʿAfia's depiction of a multiethnic society where members of religious communities crossed paths in each other's sacred spaces. Ibrāhīm evokes the common origins shared by Jews and Muslims, referring to Abraham, the father of both monotheistic religions. Other names, like Sara and Rachel, are similarly significant, referring to the biblical matriarchs and revered in Muslim and Arab circles. Jewish names in literary texts published after the 1948 War, however, had only negative connotations. Sasson Somekh notes that Rachel is one of two common names employed in modern Arabic literature to represent the Israeli Jewess,[35] and that, as a rule, in Arabic literary works produced between the establishment of Israel and the 1980s, the name has mostly negative connotations, being associated with the girl soldier and cunning Jewess.[36] The intentional use of the name Rachel to indicate a comforting, counseling, and even righteous character in *Ḥadd al-ghawāyah* signals a shift from the demonization of Jewish characters toward acceptance and appreciation. Besides Rachel being presented as a genuinely helpful character who bridges Jewish and Muslim knowledge, Sara also calls herself Rachel when speaking to the imam, an indication that even a woman with an evidently Jewish name could access Muslim sacred spaces without worry of exclusion.

The depiction of this shared world does sometimes refers to occasional tension. For instance, the relationship between Muslims and Jews in Egypt occasionally grows tense when the religious identity of a Jew is revealed in a secular setting. In *Yahūd al-iskandariyyah*, Maẓlūm is approached in a nightclub by a female sex worker. He had seen her being ridiculed by other customers for her physical appearance before turning to him. When she discovers Maẓlūm is Jewish, she leaves him immediately, exclaiming, "Are you Jewish?[37] Later, recalling what happened that night, Maẓlūm wonders why she put up with her humiliation by several lower-class men but ran away from him the moment she discovered his Jewishness.[38] Maẓlūm's resentment of her rejection shows his struggle with acceptance. But it should be highlighted that this rejection takes place in a secular space and by lower-class members of the society, who are depicted as easy targets for stereotyping.

INTERFAITH MARRIAGE

A characteristic of multiethnic Egypt that emerges from the narratives studied here is the tolerance of interfaith marriage and the acceptance of children with hybrid religious identity. Unlike Judaism, which contains explicit injunctions forbidding marriage between Jews and non-Jews, Islam permits matrimony between Muslims and non-Muslims, especially the people of the book (that is, Jews and Christians), albeit with restrictions.[39] Despite the implications of such marriages, the authors considered here all assign a central role to figures involved in them.[40] Differences in religious identity do not prevent romantic relations between members of various religious communities. Indeed, this sort of relationship crosses religious and communal boundaries and contributes to an inclusive multiethnic and multireligious society that subscribes to norms of tolerance and acceptance, a society that values individual freedom and does not relate to these individuals with strictness and rejection. From the perspective of the authors, the inclusion of intermarriage between Jews and Muslims is a confirmation of the ideals of the Egyptian society as accepting mixed marriage (though not necessarily welcoming it, as we will see) and compliance with the religious principle found in the Qur'ān, "no compulsion in religion" (2:256).

Intermarriage between a Muslim woman and a non-Muslim man, irrespective of his religion, is forbidden according to the traditional understanding of Islamic law, and the novels conform to this point by pairing Muslim men with Jewish women, which is legally permissible. In *Ḥadd al-ghawāyah,* Maḥmoūd Ḥanafī marries Samīḥa, a Jewish woman who left Egypt for British Palestine in the 1940s and left shortly after the birth of the State of Israel in 1948.[41] The relationship between the couple is portrayed as the result of mutual affection, devoid of hidden motives, in stark contrast to earlier literary works, where intermarriage was a means for the Jewish spouse to take advantage of the Muslim spouse. For example, in Iḥsān ʿAbd al-Quddūs's novel *Lā tatrukūnī hunā waḥdī* (Do not leave me here alone; 1979), Lucy decides to convert to Islam to marry the rich Muslim Shawkat bey not out of romance, but out of commitment to the Zionist project.[42] *Ḥadd al-ghawāyah* departs from this conventional negative portrayal of mixed marriage between Jews and Muslims to depict both sides as sincerely engaged in a genuine relationship.

Since cosmopolitanism, from the perspective of the authors, entails the active participation of social actors in enduring acceptance and contributing to diversity, cases of mixed marriage are extended to include Jews and Christians as a way to reflect the representation of the three religious communities in Egyptian society. The narrator in *Yahūd al-iskandariyyah* indicates that Maẓlūm, a personal adviser to a wealthy Muslim pasha, was born to a mixed marriage between a Jewish man and a Christian woman in Egypt.[43] However, the narrator does not reveal to us why Maẓlūm became a Jew and not a Christian after his mother's faith.

On some occasions, however, a Jewish character's religious identity creates a barrier to interfaith marriage. In *Yahūd al-iskandariyyah,* Kamāl's mother opposes marrying Gawhara, a Jewish woman, to her son Kamāl, a Muslim, specifically because of Gawhara's religion. When Muḥsin, Kamāl's father, reminds his wife that Gawhara was raised among them and "acquired our morals,"[44] the mother attempts to justify her opposition by recalling how Gawhara was too liberal in expressing her feelings toward Kamāl, including by sneaking into his room at night.[45]

In novels published between 1948 and the signing of peace accords (1978–79) between Israel and Egypt, mixed marriage is treated as foreign to Egyptian identity and a threat to society. In more recent novels, like the ones studied here, mixed marriage, not only between Jews and Muslims but between Jews and Christians and Muslims and Christians, is shown as enriching the pluralistic nature of Egyptian society in the past.[46]

THE STRUGGLE FOR POWER

In steering away from the stereotypical representations of Egyptian Jewry that dominated literary works published from 1948 to 1981, the novels studied here show understanding of the vulnerability of Jews as a religious minority contributing to the larger Egyptian society. Jewish characters in the novels search for political and economic power either to fulfill their communal objectives and needs or to secure self-protection out of the awareness of their minority status.

In *Yahūd al-iskandariyyah*, Sa'īd Pasha (1822–1863), the viceroy of Egypt, is suffering from a fatal disease, leaving the leaders of the Jewish community in Egypt, Dov, 'Āmīr, and Zakāy, very concerned that he might die without granting "Egyptian Jewry more privileges."[47] To remedy this, they recruit Jews for "a mission that benefits Egypt Jewry."[48] Historically, Sa'īd Pasha released non-Muslim communities in Egypt from paying *al-Jizya* (certain payment in exchange for military service) in 1854. Due to his tolerant policies toward Jews and Christians, the Jews of Alexandria were involved in tax collection and customs clearance in the late nineteenth and early twentieth centuries.[49] The novel, however, shows that some figures were not attentive to the sensitive status of Jews and plotted to sever relations between them and the palace. The viceroy's Muslim secretary realizes that the Jews' self-oriented political agenda and he acts to undermine the relationship of the three Jewish leaders with the viceroy.[50]

The third chapter of *Yahūd al-iskandariyyah* portrays another episode in the Jewish search for power in Egypt. It is the reign of al-Sādāt, the Egyptian president who achieved peace with Israel. Upon his becoming president, the Jewish woman Gawhara writes a letter to him reminding him of how her family housed and protected him in 1942 when the British authorities were searching the village for him. When al-Sādāt learns about her impoverished status, he decides to return the favor and pay a visit to the daughter of "the patriot Munīr," who died manufacturing bombs and explosives for the armed resistance movement to confront British troops in Egypt.[51] From then on, Gawhara uses her personal connection with al-Sādāt to consolidate the status of Jews in Egypt. At times she even threatens local authorities for opposing her plans to restore the Jewish cemetery in Alexandria.[52]

The place of economics in Jews' lives in Egypt is not pushed to the sidelines in theses novels. Munīr, Gawhara's father, is criticized for his love of money at the cost of meeting his wife's emotional needs. Wiṣāl complains to Naẓīra, Munīr's mother, saying, "Your son does anything for the sake of money."[53] Scoffing at him for not paying attention to his health, Munīr's mother says to him, "Your love for wealth has caused you to lose everything."[54] Elsewhere, Jews are told to be successful merchants. Speaking to a group of merchants in a local market about the privileges of trading in pepper, a spice seller tells them, "Jews became rich trading in pepper, and you know that Jews never trade in something that is not successful."[55]

ARAB-ISRAELI CONFLICT

While the works studied here do not belong to the literary genre of *riwāyah siyāsiyyah* (political novel), which means "a literary product in which political events play a central role,"[56] contemporary literature does frequently engage political events, notably in stories related to the Arab-Israeli conflict. Unlike the strong tone in which *adab al-muqāwamah* (resistance literature), such as Alfred Farag's *Al-Nār wa-al-zaytūn* (Fire and olives; 1970),[57] addressed the conflict, contemporary Arabic works are less strident in their tone and incorporate political events as far as the case of Egypt is concerned. As opposed to the embrace of a multiethnic model within which Jews are recruited to strengthen and support the model, ethno-religious nationalism is strongly less favored by these three novelists. As Yaron Shemer has remarked, the moment a Jewish character is perceived as participating in parochial nationalism, in this case Zionism, they are excluded from the cosmopolitan model.[58]

The emergence of Zionism and its dissemination among Egyptian Jews casts a shadow on cosmopolitan Egypt and causes tension not only between Jews and non-Jews but between pro-and anti-Zionist Jews. In *Ḥadd al-ghawāyah*, Ephraim explains to Samīḥa that the reason underlying his resistance to going to Schlesinger's palace is Schlesinger's involvement in Zionist activities. Without the insistence of Samīḥa's brother Yosef, an ardent Zionist, neither Ephraim nor Samīḥa would have gone to the palace.[59] Discontented with the Zionist movement, Ephraim joins the Jewish Anti-Zionist League, which was established by members of the Iskra organization and resorted to militant agitations in Jewish neighborhoods in Cairo.[60] Shortly afterward, the Egyptian government bans the activities of Iskra and detains and deports its members, with the consideration that the communists constitute a greater threat to public security than the Zionists.

JEWISH DEPARTURE FROM EGYPT

The most important episode in the Arab-Israeli conflict was the 1956 War. In *The Jews in Modern Egypt*, Gudrun Krämer estimates that some fifty thousand to fifty-five thousand Jews remained in Egypt during the war.[61] This estimate contradicts the prevailing assumption that the creation of the State of Israel in 1948 marked the end of Jewish presence in Arab states, including Egypt. The novels also attest to the continued existence of the Jewish community in Egypt after World War II, which had forced a sizable number of Jews to leave Egypt out of fear that the German army would invade Egypt and annihilate the Jews as they had done in Europe.

The triple invasion of 1956 resulted in the expulsion of British and French subjects who had lived in Egypt for many years. "Alexandria was not disturbed by their expulsion," the narrator relates in *Ṭuyūr al-'anbar* (129).[62] While the British and French are depicted as detached from Egyptian society and its people, the disappearance of the Jews in the wake of the 1956 War echoes through the three novels, which note that their absence caused remarkable changes to Egyptian society. The authors refer to the state of perplexity that clouded the community in Alexandria regarding the absence of its Jews. ʿArabī, one of the main characters in *Yahūd al-iskandariyyah*, wonders why Jews would leave despite the fact that local authorities did not expel them, save for those who were involved in antagonistic activities against the state and cooperated with the British (130). The narrator of *Ṭuyūr al-'anbar* explains two factors that caused the departure of the Jews. First, he points out that rumors had spread everywhere that the authorities would confiscate Jewish property and Jews would be put in detention because of what Israel had done to Egypt (130). These rumors have created a sense of pessimism among the Jews of Egypt: "The most optimistic of Jews believed that if he did not leave today, he would be leaving tomorrow, and if he did not leave this week he would be leaving next week. None of them thought to wait for only one year. They never wait for one year" (131). Non-Jewish Egyptians express their astonishment that this could be allowed to happen to Jews who "were Egyptians who had lived here for centuries" (130). Unlike the British, French, Greeks, and Italians who lived in Alexandria, "it never occurred to [non-Jewish Egyptians] to consider Jews of Alexandria subjects of Israel" (130).

The Jews' departure caused remarkable social, economic, and political changes in the country, as reflected in all three novels. Stock prices went down in the wake of the rapid sales by Jewish owners, and moneylending in Alexandria decreased (130). The decline of moneylending businesses not only affected Egypt's economy, but also affected people's lifestyle. Moneylending had been identified with Jews in the Islamic orbit since the Middle Ages, as Haim Gerber has noted. Muslims in modern times saw no harm in adopting it after the Jews left.[63] This is expressed in *Yahūd al-iskandariyyah* through impersonation. Through proximity to and familiarity with Jewish moneylenders, Muslims acquired the accepted manners and customs of running such a business, going so far, as portrayed in the novel, as taking on the physical qualities of a Jewish businessman. To have any chance to succeed, as Annette Baier writes, an impersonator "must look and sound like the one impersonated, as well as seem to have the memories and abilities the impersonated one would have."[64] The impersonator in the novel takes over the business and talks like a Jew, walks like a Jew, looks like a Jew:[65]

> Aḥmad Ḥasan, the owner of the moneylending business in Karmūz, would talk like Jews from his nose, walk slowly in his store bending his back although he was not an old man, and look suspiciously at customers who come to pawn their personal property. . . . Aḥmad would claim that he was not interested in what the customers pawned, but after he became certain that the customer was confused, he would offer him the lowest sum and the customer would agree. At the end, the customer would leave the store cursing Aḥmad Ḥasan the Jew, even though he was a Muslim.[66]

The impersonation of Jews by Muslim characters in the novel contributes to the preservation of memory in Egyptian society. The impersonated Jew is absent from the society in which they once lived and thrived once, but their memory is active through the Muslim impersonator.

If in this case the Muslim impersonator is depicted as having usurped Jewish economic activity, in other cases the Jewish character is portrayed as trusting a Muslim character with their wealth and business. In *Yahūd al-iskandariyyah*, some Jews have left their wealth to Egyptians who worked with them. This trope bypasses literary works published from 1948 to 1981, where negative portrayals of Jews prevailed, and draws on literary and cinematic works from the 1940s. These earlier works depicted the diversity of Egypt's populace and are imbued with the language of coexistence, as Deborah Starr has indicated.[67] In the film *Li ʿbet el-Set* (The lady's puppet; 1946) the news of the arrival of the Nazis in Egypt through the western borders terrifies Jews and disturbs their social and economic life in the country. Isaac ʿAnbar, a successful Jewish businessman who owns a popular department store, decides to flee the country. Before his departure, he sells his business to his decent employee Ḥasan ʿAshūr Abū Ṭabaq, played by Nagīb al-Rīḥanī. Similarly, Rachel gives money to ʿArabī to start his own business rather than remaining an employee under the leadership of Katina, who fears that this money will drive ʿArabī away from her to start his own business at the expense of her own.[68] Other cases include Khawaja Shalom, who leaves his wealth to his private driver. Samʿān the Jew gives his bar to Khamīs, who used to work as "a carrier at the station by day and a thug by night."[69] In turn, Khamīs turns the bar into a café. Aṣlān the Jew bequeaths his clothes store to Mursī the coffee maker, who turns into a business owner. Bishr Ḥamza the shoemaker becomes the sole owner of leather factory after his four Jewish partners leave in a rush for Italy, where they establish their own factory.[70]

Aside from the elevation in economic status of non-Jewish Egyptians who inherited the businesses of their Jewish fellows, the absence of the the Jews negatively affected them. The narrator of *Ṭuyūr al-ʾanbar* discusses the loneliness and isolation felt in the country in the wake of the Jews' departure. ʿArabī walks around the Jewish neighborhood in Alexandria, which is "dark and the doors were locked." Yet the windows are only partially closed, which signals to him that the residents had not permanently left. ʿArabī says, "I am truly very sad. The residents of almost the entire neighborhood travelled abroad. It is still our Lord."[71]

The twentieth-century Jewish departure from Egypt had both a more significant and a more negative impact on Egyptian society than did the departure of other minority communities. From the perspective of the narrator of *Ṭuyūr al-ʾanbar*, it marked "the disappearance of the atmosphere of tolerance that Alexandria inhaled with its air."[72] Although the narrator seems to disagree with the policies applied to Egyptian Jewry in the wake of the 1956, he does not explicitly criticize the measures that directly or indirectly influenced their rights and lives.[73] Rather, he directs his dissatisfaction toward the *siyāsat al-tamṣīr* (policies of Egyptianization) that isolated Egypt from the world. Other characters in the novel express similar sentiments. Jean, Sulaimān's British girlfriend, sends him a letter from Australia after she arrives there following the expulsion of foreign subjects from Egypt. She writes, "I do not like the policy of Egyptianization. There is no doubt that Abdelnaser is a patriotic and honest leader, yet your country cannot survive being isolated from the world."[74]

Yet, beyond their criticism of the policy of Egyptianization, the characters of *Ṭuyūr al-'anbar* refuse to hold "the genuine leader" accountable for what happened to the Jews, blaming other powerful officials who ran the country behind Nasser's back. This perspective is echoed several times in the novel. Rachel, the daughter of Isaac, wishes that Nasser knew about their situation. Had he known, he would have protected them and defended them against the aggression they faced from the authorities. Nasser as the savior of the oppressed also appears in the story of the nurse Nawāl, whom the authorities have humiliated and imprisoned unjustly based on accusations of her being a communist. When her father learns of her disappearance, he writes a letter to Nasser, who personally intervenes and returns his daughter to him safely, though he gets his share of humiliation from the national security officer for "disturbing" the president and getting him involved in the matter of his "unworthy daughter."[75]

INTERPLAY OF RELIGION AND POLITICS

Ḥadd al-ghawāyah, *Ṭuyūr al-'anbar*, and *Yahūd al-iskandariyyah* all shed light on the intersections between religion, gender, culture, and politics in the Middle East and their relevance to Egypt. A feature of the new-consciousness novel, according to Mary Youssef, is not only "the marginality of its protagonists across the class and gender spectrum" but also the centrality of "the more complex reality of the intersections of class with race, ethnicity, religion, gender."[76] Religion is depicted as a determining factor in Egypt's and Israel's politics, and the novels indicate various levels of understanding of the relationship between politics and religion by highlighting through their characters how religious principles are transformed and incorporated into the political sphere, as well as how some of these principles are contested. While religion itself, be it Judaism or Islam, is not wholly rejected nor mocked, the combination between religion and politics appears complex and provocative. Religiosity in some cases is depicted as incompatible with modernity with its social, cultural, and technological advancements. This incompatibility is expressed in the association between a religious Jewish figure and stereotypical representations. A deeply pious lower-class Jew, the central Jewish character in *Yahūd al-iskandariyyah*, John, is appointed as Saʿīd Pasha's private doctor's assistant. John is represented as ugly, slim, hunchbacked, with rolling eyes, dressed in old clothes as if he were "semihuman."[77] He resembles in his appearance the Venetian Jewish moneylender Shylock, from William Shakespeare's play *The Merchant of Venice*. This negative portrayal, as Norman Stillman has shown, is imported from European representations of Jews, and is not simply "one of the stock images of the Jew in traditional Islamic society."[78] In part, this portrayal refers to the archaic traditional Jew whose religiosity prevents him from coping with modernity and realizing how his religious sentiments can be used by political actors to advance their agenda in reference to leaders of the Jewish community who wanted to receive favors from the khedive, as discussed earlier.

The eschewal of engaging religiosity in political matters is rewarded in the novels. While doing his job, the deeply pious John cannot bring himself to compromise his religious convictions to appease the monarch or to acquire economic or political gain from him for himself or the Jewish community. His piety and sincerity are rewarded beyond the expectations of everyone around him, who despise him for his ugly appearance. For his dedication to treating the sick monarch, Saʿīd Pasha endows John with a large territory in the eastern part of Alexandria. This land would come to be named "John's farm," and many Jews from the old Jewish neighborhood in the "fish market" would move to live there.[79]

References to the interplay of the religious and political are stressed when the events of the novels involve the Islamist movement or Zionism. The authors, most likely under the influence of the view that religion and politics should be separate, imply that the adoption of religion, whether Islam or Judaism, would necessarily produce a politics of aggressiveness and authoritarianism. In *Ḥadd al-ghawāyah* the Egyptian Jew Josef immigrates to British Palestine under the influence of his obsession with Zionism.

In prestate Palestine, Yosef becomes radical and gets into aggressive discussions with his moderate sister Samīḥa (48).[80] The combination between religion and politics manifested in the case of Zionism breeds only alienation and hostility. The embrace of Zionism severs Yosef's ties to his society and causes him to be hostile toward his sister.

A recurrent trope in contemporary Arabic fiction is the impact of the political events taking place in Palestine/Israel on the intimate relationship between two individuals, one an Arab and the other Jewish or quasi-Jewish. Political developments cause Judaism and Zionism to be seen as synonymous. A striking example of this occurs in *Ḥadd al-ghawāyah*. Hāshem, an Egyptian Muslim, falls in love with Sara, the child of a mixed marriage between Samīha, an Egyptian Jew with Moroccan origins, and Maḥmoūd. Hāshem cannot determine Sara's religious identity when they first spend time together. When her necklace accidentally reveals its Jewish star one day, he suspects her of being not only Jewish but a Zionist. Sara tries to convince him that the star is just a meaningless symbol that should not lead people to judgment (117). Hāshem has a different perspective. To him, signs are powerful. "In this case," he explains to Sara, "if one were to accept a specific symbol accepted by another group of people, that means they adhere to its meaning" (117–18). Sara disagrees, explaining that the necklace belonged to her mother and was originally a gift her father bought to her when they met each other in Al-Andalus in the 1950s (117–18).

It turns out, however that the true barrier between Sara and Hāshem is her relationship with Israel. One night as they walk the streets in Alexandria, he asks her, "Are you influenced by what is happening in Israel?" (169). Put differently: "Do you accept what Jews have been doing?" (170). Sara claims that she does not, explaining, "In my perspective, Israel is a suicide enterprise for all Jews." She continues:

> They became enemies with people who used to accept them. These Arabs among whom Jews lived have become enemies because they are simply weak. But what if the balance of power was tipped some day and the honeymoon between Israel and its former oppressors were to come to an end? Also, even though Israel's constitution is secular and guarantees the presence of others [non-Jews] and enables them to express their views freely, the foundation of their

> [nationalist] project and carrying it out is religious. . . . In other words, the seed for the corruption of Israel is within it, for they do not truly believe in the equality of all religions. (171)

Hāshem then asks, "That is to say that you hate Israel" (172). She assures him that she does. However, Sara supports the peace project that al-Sādāt had proposed. For her, "it is what annoys Israel, for it takes away from it its power, which is the military might provided by the United States" (172). Realizing how worried Hāshem is about her religious identity, Sara denounces her Jewishness, saying, "I swear by God that I am not Jewish. My mother was Jewish. I think Zionists, as British called them previously, are terrorists . . . and by the way, my mother did not recognize Israel" (172).

Hāshem's relationship with Sara causes him unexpected trouble among his friends, too. Sara's mother's religious identity makes Hāshem's friends, especially Aiman, believe that Sara is not a Muslim but Jewish too, since religious affiliation in Judaism is transmitted through the mother (150). Hāshem attempts to refute Aiman's claim by reminding him that in Islam religious affiliation comes from the father, not the mother. If so, then Sara should be Muslim. But Aiman remains committed to his belief that Sara remains Jewish because of her mother.

With the outbreak of the first Lebanese war in 1982, which resulted in part in the bloodbath in Sabra and Shatila, where thousands of Palestinian refugees were killed in a coordinated operation by the Israeli army and militia of the Lebanese forces, members of the Islamic movement mobilized public opinion through demonstrations against Jews in general, echoing calls such as "Khaybar khaybar oh Jews, the army of Muhammad will return" (136).[81] The narrator relates how the involvement of the Islamic movement turned the conflict into a religious one, concealing its true nature as a conflict between oppressor and oppressed (138).

If the engagement of religion in the Arab-Israeli conflict conceals its true nature and perpetuates the state of war between countries, what could be the best path moving forward? In *Ḥadd al-ghawāyah*, through the characters of Hāshem and Sara, the author proposes being intelligent, canny, and clever in dealing with such a situation. According to Sara, violence will yield more violence: "It is better to reach a reconciliation between Israel and Arabs" (141). The wisdom underlying her perspective is that we should not give these "fanatics the opportunity to kill us. . . . When you play with a crazy person you should be careful with him and get ready for deception and not conflict" (142).

Egypt in the twenty-first century witnessed the emergence of a new novelistic genre described as the new-consciousness novel, which included novels featuring Jewish characters, who assume a central role in the reconstruction of a multiethnic society where minorities are depicted as integral part of the country's social fabric. As contemporary Egypt faces challenges threatening its cohesion and stability, "the imagined Jew" is presented in constructing an image of Egypt as a pluralistic, open, and welcoming society in the new millennium. Cosmopolitan Egypt as it emerges in the studied works is nonetheless far from ideal.

To rewrite contemporary Egypt as a tolerant society, the authors interweave real historical events with imagined narratives. The Jewish characters are not depicted as aliens or isolated from non-Jewish communities. Rather, they share the cultural and the spiritual realm of Christians and Muslims and interact with them without seeing religious identity as a barrier to their relationship. Yet Jews are also depicted as conscious of their vulnerability as a minority; as a result, they seek power and compete with other non-Jewish communities to form alliances with the ruling political parties, as in the case of Sa'īd Pasha and al-Sādāt in *Yahūd al-iskandariyyah*.

The Jewish figures in *Ḥadd al-ghawāyah, Ṭuyūr al-'anbar*, and *Yahūd al-iskandariyyah*, furthermore, foster pluralism by assuming a negative role. Once a Jewish character displays parochial nationalism, that character is excluded from cosmopolitanism and viewed in an unfavorable way. Parochial nationalism, in the novels, transpires mainly in the form of Zionism. In them, during the years preceding the genesis of the State of Israel, Zionist sentiments among Egyptian Jews are presented as a threat not so much to Egyptian society as a whole but to the coherence of the Jewish family. Association with Zionism causes tension between parents and their children as well as between siblings. The tension escalates once the Jewish state is established and the Arab-Israeli conflict affects relations between Egyptian Jews and other Egyptians.

The display of ethno-religious sentiments as factors that weakened Egyptian cosmopolitanism is not confined to Zionism. The interplay between religion and politics among the non-Jewish population of the Egyptian society manifested in political Islamic movements, which are criticized for the dissemination of hatred of Jews and the deployment of religion for political gain.

Notes

1. Madadshahi, "Restored Alexandria Synagogue."

2. See the justification provided by antiquities minister Khāled al-ʿAnānī at Al-Najjar, "Al-Turāth al-Yahudī."

3. Al-Najjar, "Al-Turāth al-Yahudī."

4. The term "cosmopolitanism" is a reference to pluralist urbanism, where people with different religious affiliations and ethnic belongings interacted with one another. See Starr, "Sensing the City," 157.

5. This estimation is according to statements made by Magda Harun, the head of the Jewish community in Egypt ("Muslims in Egypt"). See also Israel-Pelletier, *On the Mediterranean*, 21.

6. For scholarly articles that have treated the subject of Jewish characters in Arabic literature in general, see Webman, "Image of the Jew/Zionist/Israeli"; LeGassick, "Image of the Jew"; Ballas, "Personnage israélien"; Stillman, "New Attitudes"; Alwan, "Jews in Arabic Literature."

7. Anderson, *Imagined Communities*, 25.

8. Al Aswany, *Chicago*, 35–36.

9. Sasson Somekh points out that Taklā's two collections were published in Israel since Egyptian presses, motivated by antinormalization, rejected the volumes even though the individual stories were published separately in various magazines in Egypt. For more details, see Somekh, "Dmuyot Yehudim," 239–40.

10. Youssef, *Minorities*, 1.

11. Youssef, *Minorities*, 28.

12. Youssef, *Minorities*, 19–20.

13. Youssef, *Minorities*, 20.

14. Siddiq, *Arab Culture*, 34–35.

15. See the difference between the cosmopolitan Jew and the Levantine Jew in Starr, "Masquerade," 35–36. For a detailed discussion of the cosmopolitan Jew, see Starr, *Remembering Cosmopolitan Egypt*.

16. In an interview, the Alexandrian writer Naṣr explains that one of his main sources was the local residents of al-Ṭabyyah, a neighborhood in eastern Alexandria, who were neighbors of the Jews before they left. For more details, see Shablool, "Riwayat Yahud al-Iskandariyyah."

17. See for instance a comprehensive analysis of the Jewish image in Iḥsān ʿAbd al-Quddūs's works in Al-Shami, *Al-Shakhsiyah Al-Yahudiyah*. For historicizing ʿAbd al-Quddūs's literary Jewish representation, see Starr, "Ambivalent Levantines / Levantine Ambivalences," 106–7.

18. See the seminal and problematic work by Yehoshafat Harkabi *Arab Attitudes to Israel*. Although not recent, this study covers a wide range of issues with respect to the common attitudes toward Jews and Israel and their origins. It also informs the works that appeared afterward, especially in Israel, until the work was challenged almost three decades later. For a critique of Harkabi's work, see Rejwan, *Arab Aims and Israeli Attitudes*.

19. Compare this with Starr, *Remembering Cosmopolitan Egypt*, 60.

20. De Certeau, *Practice of Everyday Life*, 117.

21. Levy, "Self and the City," 165.

22. ʿAbdelmegid, *Ṭuyūr al-ʾanbar*, 138, 39.

23. Nasr, *Yahūd al-iskandariyyah*, 303.

24. Nasr, *Yahūd al-iskandariyyah*, 303.

25. Nasr, *Yahūd al-iskandariyyah*, 9–10.

26. Nasr, *Yahūd al-iskandariyyah*, 45, 46.

27. Nasr, *Yahūd al-iskandariyyah*, 9.

28. ʿAfia, *Ḥadd al-ghawāyah*, 125.

29. ʿAfia, *Ḥadd al-ghawāyah*, 126.

30. ʿAfia, *Ḥadd al-ghawāyah*, 126–27.

31. ʿAfia, *Ḥadd al-ghawāyah*, 131. For details on Yaʿqūb Ṣannūʿ, see Benin, *Dispersion of Egyptian Jewry*, 82–83.

32. ʿAfia, *Ḥadd al-ghawāyah*, 132.

33. ʿAfia, *Ḥadd al-ghawāyah*, 132.

34. ʿAfia, *Ḥadd al-ghawāyah*, 132.

35. Somekh, "Cold, Tall Buildings," 125.

36. Somekh, "Cold, Tall Buildings," 125.

37. Nasr, *Yahūd al-iskandariyyah*, 271.

38. Nasr, *Yahūd al-iskandariyyah*, 294.

39. For a detailed discussion on interfaith marriage in Judaism, see Epstein, *Marriage Laws*, 145–219. Since observance of these regulations is strictly followed in the current

State of Israel, marriage between Jews and Arabs, be they Muslims or Christians, is not approved in Israel. Interfaith marriage, however, is performed overseas and recognized by Israel's Interior Ministry. These challenges find echo in literary works in Israel. A recent and controversial novel on intermarriage in Israel is Rabinyan, *All the Rivers*.

40. For a study on the legal regulations of interfaith marriage in Islamic law, see Leeman, "Interfaith Marriage in Islam," 754–58. On interfaith marriages and the debate between legal schools in Islam, see Friedmann, *Tolerance and Coercion*, 160–93.

41. ʿAfia, *Ḥadd al-ghawāyah*, 47–49.

42. ʿAbd al-Quddūs, *La Tatrukni Huna Wahdi*, 43–44. For a critical reading of *La Tatrukni Huna Waḥdi*, see Somekh, "Dmuyot Yehudim," 243–45. In his analysis, Somekh points out the biased representations of Jews, especially Egyptian Jews. ʿAbd al-Quddūs's renewed interest in Jews, it should be mentioned, stemmed from his rejection of the peace accord between Egypt and Israel in 1979; see Starr's discussion in "Ambivalent Levantines / Levantine Ambivalences," 106–7.

43. Nasr, *Yahūd al-iskandariyyah*, 301–2.

44. Nasr, *Yahūd al-iskandariyyah*, 443.

45. Nasr, *Yahūd al-iskandariyyah*, 443.

46. For a case of intermarriage between Jews and Muslims, see Ayoub, "Institutional Erasure."

47. Ayoub, "Institutional Erasure," 10.

48. Ayoub, "Institutional Erasure," 48.

49. For more details on the status of Jews in nineteenth-century Egypt, see Starr, *Remembering Cosmopolitan Egypt*, 19–21. See also Ackerman-Lieberman, "Taxation."

50. Nasr, *Yahūd al-iskandariyyah*, 11.

51. Nasr, *Yahūd al-iskandariyyah*, 475.

52. Nasr, *Yahūd al-iskandariyyah*, 475.

53. Nasr, *Yahūd al-iskandariyyah*, 353.

54. Nasr, *Yahūd al-iskandariyyah*, 355.

55. ʿAbdelmegid, *Ṭuyūr al-ʾanbar*, 58.

56. Snir, *Modern Arabic Literature*, 104.

57. For an analysis of the representation of Israeli Jews in Alfred Farag's works, see Ballas, "Demut Ha-Yisraeli Be-Sifrut Ha-Hitnagdut," 134–38.

58. Shemer, "From Chahine's *al-Iskandariyya*," 358.

59. ʿAfia, *Ḥadd al-ghawāyah*, 48.

60. ʿAfia, *Ḥadd al-ghawāyah*, 50–51.

61. Krämer, *Jews in Modern Egypt*, 4.

62. Parenthetical page references in this paragraph are to ʿAbdelmegid, *Ṭuyūr al-ʾanbar*.

63. Gerber, "Jews and Money-Lending," 100.

64. Baier, *Death and Character*, 33.

65. Baier, *Death and Character*, 131. In an interview with Mr. ʿAbd al-Nabi, an administrator at the Jewish Charity Orgnization, he told me that because he occupies a commonly known Jewish space many people who do not know him personally think he is Jewish. Interview, December 13, 2022, Eliyahu Hanavi Synagogue.

66. Baier, *Death and Character*, 131.

67. Starr, "Masquerade," 32.

68. Starr, "Masquerade," 86.

69. Starr, "Masquerade," 86.

70. Starr, "Masquerade," 131.

71. Starr, "Masquerade," 140.

72. Starr, "Masquerade," 130.

73. For more details on these measurements, see Laskier, "Egyptian Jewry," 579.

74. ʿAbdelmegid, *Ṭuyūr al-ʾanbar*, 190.

75. ʿAbdelmegid, *Ṭuyūr al-ʾanbar*, 366–71.

76. Mary Youssef, *Minorities*, 26.

77. Nasr, *Yahūd al-iskandariyyah*, 53.

78. Stillman, "New Attitudes," 197. The historian Jacob Landau attributes the spread of anti-Jewish stereotypes to the publication of political plays treating the subject of Palestine shortly after World War II. For more details, see Landau, *Studies in the Arab Theater*, 88–91.

79. Nasr, *Yahūd al-iskandariyyah*, 90.

80. Parenthetical references in the rest of this chapter are to ʿAfia, *Ḥadd al-ghawāyah*.

81. For a study on Sabra and Shatila bloobath, see Bayan Nuwayhed Al-Hout, *Sabra and Shatila*.

Bibliography

ʿAfia, ʿAmr. *Ḥadd al-ghawāyah*. Cairo: Dar Mirit, 2004.

ʿAbdelmegid, Ibrāhīm. *Ṭuyūr al-ʾanbar*. 3rd ed. Cairo: Dar Al-Shoruk, 2010.

Ackerman-Lieberman, Phillip. "Taxation." In *Encyclopedia of Jews in the Islamic World*, edited by Norman A. Stillman. Leiden: Brill, 2010. http://dx.doi.org/10.1163/1878-9781_ejiw_COM_0021050.

Alwan, Mohammed Bakir. "Jews in Arabic Literature, 1830–1914." *Al-ʿArabiyya* 11, nos. 1–2 (1978): 46–59.

Anderson, Benedict. *Imagined Communities: Reflections on the Origin and Spread of Nationalism*. London: Verso Books, 2006.

Aswany, Alaa Al. *Chicago: A Novel*. Translated by Farouk Abdel Wahab. New York: Harper, 2007.

Ayoub, Samy A. "Institutional Erasure: Legal Pluralism in Colonial Egypt." Canopy Forum, February 23, 2022. https://canopyforum.org/2022/02/23/institutional-erasure-legal-pluralism-in-colonial-egypt/.

Baier, Annette. *Death and Character: Further Reflections on Hume*. Cambridge, MA: Harvard University Press, 2008.

Ballas, Shimon. "Demut Ha-Yisraeli Be-Sifrut Ha-Hitnagdut." In *Ha-Sifrut Ha-ʿAravit Be-Tsel Ha-Milhamah*, edited by Shimon Ballas, 129–41. Tel Aviv: ʿAm ʿOved, 1978.

———. "Le Personnage israélien dans la littérature arabe." *Les Nouveaux Cahiers* 44 (1976): 46–52.

Benin, Joel. *The Dispersion of Egyptian Jewry: Culture, Politics, and the Formation of a Modern Diaspora*. Berkeley: University of California Press, 1998.

Certeau, Michel de. *The Practice of Everyday Life*. Translated by Steven Rendall. Berkeley: University of California Press, 1984.

Epstein, Louis M. *Marriage Laws in the Bible and the Talmud*. Cambridge, MA: Harvard University Press, 1942.

Friedmann, Yohanan. *Tolerance and Coercion in Islam: Interfaith Relations in the Muslim Tradition*. Cambridge: Cambridge University Press, 2003.

Gerber, Haim. "Jews and Money-Lending in the Ottoman Empire." *Jewish Quarterly Review* 72, no. 2 (1981): 100–118.

Goitein, S. D. *Jews and Arabs: Their Contact Through the Ages*. New York: Schocken Books, 1964.

Harkabi, Yehoshafat. *Arab Attitudes to Israel*. New York: John Wiley and Sons, 1974.

Ibrāhīm, Ṣunʿ Allâh. *Amrīkānlī: Amrī Kān Lī*. Cairo: Dal al-Mustaqbal al-ʿArabi, 2004.

Israel-Pelletier, Aimée. *On the Mediterranean and the Nile: The Jews of Egypt*. Bloomington: Indiana University Press, 2018.

Krämer, Gudrun. *The Jews in Modern Egypt, 1914–1952*. London: I. B. Tauris, 1989.

Landau, Jacob M. *Studies in the Arab Theater and Cinema*. London: Routledge, 2016.

Laskier, Michael M. "Egyptian Jewry under the Nasser Regime, 1956–70." *Middle Eastern Studies* 31, no. 3 (1995): 573–619.

Leeman, Alex B. "Interfaith Marriage in Islam: An Examination of the Legal Theory Behind the Traditional and Reformist Positions." *Indiana Law Journal* 84, no. 2 (2009): 743.

LeGassick, Trevor. "The Image of the Jew in Modern Arabic Fiction." *Shofar* 7, no. 3 (1989): 43–57.

Levy, Lital. "Self and the City: Literary Representations of Jewish Baghdad." *Prooftexts* 26, no. 1 (2006): 163–211.

Madadshahi, Carmel. "Restored Alexandria Synagogue Hosts Largest Jewish Prayer in Decades." *Jerusalem Post*, February 27, 2020. https://www.jpost.com/diaspora/restored-alexandria-synagogue-hosts-largest-jewish-prayer-in-decades-617756.

"Muslims in Egypt Are Trying to Preserve Its Jewish Heritage." *Economist*, September 9, 2017. https://www.economist.com/middle-east-and-africa/2017/09/09/muslims-in-egypt-are-trying-to-preserve-its-jewish-heritage.

Najar, Mustafa al-. "ʿAyzīn al-Galalīb todkhol al-Mathaf wa al-Turāth al-Yahudī awlawiyyah ʿandī." *Sout al-Omma*, December 9, 2018. http://www.soutalomma.com/Article/847164/وزير-الآثار-أمام-البرلمان-عايزين-/

الجلاليب-تدخل-المتحف-والتراث-اليهودي
?fbclid=IwAR12HNHzhy6JR38n9
szNMbNeKYrZyll1Nn1stCoVY
_7jANNnHYFvK5M2BB8.

Nasr, Mostafa. *Yahūd al-iskandariyyah*. Cairo: Al-Dar Al-ʿArabiyya lil-Kitab, 2016.

Quddūs, Ihsan ʿAbd al-. *La Tatrukni Huna Wahdi*. Cairo: Maktabet Masr, 1979.

Rabinyan, Dorit. *All the Rivers*. Translated by Jessica Cohen. New York: Random House, 2017.

Rejwan, Nissim. *Arab Aims and Israeli Attitudes: A Critique of Yehoshafat Harkabi's Prognosis of the Arab-Israeli Conflict*. Jerusalem: Leonard Davis Institute for International Relations, Hebrew University of Jerusalem, 2000.

Robbins, Bruce. "Introduction Part I: Actually Existing Cosmopolitanism." In *Cosmopolitics: Thinking and Feeling Beyond the Nation*, edited by Pheng Cheah and Bruce Robbins, 1–19. Minneapolis: University of Minnesota Press, 1998.

Shablool, Ahmed Fadl. "Riwayat *Yahūd al-Iskandariyyah* al-Murashahah li-lbokar 2017." *Bawabat al-Ahram*, November 4, 2016. http://gate.ahram.org.eg/News/1275317.aspx.

Shami, Rashad ʿAbd Allah al-. *Al-Shakhsiyah Al-Yahudiyah Fi Adab Ihsan ʿAbd Al-Quddūs*. Cairo: Dar al-Hilal, 1992.

Shemer, Yaron. "From Chahine's *al-Iskandariyya . . . leh* to *Salata baladi* and *ʿAn Yahud Misr*: Rethinking Egyptian Jews' Cosmopolitanism, Belonging and Nostalgia in Cinema." *Middle East Journal of Culture and Communication* 7, no. 3 (2014): 351–75.

Siddiq, Muhammad. *Arab Culture and the Novel: Genre, Identity and Agency in Egyptian Fiction*. London: Routledge, 2007.

Singerman, Diane, and Paul Edouard Amar. *Cairo Cosmopolitan: Politics, Culture, and Urban Space in the New Globalized Middle East*. Cairo: American University in Cairo Press, 2006.

Snir, Reuven. *Modern Arabic Literature: A Theoretical Framework*. Edinburgh: Edinburgh University Press, 2017.

Somekh, Sasson. "Cold, Tall Buildings: The Jewish Neighbor in the Works of Arab Authors." *Jerusalem Quarterly* 52 (1989): 111–25.

———. "Dmuyot Yehudim Ba-Sifrut Ha-ʿAravit Shel Yamenu." In *Sofrim Muslemim ʿAl Yehudim Ve-Yahadut*, edited by Hava Lazarus-Yafeh, 235–45. Jerusalem: Merkaz Zalman Shazar, 1996.

Starr, Deborah Ann. "Ambivalent Levantines / Levantine Ambivalences: Literary Constructions of Egyptian Jewish Identity." PhD diss., University of Michigan, 2000.

———. "Masquerade and the Performance of National Imaginaries: Levantine Ethics, Aesthetics, and Identities in Egyptian Cinema." *Journal of Levantine Studies* 1, no. 2 (2011): 31–57.

———. *Remembering Cosmopolitan Egypt: Literature, Culture, and Empire*. London: Routledge, 2009.

———. "Sensing the City: Representations of Cairo's Harat Al-Yahud." *Prooftexts* 26, nos. 1–2 (2006): 138–62.

Stillman, Norman A. "New Attitudes toward the Jew in the Arab World." *Jewish Social Studies* 37, nos. 3–4 (1975): 197–204.

Webman, Esther. "The Image of the Jew/Zionist/Israeli in the Arab World." In *Muslim Attitudes to Jews and Israel: The Ambivalence of Rejection, Antagonism, Tolerance and Cooperation*, edited by Moshe Maʾoz, 48–66. Brighton: Sussex Academic Press, 2010.

Youssef, Mary. *Minorities in the Contemporary Egyptian Novel*. Edinburgh: Edinburgh University Press, 2018.

CHAPTER 4

Al-Zaman al-Gamīl Refigured

Jews and Re-narration of the Nation on Egyptian TV

ISKANDAR AHMAD ABDALLA

It is 1948. *Ḥārat al-Yahūd,* the Jewish quarter in the heart of Cairo, witnesses the outbreak of the Arab-Israeli War. A boy warns the crowd, shouting, "Turn the lights off! There's an airstrike!" The inhabitants of the quarter, fearful, some in pajamas or half-dressed, leave their shops and homes, hurrying to their refuge: the synagogue of the *ḥārah*. Inside the synagogue, the camera continues to move hastily, capturing the troubled crowd before coming to rest on the devout faces of the scene's main protagonists—three mothers and neighbors: a Jew, a Christian, and a Muslim. The three women stand closely aligned in a row in front of the bimah and pray, each in her own way. This is the opening scene of one the most popular Egyptian TV series of the last several years. It premiered in 2015 during the holy month of Ramadan.[1]

The plot is almost entirely fictional, and only a few characters are based on historical figures; nevertheless, the series lays claim to "authenticity" and "historical precision."[2] The set and costume designers used Egyptian films as references in their urge to remain true to the fashion of the period, and "historical experts" were hired as consultants to ensure the plot's conformity with historical facts.[3] Produced by one of the biggest film and TV production companies in Egypt, *Ḥārat al-Yahūd* is characterized by costly scenery and costume design, and stars some of the region's highest-paid film actors.[4] The success of the series was reflected not merely in its high viewership ratings, but also in controversial debates and intensive media coverage in the surrounding Arabic-speaking world and—unprecedentedly for a TV series—around the world.

In the *New York Times*, Joel Benin describes *Ḥārat al-Yahūd* as "more consistent with the facts than almost anything else that has appeared in Egyptian mass media in recent decades."[5] *Le Figaro* commented, "It is the first time that the Jewish community is shown [in Egyptian cinema and television] in a positive light."[6] In Germany, *Die Zeit* described the series as "unbelievable news after 80 years of hatred" and asked if such a work could reshape (*umformen*) the allegedly anti-Semitic views of Egyptians on Jewish people, while the *Süddeutsche Zeitung* considered the series a part of the Egyptian president's new political course of rapprochement with Israel.[7]

In fact, *Ḥārat al-Yahūd* was unconventional enough to draw the attention of the media and become a topic of public debate. The series signifies a remarkable shift in the way Jews have been perceived in Egyptian popular memory and represented in its cultural artifacts. Even if the show maintains some generic conventions and stereotypical depictions associated with Jews in local films and TV productions since the 1960s, it breaks with many. Jews have traditionally been depicted as Israelis, and almost exclusively as enemies of the state, spies, or traitors, which is not the case in *Ḥārat al-Yahūd*.[8] Instead of understanding this shift in terms of potential changes in Egyptians' views of Jews or Israel or as a sign of diminishing anti-Semitism—a claim for which the series has been celebrated in Western media—I suggest understanding it as primarily concerned with viewing one's own history and embedded in national modes of self-perception and self-representation.

This chapter aims to sketch a picture of contemporary historical imagination about Jews of Egypt and the whole period under scrutiny in general, inquiring about the collective longings and visions such imagination implies. It reads *Ḥārat al-Yahūd* as an allegory for the Egyptian nation: for how it imagines itself historically and how it envisions its future.

A historical melodrama set between 1948 and 1954, *Ḥārat al-Yahūd* revolves around a love story between a Muslim military officer, ʿAli (ʾIyad Nassār), and a Jewish saleswoman, Layla (Mennah Shalabi). The families of the two lovers are neighbors and friends, and they both belong to the urban Egyptian petite bourgeoisie: Harun, Layla's father (Aḥmad Kamāl), owns a drapery shop; his son, Musa (Aḥmad Ḥātim), who is very enthusiastic about Zionist ideas, is a dancer; whereas ʿAli's father, Ḥusainy (Samy al-ʿAdl), owns a yogurt factory; his daughter Fatima (Basmah Yāssir) has just finished school and wants to be a physician. A Christian family lives in the same house: Stefanos, a civil servant, his wife, Therese (Ingy Sharaf), and their only daughter. The love affair between ʿAli and Layla is neither endorsed by their families nor wholly disapproved. Both sides cast doubt on whether this love can be fruitful. With the escalation of the political situation in the wake of the 1948 War, the doubts grow and eventually are proven valid.

The series depicts Jews as neighbors, friends, and lovers; we see them in their everyday lives, not necessarily engaging in devious political plans or evil conspiracies but doing the mundane things everyone else does. We see Jews at work, at home, dining, or listening to the radio; we see them at the coffeehouses sharing good times with friends. On a technical level, the series also breaks with the visual elements traditionally deployed in depicting Jews. The Jews of the quarter are not distinct from other characters in their performance, clothing, or accessories; they are not lit differently, or shot from a low-angle camera perspective or with specific lenses to highlight their otherness or wickedness, as is the case in many Egyptian films.[9]

The Egyptian nation, often perceived in public discourse as a combination of two elements (*'unṣuray al-ummah*)—that is, Muslims and Copts—has, through the inclusion of Jews, as shown in *Ḥārat al-Yahūd*, become a nation made up of three elements. The introductory scene of the series with the three mothers praying in the synagogue can be read as a symbolic staging of this idea: Jews are as Egyptian as Muslims or Christians. Even in that critical moment when the newly established State of Israel militarily attacks Egypt, the synagogue of the *ḥārah* becomes the shelter for all, the stage of enacting an inclusive Egyptianness that stands beyond religious difference. Such shift in perception and representation can be understood as an attempt to visually renarrate the nation and redraw its potential boundaries.[10] In contrast to their physical absence, reimagining Jews on screen serves as a narrative trope through which the story of the nation is nostalgically evoked. Jews became an object of national *nostalgia*.

In this chapter, *Ḥārat al-Yahūd* offers a case study for capturing the characteristics of a nostalgic narrative of the nation within which the Jews of Egypt are dominantly located. The content of the series is analyzed through incorporating it into the discursive spaces it creates; the spheres in which the series has been debated and commented upon; and the interpretive framework of the audience, perceived here as active decoders, who negotiate, modify, and debate the mediated content.[11]

THE NOSTALGIC GAZE: A TELEVISED JOURNEY THROUGH THE "BEAUTIFUL AGE"

One day before the airing of the first episode of the series, author and screenwriter Midḥat al-ʿAdl stated the following in a short interview on TV:

> The Jewish quarter we are going to watch resembles Egypt as it was in the past. Muslims, Christians, Jews, Armenians, etc. live there in peace together. Egypt was a cosmopolitan nation. . . . I wanted to show Egypt as it was. A nation that acknowledges and accepts the other, whatever he believes, whatever his religion is, as long as he respects this country. [In *Ḥārat al-Yahūd*] we will witness al-zaman al-gamīl [the beautiful age]. The time we usually see in black-and-white films, the time when Umm Kulthum, every first Thursday evening of the month, used to have her concert. Whatever religion one had, all Egyptians gathered and listened to her together. These were times of strong bonds and good relations that are absent today.[12]

Since the early years of cinema, motion pictures have demonstrated enormous potential to render what is deemed unattainable—whether for economic or political reasons or as a result of the physical laws of time and space—visible and accessible to a wider audience. Through motion pictures, audiences can travel through time, to the past or to the future, and perambulate up and down impossible places. Motion pictures can be "an instrument with the power to 'suture' viewers into pasts they have not lived, . . . a site in which people experience a bodily mimetic encounter with a past that was actually theirs."[13]

As the quote above suggests, Midḥat al-ʿAdl, poet, TV journalist, and screenwriter of *Ḥārat al-Yahūd*, promised viewers of the series an encounter with a past that "resembles Egypt" and a journey through a time when—

according to him—Muslims, Christians, and Jews used to live together in peace as subjects of a common "cosmopolitan nation." In *Ḥārat al-Yahūd, al-zaman al-gamīl,* the good old days of the "beautiful age," are made palpable.

Al-zaman al-gamīl is a term that has been continuously used in Egypt's public debates about culture, architecture, and politics, but also often invoked in novels and films.[14] As is the case here, its utterance usually evokes glamorous images of film classics or the memory of influential cultural personalities (like Umm Kulthum). Moreover, *al-zaman al-gamīl* is always inscribed with idealistic notions and positive attributes that are allegedly absent today. Unlike the Belle Époque, which has been constructed by Western historiography as an epochal term to mourn the lost world before the first World War,[15] the temporal contours of *al-zaman al-gamīl* in Egypt are not fixed. The term is sometimes used to describe the period before the coup d'état of the Free Officers in 1952, and sometimes it includes the period under Nasser until the war of 1967; in other cases, it can be a decade shorter or longer. *Al-zaman al-gamīl* has dynamic borders that can be adjusted to fit the ideological or political standpoint of its speaker. *Al-zaman al- gamīl* is uttered not for the sake of identifying a specific time period but to invoke an idealized past that is the antithesis of a present condition. It is a *nostalgic* utterance that can be dialectically conceptualized as "a retreat from the present [and] a retrieval for the future."[16] Al-ʿAdl's invocation of the "beautiful age," his attempt to reimagine it in the series and contrast its values, figures, and images with a present-day "absence," can be read as a mode of nostalgia. Nostalgia suggests an alternative access to history, one that acknowledges unrealized dreams and obsolete future visions and, at the same time, aspires to find a way out of a crisis-laden present, to cope with loss and absence. Made of two Greek words, *nóstos* (homecoming) and *álgos* (pain), "nostalgia" was coined in the seventeenth century to signify a pathological category describing a sort of homesickness, associated with somatic and psychological symptoms. By the nineteenth century the term almost ceased to denote any pathological conditions and had instead shifted its meaning from abundant spaces to abundant times. Since then it has come to describe an emotion of longing for lost times.[17]

Remembering "the beautiful age" in a TV series has political implications imbued with present anxieties and convictions. Witnessing it alive on screen enables a collective practice of cultural identification with the nation it allegedly belongs to. The notion of "home" here again becomes pivotal to nostalgic longings. Longings for a "home that no longer exists is . . . a sentiment of loss and displacement, but also a romance with one's own fantasy."[18]

The alternative temporality of the plot articulates, through its contrast to the present, a sense of longing for the *nóstos*, for the homecoming, for crossing the gap between the "space of experience" and the "horizon of expectation."[19] *Ḥārat al-Yahūd* is doubtless a commodified cultural product that strives to embrace generic conventions and generate profit. Yet the narrative it presents is not entirely nostalgic in the sense of what Arjun Appadurai designates a merchandised "armchair nostalgia," manipulating viewers by letting them miss what they have neither lived, nor lost, nor shaped as their collective history.[20] The nostalgic account deployed here grounds itself by reference to a historical loss, tangible in the absence of Jewish life in Egypt today. In doing so, it does not aim to compensate for what has been lost, but rather to activate national sentiments in relation to mediated perceptions of transition and loss, to stage history as a fictional lived experience with which the viewers can engage, and a loss they can contemplate, all the while reimagining the nation.

But how does this process of activation take place through narration and images? What tropes and representations are deployed to allegorize the *nóstos* and narrate the nation? What vision for the present and future is implied in this nostalgic gaze on the past? The following sections attempt to answer these questions.

IMAGINED SPACES: LOCATING THE "BEAUTIFUL AGE"

A beautiful age must have a geography. It can only be imagined in space. The Jewish Quarter still exists in today's Cairo. From the Ottoman conquest until the end of the nineteenth century, most Jews in Cairo used to live there.[21] Yet, according to the director, Muḥammad al-ʿAdl, filming in the original *ḥarah* (quarter) was out of the question. He believes that the audience has "specific references" for how Cairo would have looked during the period in which the series is set (1948–54).[22] These references are "nonexistent" in today's Jewish Quarter, and thus scenery had to be built for filming purposes. The Jewish Quarter had to be reinvented in order for "the beautiful age" to be topographically fixed.[23]

On the one hand, the new scenery introduces itself as based on references supposed to be historical, and on the other hand, it means to allegorize the nation. Scenic design in motion pictures stages the spatial setting within which the events take place, but simultaneously transforms places into narrative spaces.[24] Cinematic landscapes and designed sceneries often perform as agents in the plot, with a life of their own. They are coded with cultural and political views expressed as spatial/natural. They project visions, mediate meaning, and simultaneously create it.[25]

"Clean streets, clean cafes, no dirt, no noise. The series makes us yearn for the streets and quarters of the past. Egypt must be back as it was. As the one we saw on screen."[26] With these words, star TV presenter Poussy Chalabi commented on the series, emphasizing how, in the case under scrutiny, spatial imaginations regarding the past are closely tied to specific visions for the future and to certain sentiments of uneasiness toward the present. The scenery of the series corresponds with spatial imaginaries—predominantly envisaged by an urban middle-class elite—about how Egypt should look in the future, while, through contrast, the problems of the present moment, the troubles with "dirt" and "noise," are subtly highlighted. Already in the first two episodes of the series it is noteworthy how and where the "beautiful age" is placed. The elegance and beauty of the Jewish department store Cicurel, where Layla works, are highlighted in several panoramic long shots, tracking the crowds of neatly dressed customers, the valuable furniture, the sparkling chandeliers, and the stylishly well-mannered French-speaking salesgirls. However, and so as not to give the impression of a fully westernized Egyptian Jewry, the European aura enveloping the storehouse has been neutralized by the interiors of a house inhabited by Nahum (played by Gamīl Ratib), an old man, likely the head of the Jewish community, always wearing the traditional Egyptian ʿabāya.[27] The house is furnished with wooden Arabic-style chairs. Walls, stairs, and floors are adorned with charming arabesques, ornaments, and lattices inspired by Islamic architecture.

The pyramids, the symbol for Egypt's national pride par excellence, act as the backdrop before which the love story between the main protagonists is introduced to the audience in the first episodes. There we see ʿAli—in military uniform—and Layla together for the first time, walking arm in arm, in a monumental long shot dominated by the view of the pyramids, functioning as an associative space for national mythmaking.

THE VOICE OF EGYPT: UMM KULTHUM AS A FIGURE OF MEMORY

In his reading of Maurice Halbwachs's work on collective memory, Jan Assmann reminds us that for memories to be collective they have to be either objectified in cultural artifacts or fixed in topographical sites. However, Halbwachs's notion that in the moment when these sites disappear collective memories vanish as well seems to be incorrect.[28] Many of the tangible traces of Jewish life in Cairo have been closed, lost, demolished, or irrevocably appropriated to serve other functions, yet this very sense of loss seems to induce and simulate a collective memory of a national community, culturally and politically reinvented on screen, recaptured in symbolic sceneries and located in imagined spaces of a lost beautiful age.

Assmann expands Halbwachs's conception of collective memory by distinguishing between a communicative and a cultural memory. The former is based on everyday communications, whereas the latter is characterized by its distance from the everyday.[29] The "distance from the everyday" does not consequently signify a detachment from contemporary references, as cultural memory "always relates its knowledge to an actual and contemporary situation."[30] The distance denotes rather that the objects of memory are past events fixed in a specific horizon of time. The past events are maintained in cultural formations that Assmann calls *Erinnerungsfiguren*, or figures of memory. Figures of memory culturally objectify past events and stabilize collectively shared narratives.[31] In *Ḥārat al-Yahūd*, *al-zaman al-gamīl* is not merely captured in space or virtual sites of memory, but also in *Erinnerungsfiguren*. The legendary singer Umm Kulthum (1898–1975), whose popularity in the Arab world remains unsurpassed, operates as one such "figure of memory" in the series.

Her voice is omnipresent in the *ḥārah*; it rings continuously from radios, in coffeehouses, in homes, at private gatherings, celebrations, or dinners; it accompanies lovers in their longings and mourners in their pain. Her voice does not function merely as a sort of background music, but becomes a topic of the narrative itself. In one scene, Layla's mother disagrees with her son's claims of feeling insecure as a Jew in Egypt: "You are simply wrong. The long years I lived here peacefully with my neighbors assure me that you are wrong. Every first Thursday of the month, we all gather in one of our flats to listen to Umm Kulthum. With her voice, we all swing in happiness and shout in ecstasy, no one has ever cared who has what religion or who prays and who not."[32] The conjunction of national sentiments and the voice of Umm Kulthum becomes clearer in another instance, when the inhabitants of the *ḥārah* meet to celebrate the release of their neighbors, who were imprisoned for their guerilla activities against the British presence in Suez. The celebration takes place both privately and publicly in two overlapping scenes. The common denominator between the two scenes is the voice of Umm Kulthum. It rings loudly out of the radios in both locations and occupies the center stage. Everybody listens to her with great relish, while shouts of excitement mingle with patriotic statements about longings for home. Her voice acts both as a companion to the patriotic talks the protagonists share and as a subject of them.

Privately, the families of Harun and Ḥusainy meet in the flat of their neighbor Stefanos (Muḥammad Maḥmmūd), one of the released detainees. "You are an honor for us, Stefanos," says ʿAli, and the other attendees enthusiastically approve his praise. Only Layla is slightly dissatisfied. Certainly not because she disagrees with ʿAli or questions Stefanos's patriotism, but rather because Umm Kulthum's singing has been interrupted. "How dare you talk about politics while 'The Lady' is singing?" she says. Everyone approves her unanimously, yet ironically, instead of listening attentively, they all agree that Layla should dance to the song. After some hesitation, Layla starts dancing, while casting shy glances at her lover.

Umm Kulthum continues singing, yet the camera brings us to the next location, the coffeehouse where other inhabitants gather to celebrate the detainees publicly. The radio out of which her voice loudly rings occupies half of the frame. We see the gathering crowd, blurred at first, before the lens shifts its focus from the radio to the people. "It is worth leaving the prison, even just for listening to Umm Kulthum again. How much we missed her voice!" says one of the released "national heroes."[33]

In fact, listening to Umm Kulthum in Egypt has been a kind of participatory social practice her fans cherish beyond concert halls and long after her death. While they listen to her, their musical ecstasy is articulated bodily or verbally in gestures of admiration or yells of delight and thus communicated to the colisteners. "Home" is incarnated in these moments as a commonly shared musical excitement. Recalling these moments concurrently engenders and vocalizes the *algia,* the pains of homesickness. Umm Kulthum is what the detainees have missed most of all away from their homes, and it is her music that Layla longs for when she leaves Egypt in despair.[34] If nationalists of various backgrounds and in several contexts have used female images and characteristics allegedly understood as feminine to symbolize the nation and give it a discursive shape,[35] in *Ḥārat al-Yahūd* a similar rhetoric is formulated through the voice of Umm Kulthum acting as a national symbol, as a shared legacy that self-evidently unifies all Egyptians.

Interestingly, the long stage career of Umm Kulthum, from 1920 to 1973, seems to verify this in how her stage performances have accompanied different vital phases of modern state-building in Egypt. This fact has contributed to her artistic legacy as a figure who stands beyond time and, as it has often been said, succeeded where politicians have failed: in unifying not only Egyptians, but also all Arabs. Ifdal Elsaket notes that the engagement with the figure of Umm Kulthum can provide us with "an illuminating entry point for the study of Egyptian constructions of the nation."[36] Elsaket argues, furthermore, that Umm Kulthum's public image, often inscribed with signs of ideal femininity, has managed to define the struggle of ordinary Egyptians and to embody multiple narratives and configurations of a postcolonial Egyptian nation.[37] In the same vein, Ella Shohat underlines how Umm Kulthum's voice has "managed to transcend . . . social tensions and political conflicts" and to serve as a marker of an unquestioned national identity usually assumed by third-world nationalist discourses.[38]

Looking at it through the prism of Assmann's conception of collective memory, the legacy of Umm Kulthum functions here like "texts, rites and monuments" and other cultural formations to stabilize a collective identity, a joint experience of home, and symbolically reify the memories of the "beautiful age."[39] Yet, if the "beautiful age" is distant from the everyday life of the contemporary audience, Umm Kulthum's voice is definitely not. It is neither lost nor irretrievable. For Egyptians today, Umm Kulthum is thoroughly ubiquitous, ever-present in their daily life. Her songs have not merely been reproduced in countless copies in different formats, but the lyrics and melodies are memorized by millions upon millions of Egyptians, many of whom were born after her death. Umm Kulthum stands here as a witness to the lost "beautiful age"; her voice shapes the audiences' space of experience about the past and simultaneously alludes to their lived present, thus merging the sphere of communicative memory with that of the cultural.

THE COSMOPOLITAN NATION

As Midḥat al-ʿAdl, the author of the series, suggests, home in the beautiful age was a "cosmopolitan" nation. Al-ʿAdl locates himself within liberal traditions, which perceive the first half of the twentieth century in Egypt as "a cosmopolitan age," associated with a flourishing cultural and intellectual life, and contrasts it with a "degenerated" present dominated by Islamist modes of thought.[40] In *Ḥārat al-Yahūd*, cosmopolitanism makes itself conspicuous basically by the promotion of religious tolerance. The quarter showcases a friendly atmosphere in which peaceful relationships between the Jewish inhabitants of the *ḥārah* and their Christian and Muslim fellow citizens prevail. Like a big family, all are closely affiliated; they care for each other in times of crisis and call each other brothers and sisters. At the same time, the series tries to avoid the trivializing portrayals frequently deployed in representations of minorities on screen. Unlike Copts appearing in many Egyptian films and state-funded TV dramas, whose difference is often "silenced for the sake of national unity,"[41] the Jews of the series—as well as the Copts—are shown as equal to their fellows not by virtue of being like-minded or because of their lack of deficiencies and negative traits, but *despite* their flaws. The *ḥārah* is neither a utopia of peace and harmony, nor is flawlessness a precondition for being part of it. For instance, already in the very first scene, we notice the signs of a deep conflict between Layla and ʾIbtihal, one of the Muslim inhabitants of the *ḥārah*. "Where is the Jewess?" ʾIbtihal angrily asks her maid, while contempt fills her eyes. The conflict escalates by the end of the first episode, when ʾIbtihal tries to disfigure Layla's face through an acid attack. Soon we figure out that this conflict has nothing to do with religion, but rather with jealousy and rivalry over the love of the same man, ʿAli.

Nevertheless, religious practices and beliefs are visible in the *ḥārah* and its public life. The protagonists of the series identify themselves strongly with religious customs and symbols. ʿAli takes a Qurʾan copy he got as a present from ʾIbtihal with him to the war front. "I am sorry, my love," he says to Layla. "It is the book of God. I have to take it with me, even if it is a present from ʾIbtihal." The Jewish family of Harun observes Shabbat, and when Layla gets sick they ask the rabbi to come and bless her. Eventually he recommends she stay a whole night in the synagogue, and only the

Zionist brother Musa condemns this recommendation as superstitious behavior.

The different religious communities are visible in the public life of the *ḥārah* through their symbols and rituals. We see Jews celebrating their weddings publicly in the street, as many Egyptians traditionally do.[42] We see the bridegroom—wearing a kippah—and the bride sitting under the chuppah, according to Jewish religious custom, while some male attendees greet them with Hasidic dances.[43] Even Jewish ritual slaughters are carried out in public. It is not that religion is relegated to the private sphere, but rather that no religious community is shown to have an advantage over another in public. Public practice of religion is acceptable as far as religious differences are understood as secondary within a supreme national ethos of unity. The only valid claim to sovereignty is national affiliation. It is true that Muslims are the majority, yet "the *hārah*'s name is eventually *Ḥārat-al-Yahūd* [the Jewish quarter]," as Harun tells his wife, who thought about moving out after the political situation had escalated in Egypt and repeated incidents of attacks against Jewish property in the country had taken place.[44] "There is no difference among Egyptians," says ʿAli to his sister when she mistrusts her neighbors because they are Jews.[45] "I am Egyptian first and Jewish second," Layla asserts in another scene.[46] The visibility of religion in public is conditional on its depoliticization. Religion might be constitutive of the personal beliefs of the state's citizens and their ethical self-cultivation, but it is not fundamental to national identity. "Religion is a false standard," says ʿAli to his father when he expresses his concerns about letting him marry a Jewess.[47] In fact, their marriage eventually fails not because she is Jewish and he is Muslim, but rather when it is found out that Layla's brother is a "Zionist traitor" who planned terrorist attacks in Egypt. Patriotism, rather than religion, becomes the standard through which we can differentiate between a "good" and a "bad" citizen.

Ḥārat al-Yahūd presents to contemporary Egyptians a model for an ardent patriotism demonstrated by ancestors regardless of their religion or piety. Jews were also among the patriots. The communist Henry Curiel (1914–1978), who founded the movement known as *al-Ḥarakah al-Miṣriyyah lil-Taḥrīr al-Waṭaniy* (Egyptian Movement for National Liberation, HAMETO) in 1943 and was expelled from Egypt in 1950,[48] appears in the series in a small role as a patriotic rebel. He leads a secret group including military officers to overthrow the monarchy and proceed with the war against Israel.[49] Like ʿAli, who fought against Israel in 1948, Layla, who went to Israel for a short time, was tortured and imprisoned there as well because she disobeyed orders and defended Palestinians. She comes back to Egypt with an almost disfigured face. Her father, Harun, wants to join the volunteer militias fighting against the British in Suez. The Christian Therese and her daughter want to volunteer as well, whereas Therese's husband, Stefanos, faces imprisonment for being involved in insurgent activities against the British. Stefanos had previously appeared in the first episodes as a broken man with wounded pride after catching his wife cheating on him with Musa. At the end of the series, however, on account of his patriotism, Stefanos's wounds have been healed, revealing a sublime manhood befitting a national hero. Eventually Stefanos's wife repents of her sins and asks for forgiveness, although she seemingly remains in love with Musa until the end. Even the owner of the brothel on the margin of the *ḥārah*, named Zināt, is celebrated as a national heroine for her part in insurgencies against the British. Whether one is Muslim, Christian, Jewish, or even a prostitute, neither religion nor ethical conduct is what counts. The "good" ones are those who dedicate themselves to the nation. All these characters reveal weaknesses and flaws for which they are not necessarily condemned, as long as their unconditional love for the nation is beyond reproach. The cosmopolitanism nostalgically evoked here diminishes religious beliefs or pious conduct as markers of political identity, but, at the same time, it remains inexorably tied to national interests and affinities, to a framework of an unconditional patriotism. It thereby opposes the prevailing understanding of cosmopolitanism as the "antithesis of parochial nationalism,"[50] as it becomes entirely subsumed within the borders of national identification. Jewishness is not evoked as a means to question monotonous imaginaries about the nation and its boundaries; rather, Jewish patriotism is foregrounded to cohere the nation, to embody a difference whose inclusion is instantly hinging upon subduing it to an unequivocal national ideal of unity. Cosmopolitanism is assumed here as a currently blemished, yet innate feature of the nation. Its restaging is an attempt to recall a forgotten national history, not to unsettle its parochial foundations,[51] nor to reckon with the "historical complexities that produced Egyptianization."[52] *Ḥārat al-Yahūd* remains thus on good terms with the conventional politics of identity creation in Egyptian TV dramas in general: "to shore up the nation-state."[53]

HEROES AND VILLAINS

No melodrama can function without villains, and even in the "beautiful age" there are those who disturb peaceful life. Unlike Egyptian spy films and TV series, the villains here are not the Jews or even the Zionists, but the Muslim Brothers, represented by Khalil, a salesman in the *ḥārah*, and his son Ḥasan. The Muslim Brothers appear as traitors, those who want to damage the pillars of national unity and charge Jews with treason, religious fanatics who ignite sedition and are involved in wicked conspiracies to deceive Egyptians. Although Khalil and his son are continuously criticized and taunted by the other inhabitants of the *ḥārah*, their rhetoric finds more supporters by the end of the series with the escalation of the political situation. Even Faṭimah, ʿAli's sister, eventually supports the Muslim Brothers. Under the influence of her lover Ḥasan, who convinces her to marry him in secret, she flees her parents' house, abandoning the progressive values she used to believe in the earlier episodes. But also, beyond the *ḥārah*, the threat of the Muslim Brothers to the multireligious cosmopolitan nation looms.

Ḥasan al-Bannā (1906–1949), the founder of the Muslim Brotherhood, appears in a few scenes in the series. Deploying dramatic tools that are typically used in mainstream cinema to depict villains, the camera captures al-Bannā (played by Muḥammad ʿAbdil Ḥafiẓ) giving a speech to his supporters after the Arab defeat of 1948. The camera tilts down, showing the politely seated and attentively listening crowd from above, before it rests on the back of the speaker's head. In this moment, the lens zooms in to focus on al-Bannā's head while blurring the crowd in the background. In his speech, al-Bannā calls for jihad against Jewish properties and institutions in Egypt. "The war is not only in Palestine, but the war against Jews is here and there,"[54] he says while warning music blares.

It is interesting to contrast this scene with the opening scene in the synagogue. While in the latter an atmosphere of intimacy is created through the circular tracking shots, and the diversity of the crowd is evident in the variety of colorful outfits, the mise-en-scène of the former is rather symmetrical, rendering the gathered crowd identical and highlighting the strict hierarchy dominating the place.[55]

The series demonstrates another candid contrast that is typical for melodramas: the ruthlessness of the villain Islamists is contrasted with the heroic actions and sentiments of the military officers, who are presented as the liberators of the nation and the protectors of its integrity against enemies, whether British, Zionist, or Muslim Brother. In the series, the heroism of the officers stands beyond question, setting the standard for patriotism and love of nation. "Good" citizens, whether Muslim or Jewish, should adhere to that. "The military is a red line. Nobody is entitled to suspect it," says a Jewish activist in one episode,[56] while in another episode Layla and her father enthusiastically celebrate the Free Officers' successful coup against the king. "Of course our future will be better. It's the military! It's ʿAli and his comrades [who are in power now], not Khalil and his fellows," says Layla to her worried mother.[57]

Yet—and as is usually the case in melodramas—the future that unfolds in the later episodes inflicts agony and distress. If Musa's Zionist convictions lead to Layla's family falling apart, with the mother following her son, leaving her beloved home and going to Israel, so do Ḥasan's Islamist convictions lead to the tearing apart of ʿAli's family, with Fatima eventually fleeing her parents' house and abandoning the "cosmopolitan" values she used to endorse. The "beautiful age" is over, and Jewish existence in Egypt comes to its inevitable end. The love story between ʿAli and Layla is doomed to failure. The blame for this is laid not at the feet of the Zionists alone but also at those of the Islamists, who scatter families and demolish homes.

While the series pioneers new ways of portraying Jewish themes and characters, thereby challenging established narratives about Jews and their relationship to the nation, it remains confined to a populistic exclusionary narrative that glorifies the Egyptian military on the one hand and on the other hand replaces one enemy with another. In this changed political atmosphere, the Muslim Brothers have replaced Jews as the enemy. "What a pity! We have all lived together in peace, Jews, Christians, and Muslims, until those masons came, the Muslim Brothers, whose goal is to destroy Nations," comments a viewer on YouTube in phrasing that encapsulates this bias: the anti-Semitic trope of the conspiratorial Jew undermining nations and communities is being projected here onto the Muslim Brothers.

EPILOGUE

Narrating the past on screen engages audiences in ways intended not only to render historical events cognitively intelligible but also to affectively attach audiences to a certain narrative about history. In such an affective bonding and by virtue of the imagination, history becomes feasible and sensible, while the audience's sense of collective belonging—as sharers of a commonly staged past—is evoked and reestablished in ways that inevitably reflect current anxieties and political entanglements. In *Ḥārat al-Yahūd*, history is observed through a nostalgic gaze that seeks to bridge the gap between a lived experience and an imagined one. The lost Jews of Egypt are metonymic for a lost beautiful age, projected onto the present while also acting as its contrast, its role model, and the essence of the nation. At the very end, the analysis above can be contextualized in a framework that considers the following.

First, TV dramas in Egypt function not only as a means of entertainment but as a means of national pedagogy. They seek to "mold the national community" and convey notions of morality that are "community-oriented and thoroughly imbricated with the available political discourses."[58] Even in times of privatization and the state's retreat from TV production, the validity of this assumption remains intact as a generic convention that TV series are expected to pursue. Second, the reactions of some Western media toward the new series imply an inclination to regard Arabic TV as a priori anti-Semitic. There is already a large body of literature that engages primarily with representations of Jews in Arabic TV in its attempt to diagnose anti-Semitism in the Arab world. Though it might have been interesting to draw on this literature and analyze *Ḥārat al-Yahūd* with a focus on its role in reproducing or challenging allegedly anti-Semitic representations, I suggest instead an alternative path, shifting the focus from the Jews themselves to the Egyptian nation as the main object of representation and thus of analysis. By the same token, the public controversies that arose around the series among critics, journalists, commentators, and the audience on social networks can be regarded not primarily as an indicator of a rise or decline of anti-Semitic attitudes, but rather as a forum for debating the nation itself: the borders of its community, the political and moral concepts it was supposedly established upon, and those it should embrace in the future.

Finally, despite its unconventional treatment of a sensitive issue and the novelty it exhibits in bypassing certain taboos, *Ḥārat al-Yahūd* should not be regarded as particularly exceptional; rather, it is a part of a broader discursive shift regarding Jews and other (historical) minorities that has been taking place in Egypt over the last two decades. Jews have reappeared as significant characters in several recent productions, both fiction and documentaries. These works, though still subscribing to a rigid political framework, have tried to reimagine Jews beyond the image of the enemy without invalidating the narrative of national conflict entirely. For example, the documentary *Salāṭah baladī* (Salade maison; 2007) by Nadia Kamel features the director's mother, Mary Kamel, who tries to trace back the roots of her family and reunite with her Jewish relatives who left Egypt decades ago. In *Wilad al ʿAm* (Escaping Tel Aviv; 2009) by Sharif ʿArafa, we encounter Victor, an Egyptian Jew who lives in Tel Aviv but claims not to be a Zionist. He loves Umm Kulthum and remembers the streets of Cairo by heart. We also encounter Madam Vera in *Heliopolis* (2009) by Ahmad Abdalla. She is Jewish and still lives in Cairo, while refraining from making her identity public. She isolates herself in her old flat and hardly leaves it, as if wanting to resist the radically changed realities of Cairo. Stereotypical representations of Jews are also critically referred to in recent films. In a key scene of Amir Ramses's *ʿAn yahūd miṣr: Nihāyat al-riḥla* (Jews of Egypt: The end of the journey), Magda Haroun, the head of the Jewish community in Egypt, criticizes how Jews are perceived in the Egyptian popular imaginary and states that the time has come to challenge this perception. Finally, in 2019 and after the remarkable success of *Ḥārat al-Yahūd*, another TV series, titled *Al-Daher* (named after a district of old Cairo), features a love story between a Muslim police officer and a Jewish French girl of Egyptian origin who went to Egypt to discover her family roots.

Even if some of the Jewish characters appearing in recent productions like these adhere to the stereotypical image of Jews on screen, they reveal a broader quest for different modes of representation.

Ḥārat al-Yahūd may break with long traditions of stereotypical, ideologically restricted modes of representation, but the series can be regarded as an example of a wider transformation of Jewish representation on screen and in other cultural accounts of recent years. As previously mentioned, this transformation cannot be separated from larger shifts in the narratives through which Egyptian secular urban elites perceive their nation and articulate a nostalgic interest in relation to a lost ethnic and religious diversity—to what they deem a cosmopolitan national culture.

Notes

1. For more than half a century, Ramadan has been the main season for Arab *musalsalat* (TV series). The demand for TV shows is high, and media interest is demonstrated widely beforehand, giving rise to a public discourse about the stars and their roles.
2. CBC Egypt, "Hunā al-ʿaṣimah," June 17, 2015.
3. CBC Egypt, "Hunā al-ʿaṣimah," June 17, 2015.
4. *Ḥārat al-Yahūd* was produced by al-ʿAdl Group, a family business to which the director (Muḥammad al-ʿAdl), screenwriter (Midḥ at al-ʿAdl), and one of the lead actors (Samy al-ʿAdl) all belong.
5. Kirkpatrick, "For Egypt, TV Show's Shocking Twist."
6. Mehadji, "Le Quartier juif."
7. Joffe, "Seifenoper-Wunder"; Steinke, "Verbotene Liebe."
8. As stated by Magda Haroun, the current head of the Jewish community in Egypt, when she was interviewed by Amir Ramsis in the second part of his documentary *ʿAn yahūd miṣr: Nihāyat al-riḥla* or *Jews of Egypt: The End of a Journey*. I have tackled the question of the representation of Jews in Egyptian cinema elsewhere; see Abdalla, "Shalom, Cohen, Salome." See also Armbrust, "Political Film in Egypt," 233–38.
9. For example, Gina in *Jarimah fī al-ḥay al-hadiʾ* (A crime in the quite neighborhood) by Ḥusam al-Dīn Musṭafah, 1967, or Yussif in *Fatah min israʾil* (A girl from Israel) by ʾIhāb Rady, 1999.
10. Bhabha, "Introduction," 1.
11. Hall, "Encoding/Decoding," 128–31.
12. Al-ʿAdl, "Al-bayt baytak."
13. Landsberg, *Prosthetic Memory*, 14.
14. Starr, "Masquerade," 33.
15. Kalifa, "Belle Époque," 119–20.
16. Pickering and Keightley, "Modalities of Nostalgia," 937–38.
17. Boym, *Future of Nostalgia*, 3–7.
18. Boym, *Future of Nostalgia*, xiii.
19. Boym, *Future of Nostalgia*, 9. See also Koselleck, *Vergangene Zukunft*, 349–75.
20. Appadurai, *Modernity at Large*, 78.
21. Starr, "Sensing the City," 139.
22. Al-ʿAdl, "Al-bayt baytak."
23. Assmann, "Das kollektive Gedächtnis," 76.
24. Lukinbeal, "Cinematic Landscapes," 7.
25. Lukinbeal, "Cinematic Landscapes," 15–16.
26. Chalabi, *Khyamat al-Nahār*, June 16, 2015.
27. Without any direct claims to embody his person, this character entails references to Haim Nahum (1873–1960), the chief rabbi of Egypt (1925–60).
28. Assmann, "Das kollektive Gedächtnis," 76–79.
29. Assmann, "Kollektives Gedächtnis und kulturelle Identität," 12–15.
30. Assmann, "Kollektives Gedächtnis und kulturelle Identität," 15.
31. Assmann, "Kollektives Gedächtnis und kulturelle Identität," 15.
32. Al-ʿAdl, *Muḥammad*, episode 11.
33. Al-ʿAdl, *Muḥammad*, episode 25.
34. Al-ʿAdl, *Muḥammad*, episode 20.
35. Cf. Baron, *Egypt as a Woman*, 5.
36. Elsaket, "Star of the East," 36.
37. Elsaket, "Star of the East," 38–49.
38. Shohat, *Taboo Memories*, 306.
39. Assmann, "Das kollektive Gedächtnis," 78.
40. Bayat, "Egypt and Its Unsettled Islamism," 159–60.
41. Cf. Shafik, *Popular Egyptian Cinema*, 56.
42. For more about traditional street weddings in Egypt and their history, see Fahmy, *Street Sound*, 157–58.
43. Al-ʿAdl, *Muḥammad*, episode 8.
44. Al-ʿAdl, *Muḥammad*, episode 18.
45. Al-ʿAdl, *Muḥammad*, episode 15.
46. Al-ʿAdl, *Muḥammad*, episode 20.
47. Al-ʿAdl, *Muḥammad*, episode 20.
48. Beinin, *Dispersion of Egyptian Jewry*, 143.
49. Al-ʿAdl, *Muḥammad*, episode 18.
50. Starr, *Remembering Cosmopolitan Egypt*, 14.
51. Cf. Shemer, "From Chahine's *al-Iskandariyya*," 370–71.
52. Gordon, "Hasan and Marika," 50.
53. Abu-Lughod, *Dramas of Nationhood*, 136.
54. Al-ʿAdl, *Muḥammad*, episode 4.
55. There are longer traditions of depicting Islamists and Muslim Brothers on screen upon which the series narrative draws. Cf.

Abu-Lughod, "Finding a Place for Islam," 495–508. However, the image of Muslim Brothers as traitors in the series should not be separated from the political context in Egypt after the coup d'état of 2013 that overthrew President Muḥammad Mursi and brutally cracked down on the Muslim Brotherhood.

56. Al-ʿAdl, *Muḥammad*, episode 18.

57. Al-ʿAdl, *Muḥammad*, episode 24.

58. Abu-Lughod, *Dramas of Nationhood*, 114.

Bibliography

Abdalla, Ahmad, dir. *Heliopolis*. Film House Egypt, 2009. 98 min.

Abdalla, Iskandar Ahmad. "Shalom, Cohen, Salome and The Impossible Home." In *Cousins: Jewish-Arab Identity in Post-Colonial Cultural Discourses*, edited by Claudia Jubeh, 185–98. Berlin: Makan, 2016.

Abu-Lughod, Lila. *Dramas of Nationhood: The Politics of Television in Egypt*. Chicago: University of Chicago Press, 2005.

———. "Finding a Place for Islam: Egyptian Television Serials and the National Interest." *Public Culture* 5, no. 3 (1993): 493–513.

ʿAdl, Midḥat al-. "Al-bayt baytak. Hatifyyan | Midḥat al-ʿAdl yakshif qiṣat musalsal Ḥārat al-Yahūd al muthir lil-jadal." Aired June 17, 2015, on Ten TV. YouTube. 8:51 min. https://www.youtube.com/watch?v=_Kvd9NoLvo4&t=142s.

ʿAdl, Muḥammad al-, dir. "Ḥārat al-Yahūd." Aired March 20, 2015, on CBC Drama. 30 episodes. https://www.youtube.com/playlist?list=PLk7aOjrbxuopRLU7mIKzOSqTnaf4vsn9D.

Appadurai, Arjun. *Modernity at Large: Cultural Dimensions of Globalization*. Minneapolis: University of Minnesota Press, 1996.

ʿArafa, Sharif, dir. *Wilad al-ʿAm (Escaping Tel Aviv)*. Al majmuʿa al-fanniya al-mutaḥidah (United Art Group), 2009. 95 min.

Armbrust, Walter. "Political Film in Egypt." In *Film in the Middle East and North Africa: Creative Dissidence*, 228–51. Austin: University of Texas Press.

Assmann, Jan. "Das kollektive Gedächtnis zwischen Körper und Schrift. Zur Gedächtnistheorie von Maurice Halbwachs." In *Erinnerung und Gesellschaft: Mémoire et Société. Hommage à Maurice Halbwachs (1877–1945); Jahrbuch für Soziologiegeschichte*, edited by Hermann Krapoth and Denis Laborde, 65–83. Wiesbaden: VS Verlag für Sozialwissenschaften, 2005.

———. "Kollektives Gedächtnis und kulturelle Identität." In *Kultur und Gedächtnis*, edited by Jan Assmann and Tonio Hölsch, 9–19. Frankfurt: Suhrkamp, 1988.

Baron, Beth. *Egypt as a Woman: Nationalism, Gender, and Politics*. Berkeley: University of California Press, 2005.

Bayat, Asef. "Egypt and Its Unsettled Islamism." In *Post-Islamism: The Changing Faces of Political Islam*, edited by Asef Bayat, 185–228. New York: Oxford University Press, 2013.

Beinin, Joel. *The Dispersion of Egyptian Jewry: Culture, Politics, and the Formation of a Modern Diaspora*. Berkeley: University of California Press, 1998.

Bhabha, Homi K. "Introduction: Narrating the Nation." In *Nation and Narration*, edited by Homi K. Bhabha, 1–8. London: Routledge, 1990.

Boym, Svetlana. *The Future of Nostalgia*. New York: Basic Books, 2001.

CBC Egypt. "Huna al-ʿaṣimah. Liqaʾ khas maʿa nujum musalsal *Ḥārat al-Yahūd*." June 17, 2015. YouTube. 30:10 min. https://www.youtube.com/watch?v=2PtwchA7u2w.

Chalabi, Poussy, presenter. *Khyamat al-Nahār*. Aired July 16, 2015, on Al-Nahār TV.

Elsaket, Ifdal. "The Star of the East: Umm Kulthum and Egyptian Cinema." In *Stars in World Cinema: Film Icons and Star Systems Across Cultures*, edited by Andrea Bandhauer and Michelle Royer, 36–51. New York: I. B. Tauris, 2015.

Fahmy, Ziad. *Street Sounds: Listening to Everyday Life in Modern Egypt*. Stanford: Stanford University Press, 2020.

Gordon, Joel. "Hasan and Marika: Screen Shots from a Vanishing Egypt." *Journal of Levantine Studies* 7, no. 1 (Summer 2017): 35–56.

Hall, Stuart. "Encoding/Decoding." In *Culture, Media, Language: Working Papers in Cultural Studies, 1972–79*, edited by Stuart Hall, Dorothy Hobson, Andrew Lowe, and Paul Willis, 117–28. London: Routledge, 1981.

Joffe, Josef. "Seifenoper-Wunder: Eine populäre ägyptische TV-Serie wider Juden-und Israelhass." *Die Zeit*, August 6, 2015. https://www.zeit.de/2015/32/tv-serie-aegypten-juden-muslime.

Kalifa, Dominique. "Belle Époque: Invention et usages d'un chrononyme." *Revue d'histoire du XIXe siècle* 52 (2016): 119–32.

Kamel, Nadia, dir. *Salāṭah balādī* or *Salade maison*. Snooze Productions and Ventura Films, 2007. 105 min.

Kirkpatrick, David D. "For Egypt, TV Show's Shocking Twist Is Its Sympathetic Jews." *New York Times*, June 23, 2015. https://www.nytimes.com/2015/06/24/world/middleeast/for-egypt-tv-shows-shocking-twist-is-its-sympathetic-jews.html.

Koselleck, Reinhart. *Vergangene Zukunft: Zur Semantik geschichtlicher Zeiten*. Frankfurt: Suhrkamp, 2017.

Landsberg, Alison. *Prosthetic Memory: The Transformation of the American Remembrance in the Age of Mass Culture*. New York: Columbia University Press, 2004.

Lukinbeal, Chris. "Cinematic Landscapes." *Journal of Cultural Geography* 23, no. 1 (2009): 3–22.

Mehadji, Merwane. "Le Quartier juif: Le Feuilleton égyptien qui ne fait pas l'unanimité." *Le Figaro*, June 30, 2015.

Musṭafah, Ḥusām al-Dīn, dir. *Jarimah fī al-ḥay al-hadi*ʾ. Sharikat al-qahira lel ʾintaj al-sinimāʾyy, 1967. 94 min.

Pickering, Michael, and Emily Keightley. "The Modalities of Nostalgia." *Current Sociology* 54, no. 6 (2006): 919–41.

Rady, ʾIhāb, dir. *Fatah min israʾil*. Al-Sharikah al-ʿArabīyah lil-Intāj al-ʾiʿlāmī wa-al-Thaqāfī (Shuāʿ) (Arab Company for Information and Culture), 1999. 120 min.

Ramsis, Amir, dir. *ʿAn yahūd miṣr: Nihāyat al-riḥla / Jews of Egypt: The End of the Journey*. Daal Research and Media, 2014. 95 min.

Shafik, Viola. *Popular Egyptian Cinema: Gender, Class and Nation*, 2007.

Shemer, Yaron. "From Chahine's *al-Iskandariyya . . . leh* to *Salata baladi* and *ʿAn Yahud Misr*: Rethinking Egytian Jews' Cosmopolitanism, Belonging and Nostalgia in Cinema." *Middle East Journal of Culture and Communication* 7 (2014): 351–75.

Shohat, Ella. *Taboo Memories, Diasporic Voices*. Durham: Duke University Press, 2006.

Starr, Deborah. "Masquerade and the Performance of National Imaginaries: Levantine Ethics, Aesthetics and Identities in Egyptian Cinema." *Journal of Levantine Studies* 1, no. 2 (Winter 2011): 31–57.

———. *Remembering Cosmopolitan Egypt: Literature, Culture, and Empire*. London: Routledge, 2009.

———. "Sensing the City: Representations of Cairo's Harat al-Yahūd." *Prooftexts* 26, no. 1 (2006): 138–62.

Steinke, Ronen. "Verbotene Liebe: Israel in arabischen Fernsehserien." *Die süddeutsche Zeitung*, July 5, 2015. https://www.sueddeutsche.de/medien/israel-in-arabischen-fernsehserien-verbotene-liebe-1.2550722.

Zaid, Yāssir, dir. *Al-Daher*. Aired November 29, 2019, on WATCH IT. 30 episodes.

CHAPTER 5

Death, Burial, and Loss in Ali al-Muqri's *Al-Yahūdī al-ḥālī* (The Handsome Jew)

SARAH IRVING

The Yemeni writer Ali al-Muqri's 2009 novel *Al-Yahūdī al-ḥālī* (The handsome Jew) recounts the love story of Fatima, the daughter of the mufti of the Yemeni town of Rayda, and Salim, a boy from the town's Jewish community.[1] Having fallen in love at a young age and witnessed the various ways in which their interconnected but also deeply divided societies look upon mixed relationships, they run away together, culminating in Fatima's death in childbirth. Narrated in part by their grandson, Ibrahim, the novel depicts their relationship as an oasis of purity in a hostile society, a space of mutual respect, learning and discovery, but one that the rigidities of religious and social boundaries ultimately make impossible.

Published by Dar al-Saqi in Beirut, *Al-Yahūdī al-ḥalī* was widely reviewed in the Arabic press and was longlisted for the International Prize for Arabic Fiction in 2011.[2] Elsewhere, I have read al-Muqri's novel against theories from postcolonial studies and alongside some of the growing number of books in Arabic and by Arab writers that present themes of Arab-Jewish and Muslim-Jewish romances.[3] In that reading, I focused on the use of Romeo-and-Juliet-style plots that, in the manner of Shakespeare's original, use cross-border love and the tragic fate of lovers as a way of castigating society for its intolerance and violence. I argued that, with the temporal distance of the twenty-first century from the Nakba, or establishment of the State of Israel, and the mass migrations of Middle Eastern Jews to the new state, amatory relations involving Jewish characters within historical settings provide a language for novelists writing in Arabic to talk about questions of religion, ethnicity, and boundaries within their own societies. In this reading, the concept of postcolonial nostalgia is a useful one;[4] through this lens, images of Muslim-Jewish romance are entwined with idealized notions of history to propose that the assumption that Jews and Muslims always exist in states of conflict and hatred is fundamentally unnatural, distorted, and atypical in the long histories of both faiths. Abdulsalam al-Rubaidi, Redhwan Qasem Ghaleb Rashed, and Khaled Abkar Alkodimi have interpreted al-Muqri's writing in a similar fashion, seeing this and other contemporary Yemeni novels as part of a collective reimagining of the homeland or Islamicate societies in general in more tolerant, just, and peaceable terms.[5]

In this chapter, however, I submit a different reading of al-Muqri's work, one that contends that al-Muqri presents a very particularly *Yemeni* narrative aimed at urging radical social change. I draw on the work of historian Leor Halevi, which highlights ways in which, in Islamicate contexts, practices and discourses surrounding death and burial, with their considerable emotive and existential powers, are often tightly entwined with questions of identity, borders, gender roles, and conflict.[6] In deploying images and narratives of death and (unquiet) burial, al-Muqri exposes the reader to highly culturally and historically specific symbols and imageries, resulting in a narrative that enshrines Jewish presence as an important part of Yemen's culture and history, while also acknowledging the hardships faced by Jews under Yemeni rule. Even before the current war in Yemen, which has likely caused the final and complete demise of Yemeni Jewry,[7] only a tiny fragment of this once large and culturally significant community remained after the 1950s, with the vast majority leaving for Israel after 1948.[8] In its most overarching sense, then, personal and intimate death and loss in al-Muqri's tale speak to the broader sense of cultural and intellectual loss imposed by the absence of a once-integral part of society. In the light of this specific trajectory, therefore, and unlike many studies in Arabic literatures that adopt a corpus that spans the whole Arabic-speaking region, this chapter also argues for the utility of examining novels under a narrower focus; considering local histories and resonances adds granularity to discussions of the issue of Arab Jews and how the experiences of Jews in Arab-Muslim regions are disaggregated according to specific pasts and practices.

YEMEN, JEWS, AND AN ENTWINED PAST

The place of death and loss in works by majority world writers have been analyzed by a number of scholars. So, for instance, Ramón Soto-Crespo views Caribbean author Jamaica Kincaid's treatment of mourning—particularly in relation to the death of her brother from an AIDS-related illness—as an allegory for the colonial past of Antigua in which "her brother's subaltern body becomes bereft of life in postcolonial Antigua, just as the West Indies were depleted of their flora during colonization."[9] Grief for the dead is part of the condition of being for the hybrid writer, one's identity constantly underscored by the fact of having been torn from one's native land. References to death and the grave in such a reading—for instance in the grave dirt mixed with the rum drunk during oaths to protect rebels against enslavement—are definitively tied to colonialism.[10] Mourning for the individual dead, then, is not a matter of personal psychology, but is fundamentally political, an act of "cultural and historical memory" that draws together a colonized people to remember and condemn their past.[11] In his exploration of First Nations American writer Louise Erdrich, John Carlos Rowe executes a similar analysis. A white character of German origin, who fought as a sniper in World War I, aiming at French soldiers as they burrowed into the mud of the trenches in an act of premature self-interment, is depicted as bringing the legacy of this bloody war of colonial competitiveness with him. European violence is carried to the United States, infecting society there with alien colonial sins.[12] This character's stories are interwoven with those of his new neighbors in America, linking them all with tales of massacres of indigenous Americans by white settlers.[13] European-ness is thus linked with death and destruction, and even on the personal level is entangled with the horrors of the grave; the massacres of white expansion westward are repeated via reinfection when new generations of European immigrants settle on American soil.

Unlike the locations of the literatures outlined above, Yemen has not suffered a conventionally colonial trajectory, although its history has been significantly impacted by the imperialism of the Ottoman Empire and long history of colonial incursions by European powers.[14] Areas of southern Yemen around the port of Aden were an important stopping point for ships heading to Britain's empire in India and were claimed by Britain in 1839.[15] Following unsuccessful Portuguese attempts to establish forts and trading centers on the Red Sea, British competition with the Ottomans in the Jazeera (Arabian Peninsula) and rising Egyptian influence governed regional concerns throughout the nineteenth and first half of the twentieth centuries, whilst differences between the Zaydi Shīʿī of the uplands and Shafeʾi Sunnis of the lowlands, along with competition between local rulers, enabled a British policy of divide and conquer.[16] Lowland Yemen was also economically integrated into the British Empire, with many Yemeni men joining the merchant navy and establishing substantial diaspora communities in British port towns.[17]

On the other hand, many other connections and histories have impacts and resonances as strong, if not stronger, in Yemeni culture and society. Sheila Carapico explicitly rejects the term "postcolonial" as having "little resonance" in the Arabian Peninsula beyond the "polyglot workforce" of Aden, and emphasizes the weak impacts of both the Ottomans and Portuguese.[18] Indeed, in the eighteenth century, independent coffee trading between the Zaydi imams of highland Yemen and France was a profound annoyance to the Ottomans, who lost out on tax revenue.[19] As Jane Hathaway points out, the relationship between Yemen and Egypt in the first century of Ottoman rule could be termed "symbiotic";[20] while we are accustomed to seeing Egypt as the more powerful and influential of the two, Yemeni political and social groupings, and myths and memories drawing on them, played an important part in Egyptian politics, even until the early twentieth century.[21] Yemen tends in modern writings to be relegated to the peripheries of Arabophone culture and history, but until not long before the time of the Prophet it was one of the main economic and cultural centers of the Arabian Peninsula, and references to it resonated for centuries in the names of the Qaysi and Yemeni political factions.

In considering early histories of Yemen, we are also by definition drawn into histories of Jewishness in the Jazeera, with biblical connections (including the incense trade) between the lands of the Queen of Sheba, via the chain of Red Sea and Nabataean cities, which included Mecca, Yathrib (Medina), and Petra, to the eastern Mediterranean.[22] The origins of the Jewish presence in the Arabian Peninsula are still a matter of considerable debate among scholars, although it certainly precedes the existence of both Islam and Christianity,[23] with communities perhaps taking on the forms in which they were known until the early twentieth century at around the time of the destruction of the Second Temple.[24] Jews, some of them "Bedouinized" and others resident in cities such as Medina, play a large role in the Qurʾan, highlighting the fact that significant communities existed across the Jazeera, not just in Yemen. In the latter, however, there seems to have been a particularly large Jewish community by the fourth century CE, and (to at least some extent for reasons to do with the regional geopolitics of early Christianity) for a while the rulers of the kingdom of Himyar converted to Judaism.[25] While the presence of Jews in the rest of the Jazeera remains a complex historical and archaeological question,[26] in Yemen they became a separate but highly integrated part of the country's social and economic framework, which was dominated from the ninth century by Zaydi (Shīʿī) rulers with, from 1530 onward, periodic Ottoman invasions. Within a castelike social system, Jews occupied a low status, forbidden, for example, to ride horses or build homes higher than those of Muslims, but protected both under formal Islamic *dhimmī* (protection of non-Muslims) rules, and customary (*ʿurf*) and tribal law, which bound them tightly into honor codes under which anyone who harmed a Jew might well be pursued and violently punished by their patrons.[27] The Jews and Muslims of Yemen were also rendered interdependent by an economic system in which many specialized crafts and manufacturing skills were in Jewish hands, whilst Muslims farmed and produced the country's food. As well as entwining their livelihoods, this also ensured that Jews and Muslims had to be in regular, cooperative contact, with the result that although there were Jewish neighborhoods, sharply defined and walled areas like the Moroccan *mallāḥ* did not develop.[28]

This broad social system started to fragment in the nineteenth century, however; growing trade links and Ottoman political intervention affected the Jews' specialized craft role and their position within power networks, as well as strengthening their previously sporadic links with other Jewish communities in the Arabic-speaking world and beyond.[29] The political and theological complexities—including several messianic movements—that impacted Yemeni Jews in the late nineteenth and early twentieth centuries are beyond the scope of this essay, but one of their results was large-scale Jewish migration to East Africa and, from 1881, to Ottoman Palestine.[30]

Although accounts of Jewish migration to Palestine before World War I largely focus on European Ashkenazim, Yemenites actually represented the largest body of Jewish immigrants to Ottoman Palestine.[31] Despite official bans and Imam Yahya's entreaties to Yemeni Jews to stay, both as part of the nation's fabric and in deference to Palestinian Arab leaders who asked the Zaydi leader to prevent his subjects adding to Zionist numbers, migration continued throughout the interwar period.[32] In the British colony of Aden in southern Yemen, anti-Zionist anger combined with social tensions stemming from British ethnic policies resulted in riots against the UN's 1947 announcement of partition in Palestine. The worst in any Arabic-speaking country, they left scores of Jewish dead and injured.[33] However, unlike many other Arab leaders, after 1948 the new Imam Ahmed opened up Jewish emigration from Yemen to Israel, apparently for genuine reasons of faith and benevolence toward the community and its aspirations. A moment of immense social and cultural rupture for the country, the resulting departure of approximately 90 percent of the Jewish population is usually portrayed solely in relation to Zionism, but after years of famine and a civil war, large numbers of Shāfiʿi Muslim Yemenis also left in this period.[34] Israeli airlifts from Aden, dubbed—with heavy overtones of Orientalism—Operation Magic Carpet, carried just under fifty thousand Jews to Israel in 1949 and 1950, leaving several thousand who chose to remain in Yemen, the vast majority of whom also left in the ensuing decades.[35]

The complexities of southern Arabian history thus raise many questions about the applicability of homogenizing narratives to Yemeni literature, be they postcolonial or focused on Arabic literatures.[36] Al-Muqri's dissections of Yemeni society in *Al-Yahūdī al-ḥālī*, as well as his other works, *Ṭaʿm aswad, rāʾiḥa sawdāʾ* (Black taste, black smell), *Ḥurma*, and *Bukhūr ʿadanī* (Adeni incense), all highlight its complexity and diversity whilst also condemning inequality and prejudice arising from multiple roots.[37] In terms of the themes of Muslim-Jewish relations foregrounded in *Al-Yahūdī al-ḥālī*, there are many instances in which the position of Jews in the Islamicate world in the nineteenth and twentieth centuries was closely entangled with European colonialism, and in which discussions of representations of Jewish figures in literature can benefit from postcolonial analysis.[38] Indeed, Al-Muqri highlights such relations in *Bukhūr ʿadanī*. He is unsparing in his portrayal of the oppression imposed on Yemenite Jews in the mid-seventeenth century, in a context of particular social and political upheaval, but he is also careful not to reduce their situation to a victim narrative. In so doing, he mirrors accounts from ethnographic and historical studies that point out the respect and value accorded to the Jewish population by many Muslims for their craft skills and literacy, in a society that greatly valued books but in which the ability to read and write was often confined to the elites and to Jews.[39] As such, *Al-Yahūdī al-ḥālī* highlights the value of a more specific and historically informed field of analysis.

AL-YAHŪDĪ AL-ḤALĪ AS A YEMENI NOVEL

I thus argue that the specifics of history, setting, and style are a vital feature of *Al-Yahūdī al-ḥālī*. The historical genre fulfills three functions in this respect: first, a temporal distancing permits relationships and events to be portrayed that would not be feasible in a contemporary novel. Second, it allows real events that, for their historical importance, already carry cultural weight and allow memory work to be incorporated into the narrative, increasing its ideological and emotional impact. And third, the tendency inherent in the genre toward detailed description and place-making allows the writer to evoke and deploy a wide range of symbols and images that again carry both emotional and political weight. In order to fully appreciate how al-Muqri achieves this, I argue that a detailed understanding of the way in which he uses Islamicate and specifically Yemeni motifs, ideas, and meanings is necessary. While it remains imperative that we reject overly deterministic and monolithic ideas of the influences of Islam and Islamicate culture, it is still possible to regard them as rich traditions on which Arabophone authors might draw. In this chapter, I therefore explore al-Muqri's use of motifs of death and burial in *Al-Yahūdī al-ḥālī*, and consider how readings drawing on a combination of Islamic legal, theological, and social contexts, alongside representations drawn from Islamic and Jewish Yemeni folklore and social practice, elucidate our understanding of the novel.

In terms of the specific Yemeni-ness of the novel, it is worth first noting the title itself, which uses an unusual term for "handsome"—*ḥālī*, derived from the root more common in *ḥilū/ḥilwa* (sweet/pretty)—that is unfamiliar even to speakers of other regional forms of Arabic and is glossed with *malīḥ* (handsome/good) when first used in the text, apparently to clarify al-Muqri's meaning.[40] Although the novel itself is written in a clear, uncluttered modern standard Arabic, linked perhaps to al-Muqri's background in journalism, other key words have specifically Yemeni connotations. The most prominent example is the term used for Salim's *peyot* or sidelocks; *zunnār* was a word widely used across the Ottoman Empire to denote the belt that *dhimmīs* had to wear to indicate their non-Muslim status, but in Yemen it also meant Jewish men's sidelocks, and appeared in the customary phrase *Abu Zunnār* (wearer of sidelocks) to denote a Jew.[41] In Persian Sufi poetry, though, the term also refers to the beloved's hair, conveying the sense that the lover might be bound by it; given the learning displayed in the novel by the character of Fatima, this builds further on al-Muqri's polysemic writing.[42] Many items in the novel also evoke the Yemeni genre of poetry known as *ḥumaynī*, from the use of Yemeni dialect words, via the cameo role of the poet-rabbi Shabazi (and his first name which he shares with the central character), to the overarching theme of the intertwined and symbiotic nature of Arab and Jewish culture in Yemen.[43] The name of the central character and, for much of the novel, first-person narrator, Salim, is also a characteristically Jewish-Yemeni one.[44]

A number of events in the novel echo historical occurrences, further affirming its Yemeni setting. The reigning imam is Al-Imam al-Mutawwakil Isma῾il bin al-Qasim, who reigned from 1644 to 1676 and is said to have been one of Yemen's more anti-Semitic rulers.[45] Al-Muqri mentions that Salim's Jewish relatives in Ṣan'ā' worked at the royal mint, a matter of record from the late seventeenth century.[46] And a riot in Rayda in which Muslims smash containers of wine in Jewish houses and shops, accusing the Jewish community of illegally selling it to Muslim youths, hearkens back to genuine disputes from a little later than the novel's setting, in the eighteenth century.[47] The deployment of the 1679–80 Mawza᾽a Exile as a significant event in the novel affixes it most firmly in time and place; this effort by the imam to evict the entire Jewish population from Sana᾽a and the highland towns and force them into arid land toward the Red Sea, where many died, is a focal point in Jewish-Yemeni memory. The poet Shalom (Salim) Shabazi, who witnessed the Exile and who makes several cameo appearances in the novel,[48] is celebrated as one of the greatest voices of Yemenite Jewish literature. Although many accounts of the Exile focus on its place in a broader rise in anti-Jewish sentiment from Yemen's rulers at the time, Jewish folklore from Yemen contextualizes it as part of "those hard times when the Arabs drove the Turks out of Yemen by decade-long wars and when hunger, pestilence and famine ruined the land."[49] As Shlomo Goitein, perhaps the best-known scholar of Yemenite Jewry, observes, while the period from the seventeenth-century expulsion of the Ottomans to the mass exodus of Operation Magic Carpet had been the worst for Yemen's Jews, it had also been a difficult time for the area's Muslims, who also suffered from the wars, occupations, famines, and harsh rulers that characterized the previous three centuries.[50] Jewish traditions, therefore, affirm the interconnectedness of the community's existence in Yemen, offering a more nuanced view than decontextualized portrayals that focus on Jews to the exclusion of the peoples among whom they lived and worked.

DEATH AND BURIAL IN *AL-YAHŪDĪ AL-ḤALĪ*

What work, then, do depictions of death and loss in *Al-Yahūdī al-ḥālī* perform? This section tracks and analyzes the occurrences of death and loss as they occur through the novel, applying to them the lessons drawn from theories of minor literature and my arguments regarding the necessity of understanding much of the symbolism and imagery as specifically Yemeni or linked to particular aspects of Islamicate or Jewish-Yemeni culture. Many of these are themes evoked by other aspects of the novel; I suggest, though, that death and burial, as profoundly emotional and primal experiences, are especially forceful means which intensify the impact of these key motifs.

The novel's first representation of death and loss is the disappearance of ʿAllūs, Salim's beloved dog. Finding ʿAllūs as a stray on the streets, Salim raises him and becomes inseparable from him. Al-Muqri's character wonders whether the insults hurled at them are at the dog as an unclean animal for Muslims, or at him as a Jew, allowing the issue of Jew hatred to be raised at an early stage in the novel, but in a culturally complex and ambiguous way: "'Hey, dog.' Who did they mean? ʿAllūs, or Salim his owner? Their eyes were fixed on me as they spoke."[51] We never find out ʿAllūs's exact fate: he vanishes, resulting in an agonizing ambiguity that prefigures Fatima's unquiet burial, the repeated destruction of her and Salim's graves, and the mysterious disappearance of Saʿīd, their son, leaving the latter's child to narrate this multigenerational loss. Meanwhile, Salim's father's attitude to the dog's disappearance anticipates the ways in which his son will be unwelcome in the Jewish community's homes: "Four months went by, and I kept hoping I would find him. Every morning I went to see if he had returned in the night to the kennel which I had made for him, in front of our home, out of wooden boards and dry sticks. My father did not forget that there was room for two dogs and kept saying, every evening when he was angry with me, 'Go and lie with your friend,' until long after my friend's loss, when his house was rotting under the strength of the wind and rain."[52] However, in seeking to console Salim for his loss, Fatima gives him a copy of the tenth-century *Faḍl al-kilāb* (Book of the superiority of dogs over many of those who wear clothes) by al-Marzuban, a gift that advances their relationship and opens Salim's eyes to the possibility of questioning many of the social rules he has hitherto accepted.[53] The subject of the book itself, which challenges stereotypes about Islamic attitudes to dogs and highlights examples of their positive portrayal, alerts the reader to the constructed nature of Jews' position in society, discursively disrupting imposed inferiorities, highlighting the iniquities of those who assume themselves to be superior,[54] and providing such debates with a long and learned lineage. By placing these episodes early in his narrative, al-Muqri ensures that his complex, counter-hegemonic portraits of Salim, Fatima, and their relationship are foregrounded, influencing the way in which readers receive the rest of the book.

Later in his boyhood, Salim's older brother Hazaa dies of a raging fever, raving about the Holy Land and speaking of Yerushalayim (spelled as such in the Arabic, in contrast to elsewhere, where al-Quds is used) as a "luscious beauty, fascinating in mind and spirit, a refuge to orphans, a haven for wanderers, kind, affectionate, the wine of life."[55] Salim laments how his brother would never reach Jerusalem, "for he would not go as far as the outskirts of Rayda." Hazaa's delirium is linked to conversations in Rayda's Jewish community about the coming of the Messiah and other mystical themes; kabbalistic literature and beliefs underwent a major growth in seventeenth-century Yemen,[56] and al-Muqri seems to be aware of this and to be referencing it in Hazaa's fate. This trend included the widespread following of Sabbatai Sevi, a messianic figure whose movement, which galvanized Jews from northern Europe to the Arabian Peninsula, reached Yemen in 1666. In many places, including Yemen, the idea of spiritual redemption was combined with an earthly and warlike manifestation of the Messiah as a figure who would lead the Jewish people out from the clutches of other religions and form them into an army that would wipe out oppressive rulers.[57] As Yosef Tobi notes, however, messianic and apocalyptic themes, especially in literature, were common to both Jews and Shiʿi Muslims in

Yemen, highlighting their cultural entanglement.[58] As well as emphasizing the psychological and material oppressions of Jewish life in Yemen under at least some of the imams, the shades of Sabbateanism also emphasize the extent of the connections and entanglements even for a community that in many respects is portrayed as remote and insular. The Sabbatean movement was rooted in the Ottoman Empire, spreading along trade and pilgrimage routes, reminding the reader that Salim and Fatima's story does not take place in a timeless, unchanging setting but in a political environment of which the ruler had comparatively recently, and temporarily, thrown off Ottoman rule, and where Jews were suspect not just for primordial religious reasons but because of allegations that they had collaborated with the Ottoman conquerors. On one hand, Hazaa's dying references to Jerusalem echo long-standing mentions of the holy city in Jewish ritual, but they are also tied up with events which reinforce the dynamic nature of seventeenth-century Yemeni society and ideas. Meanwhile, in the present-day political context of al-Muqri's book, the Sabbatean movement carries an anti-Zionist message, reflecting the unmet hopes of Yemeni Jews who went to Israel, the promised land, after 1948 but were met with discrimination and mistreatment.[59]

As Salim and Fatima's friendship develops, the Jewish community witnesses warnings against love and sex between Muslim and Jew. First, Salim's Jewish neighbor, Nashwah, and Qasim, the son of the town's muezzin, attempt suicide together when their families forbid their marriage: the boy dies, but the girl lives.[60] The message that relationships that cut across community boundaries are forbidden to the point of fatality is thus reinforced, although from the dominant social perspective this permutation of Muslim man and Jewish woman is the more acceptable and less unusual. Brides who converted to marry into Muslim families were fairly well known across Yemen and accepted by Islamic society because the father dictated the religion of any offspring; Fatima and Salim's example would be the least acceptable configuration to both faiths because it contradicts both Islamic and Jewish rules of descent.[61] In a broader sense, al-Muqri foregrounds the significance of relationships that cross divisions as a source of vitality and regeneration in their subversion of religious authority and social restrictions—the building of a new society, in al-Rubaidi's terms.[62] Salim and Fatima's love, as the most transgressive possibility according to religious law, is thus in al-Muqri's terms the most potentially vibrant and fertile in its results, but also the most vulnerable to foreclosure by mainstream forces.

Second, when several Jewish women working as prostitutes, having been driven out of Ṣan'ā', arrive in Rayda and attract Jewish and Muslim men alike, the authorities of both religions threaten the women with death if they continue to practice their trade. Although al-Muqri's depiction of the sex workers as Jewish seems to follow imaginings of Jewish space as transgressive and sexualized from other parts of the Islamicate world,[63] this is complicated by the fact that the key act of sexual transgression in the novel, Fatima and Salim's romance, takes place in the house of her father, the mufti. While two of the sex workers choose to marry and become "respectable," two others, including the most desired of the group, choose death over domestic confinement and masculine control of their sexuality.[64] Al-Muqri's framing of the women's decision, in which one is offered possible redemption by a young Muslim man who wants to marry her but who "wanted to possess her forever," makes it clear that it is not only barriers between Jewish/Muslim love that the novel is critiquing, but also the gendered exercise of gendered power.[65] Indeed, when the woman who refuses to give up her work is finally stoned to death, al-Muqri depicts this as one of the few times at which the young men of Rayda's Jewish and Muslim communities are united, some even begging to be stoned alongside her, although it is also noteworthy that the unifying effect of a woman's death has a shorter-lived effect than competition for possession of her living body: "All who knew her were sure that she preferred to be stoned to death for giving her erotic nature free rein, than to be the possession of a husband. . . . Young men from both faiths asked to be stoned with her as fornicators. . . . Her spellbinding beauty died, in this way, painful to both Jewish and Muslim young men, and crying over her united them for several days as [competition over] her enchantments had separated them for several months."[66] That the woman in this situation is Jewish, resisting the advances of a Muslim man, also suggests a parallel with the Jewish situation in Yemen itself during the novel's historical period, when in the wake of the imam's reconquest of the Yemeni highlands from the Ottomans, official attitudes toward the Jewish population shifted from tolerance of *dhimmīs* to active oppression and the prospect of exile or coercive conversion. On the micro-level, the ambivalent attitudes of both Muslims and Jews in the novel echo both evidence of complex and highly variable attitudes to sexuality amongst Muslim tribes in Yemen and Jewish folktales, in which women openly offering sex for sale are accorded a certain respect, despite overarching condemnation from religious and patriarchal discourses.[67] At the level of local detail we thus find narratives that mesh with al-Muqri's novel, rather than fitting with dominant theories and perspectives, while in relation to literary theory we witness a clear commitment to minor literature's call for revolutionary social change.

Salim and Fatima's relationship—and, indeed, romantic love generally—acquire overtones of the funereal through the woman who passes their covert notes; a *muzayyina,* in the Yemeni context she helps to beautify women before their weddings, but also prepares corpses for burial and might work as a funeral wailer.[68] In a postcolonial sense, one might see this as part of Salim's increasing experience of his home environment as uncanny, as social changes both immediate and hinted at, epitomized by a destabilizing combination of love and death, disrupt the Jewish community of Rayda and his own personal life. The inclusion of a *muzayyina* in this process, however, extends beyond these themes and is particularly resonant in Yemeni cultural practices and in debates and changes around both Islamic and Jewish funereal habits from early Islam to the contemporary period. In the first centuries of Islam, attitudes toward wailing were divided along theological lines between Sunni and Shiʿa schools of law, but also along gendered lines.[69] Even in the present day, there is no uniform position, but Shiʿites such as the Zaydis of upland Yemen are more tolerant of wailing and other performative rituals than Sunni Islam.[70] Funeral wailing was also an important social event for some Jewish-Yemeni women, in practices which have shifted in meaning as societies change in both Yemen and Israel.[71] Importantly, in the role of the distinctively Muslim-Yemeni *muzayyina,* the historic Muslim wailing woman and the Jewish-Yemeni wailer cross community barriers, as we find historical examples of Jewish women providing for the costs of Muslim wailers at their funeral, and linkages between women's wailing, funeral practices, and vernacular poetry in Yemen.[72] But efforts by the establishments of both Islam and Judaism to suppress women's funeral wailing have been read as attempts to reduce women's public roles and visibility,[73] a message that chimes very much with al-Muqri's critiques of gendered power in society.

Among the many factors that propel Fatima and Salim to flee Rayda and settle in Ṣan'ā' are the deaths of Salim's parents. In the narrative itself, these deaths are given strangely little prominence but are embedded in a series of social disturbances including the stoning deaths of the sex workers. Parental mortality, though, mirrors the other emotional and moral ways in which Salim is severed from the town of his birth. In addition, the death of his father signals the cutting off of Salim from the traditional craft his father practiced, highly skilled woodworking, which is described in loving detail earlier in the book. As Jalal Toufic has elaborated, disaster is often accompanied by "withdrawal of tradition," the loss of knowledge and skills, of intellectual content and the muscle memories of expert artisans, so that the death of an individual has repercussions for cultural losses across time and space.[74] Salim does not return to his father's craft but embarks on a more cerebral career, ending as an employee of the imam, signaling both a rupture from his upbringing and a reflection of the way in which the Yemenite Jewish community has been cut off from its customary, valued role as skilled artisans in Yemeni society.[75]

Finally, Fatima and her son ultimately meet strange and uncanny endings. Fatima dies in childbirth, a common enough occurrence for women before the discovery of antibiotics. Those surrounding the couple initially bury her on the Jewish side of the cemetery; during the night her body is moved to the area for Islamic burials, after the community discovers that not only was she born a Muslim but that she and Salim both rejected the idea of conversion when they married. Muslim neighbors, however, also reject her and open this grave too, moving Fatima's body to a new site away from each of the designated zones for Jews or Muslims.[76] When, years later, Salim places his bride's grave again among the Muslims so she will not be lonely, her remaining relatives dig up the bones and again move them to the Jewish cemetery, branding her a heretic. After this, Fatima's bones are mysteriously moved again to the isolated grave, and finally they disappear; the imposition of the rigid bounds of identity are captured in the mental collapse of Fatima's son after his father's bones have also been denied a final resting place, with separation and conflict seen as carrying on into the afterlife: "That night, my father [Sa'īd] kept raving on and on: 'what is this? How? No one permits them any place in the earth . . . no-one . . .' He talked about the wars of the dead. He said that they came out at night, shouting at one another and fighting with axes and swords."[77]

In a society in which Jewish and Muslim identities are depicted as clearly bounded and separate from one another, allowing for no gray areas, Fatima's position as the Muslim wife of a Jew, mother of a Jewish-Muslim child, and rejecting the strictures of both religions, has to be disallowed in order for the two mainstreams to preserve their own stern borders. Mary Layoun, for example, discusses Maria Abraamidou's 1979 short story "Paralogismos," set during the 1974 invasion of northern Cyprus by Turkish troops. The story's protagonist, the Greek-Cypriot woman Evtuxia, murders her lover, a Turkish soldier whose child she is carrying and whose body she buries in the contested ground. Fatima's existence likewise represents a level of complexity which her polarized society cannot tolerate. Indeed, al-Muqri's shadowy grave robbers impose an even more radical solution than Evtuxia; whereas she digs her dead lover's body into the earth and then arranges for her and her mother to leave as refugees, granting him a more permanent presence on their disputed land than the living,[78] Fatima, her husband, and their border-crossing son disappear completely, eradicated from both societies, although perhaps eerily and eternally present in the dusty wind.

In much thought from both Islam and Judaism on the body after death, probably developed through theological interactions between the two faiths, the continual disturbance of Fatima's grave is a very serious matter. For Jews, interred bodies must remain physically intact in order to be properly resurrected at the end of days, while in many Islamic writings, dead bodies can experience severe pain and torture in the tomb, not just as part of purging and testing before being permitted to ascend to heaven, but also as a result of bad behavior by relatives and other humans above ground.[79] Al-Shāfiʿī, whose *madhhab* (school of Islamic jurisprudence) is followed by most Yemeni Sunnis, wrote that graves should be placed within a graveyard or other collection and not alone or isolated, as this renders them vulnerable to being desecrated by accident or design.[80] The *ḥadīth* collector al-Bukhari (d. 256/870) also recorded the story of a Christian who converted to Islam and then apostatized; his corpse was rejected by the earth as punishment, a tale that eerily echoes Fatima's unquiet burial and ambiguous status vis-à-vis Islam.[81] A less doom-laden resonance, though, is found in the Jewish-Yemeni history of the holy man Mori Salim, who, having led a humble life, equally in death refused grandeur, so that "as often as they would whitewash his grave or set a dome over it, the lime would flake off and the building disintegrate."[82] Read alongside this example, rather than the tortures of the tomb, Fatima's disturbed burial becomes the continuation of her deeply thoughtful, humble philosophy of life.

Like Fatima's, Salim's body is moved from his initial tomb where, having converted after Fatima's death, he is buried as a Muslim.[83] Both Jewish and Muslim men appear in the graveyard at various times and exhume Fatima's and Salim's bodies, emphasizing al-Muqri's point that intolerance can be found within both communities. The endless rejection and confusion over his parents' identities eventually sends their son Sa'īd mad, until he chants, waving his hands: "'Here . . . there . . . here . . . there . . . I don't know . . . The Handsome Jew and Fatima don't meet except in the grave. What? What? How . . . ? Their bones are ground and scattered in the wind . . . like this in the wind . . . with no tomb . . . and no country.' . . . We found their tombs open and empty of them."[84] Sa'īd's son, Ibrahim, similarly finds his father vanished and no one able to give an account of the direction in which he was last seen heading. The drawn-out debates over Fatima's and Salim's graves again echo theological debates intertwining Judaism and Islam over the correct way to bury the dead, arguing over the acceptability of decorated tombs, grave mounds that rise above the flat, and the more permissive doctrines of Zaydis over Sunni Muslims on this subject.[85]

However, in Ibrahim's postscript to the novel, we may productively turn to postcolonial readings. He admits that for much of his youth he "didn't know how to categorize [him]self,"[86] knowing that both of his parents were of mixed Jewish-Muslim parentage, but that he reached a point of satisfaction after his grandfather, Salim, taught him "the two languages Hebrew and Arabic, and the religions of Judaism and Islam and Christianity, and some of what was known of Buddhism, Taoism and Confucianism, and Babylonian legends, and Greek, and also Arabic and Persian and Indian literature."[87] Ibrahim, and the fates of his father and grandparents, epitomize the debates found within postcolonial studies of nomadism and its positive and negative connotations. Ibrahim represents the form given a political and ethical glamour by those who romanticize movement, the mobile figure unbound by corrupting loyalties or the hidebound constraints of the state. But at what cost? As subsequent commentators have discussed, the uncritical adoption of the notion of nomadism—especially in a literal sense of a footloose global elite—ignores the privileges it entails, implying access to certain passports, white skin, finances, and linguistic skills.[88] In Ibrahim's case, the road to his unspecified location, where his hybrid descent allows him to make choices about how he defines and projects himself, is paved with the ground and scattered bones of his ancestors.

In his macabre, almost gothic, depiction of Salim's, Fatima's, and Saʿīd's unquiet ends, al-Muqri thus intervenes in live contemporary debates about the extent of individual agency in determining identity and the limitations imposed by both institutions and by perception and imposed Othering. But his means of doing so also reinforce particular images of Yemeni Jews and wider society as laid out above. In contrast to the rhetorics of timelessness and isolation often attached to this community, al-Muqri's account stresses intellectual, political, and geographical entanglements, whether through Ibrahim's acquisition of knowledge from myriad cultures via his grandfather, himself tutored by his lover Fatima, through Salim's career as a scribe to the imam's traveling armies, or through the ultimately unknown whereabouts of the Jewish-Muslim couple and their son, literally scattered in the wind to eternally exist in their refusal to be tied to a single belief or identity.

I have attempted to foreground the complexities of thinking about the case of the Jews of Yemen and Ali al-Muqri's novel *Al-Yahūdī al-ḥālī*, which engages with the subject of relations between this community and the dominant Muslim society at a time of particular turmoil in upland Yemen. While the kind of postcolonial analyses to which contemporary Arabic novels are often subjected bears some fruit when applied to al-Muqri's work, this case also exposes some of the limitations of this theoretical framework in approaching literature of Middle Eastern origin and/or portraying the experiences of Arab Jews. The approach I have taken is not necessarily one that would work for all literatures; al-Muqri's copious research and the historical setting of the story permit a specific unpacking of his novel. But my analysis is not simply a matter of identifying factual correlations in al-Muqri's work; in writing a deeply investigated historical novel, the author creates the possibility of embedding his narrative in a solidly local, specific south Arabian/Yemeni cultural matrix that allows him to occupy the role of a minor voice in making social and political points about both Yemeni society and history and about the broader trajectories of the region's Jewish populations.

Historical fiction, like many genre fictions, allows al-Muqri to critique his own society and the relationship of Jewish communities to Zionism and the State of Israel without being didactic or simplistic. By referring to the themes, characters, and settings of Islamic- and Jewish-Yemeni histories, literatures, and folklore, *Al-Yahūdī al-ḥālī* is interlinked with other Yemeni literary genres, such as *ḥumaynī* poetry, which also played a role in the complex relationships between Jews and Muslims. And in exploring the local, the specific, and the micro-scale, we can observe how al-Muqri embeds his work in debates and discourses that are not necessarily postcolonial in nature, but that tackle interactions and conflicts that—in changing and dynamic ways—predate the colonial setting. Where, in simplified accounts of the history of Jews in Yemen, should we place the writings of the twelfth-century Nethanel ben Fayyumi, who argued that Muhammad was a true prophet and should be recognized as such by Jews?[89] An approach drawn from al-Muqri's novel seems like a good place to start thinking about an answer.

The interweaving of instances and images of death and loss throughout *Al-Yahūdī al-ḥālī*, though, must be seen not only as plot devices but as central to the ways in which al-Muqri enforces the emotive and thus ideological impact of his work. A sense of pain and absence permeates Fatima and Salim's romance and marriage, love and sex between other Muslim-Jewish couples, Salim's relationships with his blood family and the most significant aspects of the environment in which he grows up (Allūs; his craftsmanship), and Jewish aspirations to the Holy Land. As such, al-Muqri sets up an atmosphere of fragility and intangibility. Whether it is the prospect of respectful and loving cohabitation between Jew and Muslim, the notion of female empowerment and independence, or the promises of Jewish power and splendor offered by messianic movements, the Yemeni environment—so lovingly, richly, but damningly evoked—eventually curtails them, inevitably ending in unquiet death and dust in the wind. Only by leaving for the unspecified destination from which the narrator of the final paragraphs speaks can social liberation be achieved, but—as evoked by the chain of cultural and material losses with which parental death is linked in the novel—only at the cost of the local, vital sense of community from which Salim and Fatima emerged.

Notes

1. Al-Muqri, *Al-Yahūdī al-ḥālī*.
2. "*The Handsome Jew*—Ali al-Muqri."
3. Irving, "Gender, Conflict, and Muslim-Jewish Romance."

4. Walder, *Postcolonial Nostalgias.*

5. Al-Rubaidi, *Imagining an Alternative Homeland*; Ghaleb Rashed, "Fictional World of Ali Al-Muqri"; Alkodimi, "Al-Muqri's Anti-Religious Stance."

6. Halevi, *Muhammad's Grave.*

7. See, e.g., Joffre, "Yemen's Remaining Jews"; Kershner, "19 Yemeni Jews Arrive in Israel."

8. Meir-Glitzenstein, "Operation Magic Carpet."

9. Soto-Crespo, "Death and the Diaspora Writer," 343.

10. Soto-Crespo, "Death and the Diaspora Writer," 343–46, 356.

11. Soto-Crespo, "Death and the Diaspora Writer," 370–71.

12. Rowe, "Buried Alive," 198–99.

13. Rowe, "Buried Alive," 199.

14. As noted above, I have applied postcolonial readings to *Al-Yahūdī al-ḥālī* in a previous publication; Khaled Abkar Alkodimi also does so to good effect in his comparison of this novel with al-Muqri's latest, *Bukhūr ʿAdanī*, which explicitly deals with British colonialism in southern Yemen (Alkodimi, "Concept of Nation").

15. Jones, *Britain and the Yemen Civil War*, 9, 11.

16. Jones, *Britain and the Yemen Civil War*, 12, 28.

17. Halliday, *Britain's First Muslims.*

18. Carapico, "Arabia Incognita," 17–19.

19. Hathaway, *Tale of Two Factions*, 91.

20. Hathaway, *Tale of Two Factions*, 79.

21. Hathaway, *Tale of Two Factions*, 34, 36, 62.

22. Hathaway, *Tale of Two Factions*, 32–33, 36, 48; Carapico, "Arabia Incognita," 14; Goitein, *From the Land of Sheba*, 4.

23. Newby, *History of the Jews of Arabia*, 14–20.

24. Newby, *History of the Jews of Arabia*, 22–23, 32.

25. Newby, *History of the Jews of Arabia*, 34–43.

26. Newby, *History of the Jews of Arabia*, 100–104, 108.

27. Klorman, *Traditional Society in Transition*, 4–9.

28. Klorman, *Traditional Society in Transition*, 10–11.

29. Klorman, *Traditional Society in Transition*, 12–19.

30. Klorman, *Traditional Society in Transition*, 89. Klorman has a detailed discussion of the influence of the Haskala, the *Alliance israélite universelle*, and other aspects of wider Jewish modernity in Yemen, in particular the Kabbala dispute that exploded in Sanaʾa just before World War I (*Traditional Society in Transition*, 15–69). See also Ariel, *Jewish-Muslim Relations.*

31. Klorman, *Traditional Society in Transition*, 90–91.

32. Klorman, *Traditional Society in Transition*, 93–97.

33. Klorman, *Traditional Society in Transition*, 106–8.

34. Wagner, *Jews and Islamic Law*, 13.

35. Klorman, *Traditional Society*, 191–92; Meir-Glitzenstein, "Operation Magic Carpet," 150–53, 159–61.

36. See also Ariel's critique of what he terms the "overgeneralized" and "polemic" nature of much writing on the emigration of Jews in the Arab world to Israel and his call for attention to the specificities of each case (*Jewish-Muslim Relations*, 137–38).

37. Al-Muqri, *Ḥurma*; Al-Muqri, *Bukhūr ʿAdanī.*

38. For instance, Sarah Abrevaya Stein's study of the position of southern versus northern Algerian Jews under French colonialism (*Saharan Jews*); see also Hesse, "From Colonised to Coloniser," 1–2.

39. Goitein, *Land of Sheba*, 9, 24, 28, 61; Wagner, *Like Joseph in Beauty*, 7–8, 71–86, 147; Messick, *Calligraphic State.*

40. My thanks to Brahim El Guabli for highlighting this.

41. Parfitt, *Road to Redemption*, 89.

42. Tritton, "Zunnār."

43. See Wagner, *Like Joseph in Beauty*, for a wide-ranging discussion not only of *ḥumaynī* poetry but also of its historical relationship with Yemenite Jewish culture.

44. Parfitt, *Road to Redemption*, 89.

45. Tobi, "Attempts to Expel the Jews," 43.

46. Al-Muqri, *Al-Yahūdī al-ḥālī*, 77; Wagner, *Like Joseph in Beauty*, 52.

47. Tobi, "Attempts to Expel the Jews," 44, 59.

48. Al-Muqri, *Al-Yahūdī al-ḥālī*, 47–48, 137–38. All translations from al-Muqri's novel are mine.

49. Goitein, *Land of Sheba*, 119.

50. Goitein, *Land of Sheba*, 24.

51. Al-Muqri, *Al-Yahūdī al-ḥālī*, 20.

52. Al-Muqri, *Al-Yahūdī al-ḥālī*, 20.

53. Al-Muqri, *Al-Yahūdī al-ḥālī*, 20.

54. The theme of al-Marzuban's work was not actually the inherent qualities of dogs, but a commentary on the decline of Islamic society at the time and a criticism of the men leading it.

55. Al-Muqri, *Al-Yahūdī al-ḥālī*, 31.

56. Goitein, *Land of Sheba*, 22; Wagner, *Like Joseph in Beauty*, 156.

57. Gershom Scholem's *Sabbatai Ṣevi* is the most comprehensive study of Sabbatai Sevi and Nathan of Gaza's messianic movement.

58. Tobi, *Jews of Yemen*, 48–49.

59. See Madmoni-Gerber, *Israeli Media*; Meir-Glitzenstein, "Operation Magic Carpet"; Bashkin, *Impossible Exodus*; Shohat, "Sephardim in Israel." Inbari's article "Uzi Meshulam" usefully locates the impact of this long-term trauma in a Hasidic environment.

60. Al-Muqri, *Al-Yahūdī al-ḥālī*, 61–62.

61. Klorman, "Muslim Society as an Alternative," 95–96; Hollander, *Jews and Muslims*, 142–51.

62. Al-Rubaidi, *Imagining an Alternative Homeland*.

63. See, e.g., Gottreich, *Mellah of Marrakesh*.

64. Al-Muqri, *Al-Yahūdī al-ḥālī*, 72–78.

65. Al-Muqri, *Al-Yahūdī al-ḥālī*, 73.

66. Al-Muqri, *Al-Yahūdī al-ḥālī*, 77–78.

67. Goitein, *Land of Sheba*, 34; Wagner, *Jews and Islamic Law*, 4.

68. Al-Muqri, *Al-Yahūdī al-ḥālī*, 75–76.

69. Halevi, *Muhammad's Grave*, 114–16, 119–25, 131.

70. Halevi, *Muhammad's Grave*, 133–35.

71. Gamliel, *Aesthetics of Sorrow*.

72. Halevi, *Muhammad's Grave*, 90, 136; Gamliel, *Aesthetics of Sorrow*, 18, 282–85.

73. Halevi, *Muhammad's Grave*, 114–42.

74. Toufic, *Withdrawal of Tradition*. Heghnar Watenpaugh also conveys this strongly in her social history of the Zeytun Gospels, an illuminated manuscript displaced and divided during the Armenian Genocide (Watenpaugh, *Missing Pages*).

75. Klorman, "Muslim Society as an Alternative," 90, 93–94.

76. Al-Muqri, *Al-Yahūdī al-ḥālī*, 95.

77. Al-Muqri, *Al-Yahūdī al-ḥālī*, 148–49.

78. Layoun, *Wedded to the Land*, 96–102.

79. Smith, "Concourse between the Living," 229; Halevi, *Muhammad's Grave*, 219–25; Smith and Haddad, *Islamic Understanding of Death and Resurrection*, 41–59.

80. Halevi, *Muhammad's Grave*, 146.

81. Halevi, *Muhammad's Grave*, 233.

82. Goitein, *Land of Sheba*, 122.

83. Al-Muqri, *Al-Yahūdī al-ḥālī*, 148.

84. Al-Muqri, *Al-Yahūdī al-ḥālī*, 149.

85. Halevi, *Muhammad's Grave*, 33–39.

86. Al-Muqri, *Al-Yahūdī al-ḥālī*, 142.

87. Al-Muqri, *Al-Yahūdī al-ḥālī*, 142.

88. Hanley, "Grieving Cosmopolitanism in Middle East Studies," 1347–48; Georgiou, "Between Strategic Nostalgia and Banal Nomadism," 25–26.

89. Goitein, *Land of Sheba*, 15.

Bibliography

Alkodimi, Khaled Abkar. "Al-Muqri's Anti-Religious Stance: A Call for Moderate Islamic Discourse." *International Journal of Language and Literature* 7, no. 1 (June 2019): 38–47.

———. "The Concept of Nation in al-Muqri's Novels." *Interventions* 22, no. 8 (2020): 1079–94.

Ariel, Ari. *Jewish-Muslim Relations and Migration from Yemen to Palestine in the Late Nineteenth and Twentieth Centuries*. Leiden: Brill, 2014.

Bashkin, Orit. *Impossible Exodus: Iraqi Jews in Israel*. Stanford: Stanford University Press, 2017.

Carapico, Sheila. "Arabia Incognita: An Invitation to Arabian Peninsula Studies." In *Counter-Narratives: History, Contemporary Society, and Politics in Saudi Arabia and Yemen*, edited by Madawi al-Rasheed and Robert Vitalis, 11–34. Basingstoke: Palgrave Macmillan, 2004.

Gamliel, Tova. *Aesthetics of Sorrow: The Wailing Culture of Yemenite Jewish Women*. Detroit: Wayne State University Press, 2014.

Georgiou, Myria. "Between Strategic Nostalgia and Banal Nomadism: Explorations of Transnational Subjectivity among Arab Audiences." *International Journal of Middle Eastern Studies* 16, no. 1 (2012): 23–39.

Ghaleb Rashed, Redhwan Qasem. "The Fictional World of Ali al-Muqri as Seen in *The Handsome Jew*." *Contemporary Review of the Middle East* 8, no. 1 (2021): 1–20. https://www.doi.org/10.1177/2347798920976285.

Goitein, Shlomo. *From the Land of Sheba: Tales of the Jews of Yemen*. New York: Schocken Books, 1973.

Gottreich, Emily. *The Mellah of Marrakesh: Jewish and Muslim Space in Morocco's Red City*. Bloomington: Indiana University Press, 2007.

Halevi, Leor. *Muhammad's Grave: Death Rites and the Making of Islamic Society*. New York: Columbia University Press, 2007.

Halliday, Fred. *Britain's First Muslims: Portrait of an Arab Community*. London: I. B. Tauris, 2010.

The Handsome Jew: Ali al-Muqri." International Prize for Arabic Fiction. Accessed April 2019. https://www.arabicfiction.org/en/The%20Handsome%20Jew.

Hanley, Will. "Grieving Cosmopolitanism in Middle East Studies." *History Compass* 6, no. 5 (2008): 1346–67.

Hathaway, Jane. *A Tale of Two Factions: Myth, Memory, and Identity in Ottoman Egypt and Yemen*. Albany: State University of New York Press, 2003.

Hesse, Isabelle, "From Colonised to Coloniser: Reading the Figure of the Jew in Edgar Hilsenrath's *Der Nazi und der Friseur* and Jurek Becker's *Bronsteins Kinder*." *Postcolonial Text* 9, no. 4 (2014): 1–16.

Hollander, Isaac. *Jews and Muslims in Lower Yemen: A Study in Protection and Retraint, 1918–1949*. Leiden: Brill, 2005.

Inbari, Motti. "Uzi Meshulam and the 'Mishkan Ohalim' Affair: The Influence of Radical Ultra-Orthodoxy." *Israel Studies Review* 32, no. 2 (2017): 21–42.

Irving, Sarah. "Gender, Conflict, and Muslim-Jewish Romance: Reading ʿAli Al-Muqri's *The Handsome Jew* and Mahmoud Saeed's *The World Through the Eyes of Angels*." *Journal of Middle East Women's Studies* 12, no. 3 (2016): 343–62.

Joffre, Tzvi. "Yemen's Remaining Jews to Be Transferred to UAE—Report." *Jerusalem Post*, August 16, 2020. https://www.jpost.com/diaspora/yemens-remaining-jews-to-be-transferred-to-uae-report-638831.

Jones, Clive. *Britain and the Yemen Civil War, 1962–65*. Brighton: Sussex Academic Press, 2010.

Kershner, Isabel. "19 Yemeni Jews Arrive in Israel, Ending Secret Rescue Operation." *New York Times*, March 21, 2016. https://www.nytimes.com/2016/03/22/world/middleeast/yemen-jews-israel.html.

Klorman, Bat-Zion Eraqi. "Muslim Society as an Alternative: Jews Converting to Islam." *Jewish Social Studies* 14, no. 1 (2007): 89–118.

———. *Traditional Society in Transition: The Yemeni Jewish Experience*. Leiden: Brill, 2014.

Layoun, Mary. *Wedded to the Land: Gender, Boundaries, and Nationalism in Crisis*. Durham: Duke University Press, 2001.

Madmoni-Gerber, Shoshana. *Israeli Media and the Framing of Internal Conflict: The Yemenite Babies Affair*. Basingstoke: Palgrave Macmillan, 2009.

Meir-Glitzenstein, Esther. "Operation Magic Carpet: Constructing the Myth of the Magical Immigration of Yemenite Jews to Israel." *Israel Studies* 16, no. 3 (2011): 149–73.

Messick, Brinkley. *The Calligraphic State: Textual Domination and History in a Muslim Society*. Berkeley: University of California Press, 1992.

Muqri, Ali al-. *Bukhūr ʿAdanī*. Beirut: Dar al-Saqi, 2014.

———. *Ḥurma*. Beirut: Dar al-Saqi, 2012.

———. *Ṭaʿm aswad, rāʾiḥa sawdāʾ*. Beirut: Dar El-Saqi, 2008.

———. *Al-Yahūdī al-ḥālī*. Beirut: Dar al-Saqi, 2009.

Newby, Gordon. *A History of the Jews of Arabia, from Ancient Times to Their Eclipse Under Islam*. Columbia: University of South Carolina Press, 1988.

Parfitt, Tudor. *The Road to Redemption: The Jews of the Yemen, 1900–1950*. Leiden: Brill, 1996.

Rowe, John Carlos. "Buried Alive: The Native American Political Unconscious in Louise Erdrich's Fiction." *Postcolonial Studies* 7, no. 2 (2004): 197–210.

Rubaidi, Abdulsalam al-. *Imagining an Alternative Homeland: Humanism in Contemporary Yemeni Novels as a Vision for Social and Political Reform*. Bonn: CARPO, 2018.

Scholem, Gershom. *Sabbatai Ṣevi: The Mystical Messiah, 1626–1676*. Princeton: Princeton University Press, 1973.

Shohat, Ella. "Sephardim in Israel: Zionism from the Standpoint of Its Jewish Victims." *Social Text* 19–20 (1988): 1–35.

Smith, Jane Idleman, and Yvonne Yazbeck Haddad. *The Islamic Understanding of Death and Resurrection*. Albany: State University of New York Press, 1981.

Smith, Jane. "Concourse Between the Living and the Dead in Islamic Eschatological Literature." *History of Religions* 19, no. 3 (1980): 224–36.

Soto-Crespo, Ramon. "Death and the Diaspora Writer: Hybridity and Mourning in the Work of Jamaica Kincaid." *Contemporary Literature* 43, no. 2 (2002): 342–76.

Stein, Sarah Abrevaya. *Saharan Jews and the Fate of French Algeria*. Chicago: University of Chicago Press, 2014.

Tobi, Yosef. "The Attempts to Expel the Jews from Yemen in the Eighteenth Century." In *Proceedings of the Second International Congress of Judaeo-Yemenite Studies*, edited by Ephraim Isaac and Yosef Tobi, 41–64. Princeton: Institute of Semitic Studies / Princeton University, 1999.

———. *The Jews of Yemen: Studies in Their History and Culture*. Leiden: Brill, 1999.

Toufic, Jalal. *The Withdrawal of Tradition Past a Surpassing Disaster*. Beirut: Forthcoming Books, 2009.

Tritton, A. S. "Zunnār." In *Encyclopaedia of Islam*, 2nd ed., edited by P. Bearman et al. Leiden: Brill, 1960–2005.

Wagner, Mark. *Jews and Islamic Law in Early 20th-Century Yemen*. Bloomington: Indiana University Press, 2015.

———. *Like Joseph in Beauty: Yemeni Vernacular Poetry and Arab-Jewish Symbiosis*. Leiden: Brill, 2009.

Walder, Dennis. *Postcolonial Nostalgias: Writing, Representation, and Memory*. Abingdon: Routledge, 2011.

Watenpaugh, Heghnar. *The Missing Pages: The Modern Life of a Medieval Manuscript, from Genocide to Justice*. Stanford: Stanford University Press, 2019.

CHAPTER 6

Bearing Witness and Resurrecting Kurdish-Arab-Jewish Memory in *Mādhā ʿan al-sayyida al-yahūdiyya rāḥīl?*

STEPHANIE KRAVER

In Salīm Barakāt's 2019 novel *Mādhā ʿan al-sayyida al-yahūdiyya rāḥīl?* (What about Rachel, the Jewish lady?), the Kurdish-Syrian author highlights the ways in which minority identities are constructed and delineated in twentieth-century Syria. Barakāt writes to honor and preserve vestiges of this nearly forgotten Kurdish-Arab-Jewish urban and national history, illuminating the multicultural and interreligious relationships that existed before the Jewish exodus from the country. Through the eyes of a sixteen-year-old Kurdish protagonist, Kīhāt, Barakāt offers an intervention, subverting the ways in which Syria's history is customarily told and bringing to light a more inclusive landscape of life stories. The author invites his readers to navigate the ethnically diverse border town of Qamishli in northern Syria and interrogate the impetus behind the tragic loss of Syria's Jewish community.[1] However, through Barakāt's digressive storytelling—as well as his portrayal of inconclusive and circular dialogic exchanges—the author ironically obfuscates his meaning. Namely, by incorporating silences and "deferrals" in the novel, he summons the reader to bear witness to the sudden and painful departure of Kīhāt's Jewish neighbors while simultaneously underscoring the impossibility of knowing the full tale.[2]

Although the story serves as a chronicle of minority solidarities within Syria, as Kīhāt aims to understand the traditions and rituals, as well as the insecurity, of Qamishli's Jewish residents in the post–1967 War period, Barakāt foregrounds the difficulty of retelling this tragic history. In particular, the novel's anticlimactic and abrupt ending leaves the story wanting—and exhibits a continuity between the novel and traumatic experience.[3] In other words, as scholar Ann Cvetkovich explains, "because trauma can be unspeakable and unrepresentable and because it is marked by forgetting and dissociation," Barakāt's tangential narrative and the lack of closure at the story's denouement exemplify how loss and grief animate the text.[4]

In a manner redolent of the bildungsroman genre, Barakāt juxtaposes Kīhāt's emotional development and growth with the social and political transformations that occurred in Syria following the Baʿath Party's military coup in 1966, as well as the 1967 War. Notably, the perpetual fear instilled by the Baʿath regime, along with Kīhāt's inability to comprehend the ensuing rifts between Syrian Jews and their Arab and Muslim neighbors, set the tone for the novel and foreshadow the devastating loss of the country's Jewish community.

In the twentieth century, in light of Syria's political instability following the Baʿath Party's ascendancy and the anti-Zionist riots that erupted around the time of the 1948 War, Jews began to seek homes elsewhere. According to historian Walter Zenner, in the post-1948 period the situation for Jews in Syria alternated between severe restriction of their mobility and relative liberty.[5] "It was reported that in March 1964, Jews were forbidden to travel more than three miles from home without permits. Those who were able to leave the country could take only one hundred dollars with them and had to abandon all other belongings."[6] During these intervals of curtailed travel, Jews were clandestinely smuggled out of the country. The Ottoman census of 1893 reports that there were more than seventeen thousand Jews in the province of Aleppo, Damascus, and the vicinity.[7] However, in the twentieth century, with the rise of Arab nationalism and its antithetical enterprise, the Zionist movement, Syria's Jewish community practically disappeared. By 1967 the majority of Jews had left the country, marking what Norman Stillman soberly describes as the "end of a history that extended back more than a millennium."[8]

By focusing on this historical moment and analyzing the ways in which a Kurdish character resurrects Jewish memory in an Arabic text, this essay will invoke Michael Rothberg's nuanced schema on multidirectional memory, or the productive interaction of various histories, which are "subject to ongoing negotiation, cross-referencing, and borrowing."[9] Specifically, Barakāt evinces a polyphonic world of sundry voices in a monolingual work, revealing the fraught and intricate relationship between minor languages and identities—and Arabic's hegemonic character. Although the novel is solely intended for and accessible to Arabic readers, it nevertheless depicts a rich community of Jews, Kurds, and Armenians, negotiating multilingual interactions as neighbors. Barakāt illustrates the distinctively textured town of Qamishli—the city of his own childhood—in order to privilege cultural hybridity and multiethnic stories within Syria's national sphere. By spotlighting Qamishli's vibrant population in his novel, Barakāt ultimately comments on the city's fateful loss of its heterogeneous character. Throughout the story we watch as this loss slowly unfolds, and by the book's final harrowing scene we observe how the Jewish residents' departure culminates in calamity and rupture.

Barakāt's portrait of Syria's multiplicity of voices and identities often reads as a meandering and largely descriptive stream of consciousness that becomes difficult to pin down and examine. In reflecting upon the author's compositions in both poetry and fiction, literary scholar Huda Fakhreddine underscores that "Barakāt does not subscribe to genre limitations and portrays the act of writing, whether poetry or novel, as a retrieval of language's initial power to fascinate. . . . Barakāt's posture towards language involves processes of uncovering, reclaiming and de-familiarizing. He does not deny that it is also a difficult posture, one that does not come easy either to him or his reader."[10] Fakhreddine's impressions of Barakāt's poetry and prose are instructive here, as they help us discern the ways in which the novel is not a straightforward or transparent text.[11] While Barakāt sets out to disrupt the silence surrounding the Jewish exodus from Syria and the subjugation of minority cultures and life in Qamishli, his revival of this history is also imbued with departures. Kīhāt propels the narrative through his quest to unveil what encompasses the essence of Syrian identity and minority experience. However, given the oppressive and stifling presence of the military government and the boy's inability to accomplish what Shoshana Felman outlines as the "transition from a perception of the equivocal to the establishment of meaning as univocal," our search for understanding is perpetually upended.[12]

The novel highlights Kīhāt and his family during a period of severe austerity in the wake of the June 1967 War and offers a sensory-laden depiction of daily life and customs, elucidating everyday experiences with embellished detail. Barakāt sketches numerous iterations of Kīhāt and his younger brother, Mūsā, wandering around their neighborhood, which is directly parallel to the Jewish quarter—a sector marked by fragrant perfume (*ʿiṭr*) and spices (*al-afāwīhī*), as well as the meat seller Rāhīl's shop.[13] As part of Kīhāt's feeble attempt to become closer with Rāhīl's daughter Līnā, the boy volunteers to assist the two women with daily chores on Shabbat.[14] When Kīhāt is not lingering around the Jewish quarter, he and his brother habitually frequent the cinema. Barakāt provides long and elaborate descriptions of the foreign films playing in Qamishli as well as Mūsā's boundless admiration for Charlie Chaplin.

The cinema serves as a welcome distraction from Syria's tense political climate before the government staunchly censors American films and products. This caesura is poignantly felt in the story when Mūsā is punished for writing "ʾāsha Sharlī Shāblin" (Charlie Chaplin lives) on his classroom's blackboard.[15] Not only is Mūsā harshly reprimanded for this seemingly subversive deed, but his father, Awsī, is also fired from his job.[16] Through incidents such as this one, we can observe how the repressive influence of the military regime infiltrates daily life—or what Ann Cvetkovich describes in *An Archive of Feelings* as "the persistence of the everyday in [an] encounter with trauma." As Cvetkovich suggests, traumatic accounts are typified by the ordinary just as they are by the catastrophic, and thus, in this disquieting scene, we can identify how the prosaic and the eventful converge in the novel.[17]

Despite the author's preoccupation with seemingly superfluous and repetitive descriptions such as the pungent smell of tobacco (*tibgh*), which emanates throughout the story, and the extensive characterization of the emaciated chickens (*dajājāt hazīla*) that Kīhāt acquires from Rāḥīl, Barakāt avoids a more direct and clear representation of the ominous events that precipitate the Jewish community's eventual emigration.[18] In many ways, the continuous smoke exuding from the *tibgh* in the novel contributes to and affirms the narrative's ambiguity, muddling the legibility of Barakāt's text. As Cathy Caruth relates, paradoxically, the literary language in which trauma narratives are expressed "simultaneously defies and demands our witness." That is to say, experiences marked by crisis require our attention, but are not fully known through their representation.[19] Hence, using his discursive style of writing, Barakāt accents the "disorder" of the postmodern era, or how "meaning and coherence are systematically undermined, and reality is unstable."[20] The persistence of "gaps and silences [and] the repeated breakdown of language" within the work highlight how this distressing history about the loss of Jewish life in Qamishli eludes our immediate comprehension and is not easily narrated.[21]

HISTORICAL BACKGROUND: SYRIA'S JEWS, THE BAʿATH PARTY, AND THE 1967 WAR

Barakāt's novel begins in the tumultuous days leading up to the 1967 War, specifically, with Kīhāt and Mūsā painting the windows of their family home blue. Although not articulated explicitly, it can be inferred that they are camouflaging their house with paint in order to prevent it from becoming a potential target for Israeli war planes.[22] This unsettling moment exposes the political unrest that was erupting between Syria's leadership and the nascent Israeli state.

After centuries of Jewish presence and cohabitation in the region, 1967 is documented as a turning point for Syrian culture. Even though Jews in the region had coexisted and collaborated with their Muslim and Christian neighbors since the days preceding the Arab conquests, and throughout much of Islamic civilization, the twentieth century brought an end to these relatively peaceful conditions.[23] The proliferation of Arab national sentiments, as well as the creation of Israel, dramatically altered the circumstances for Jews living in Arab lands, culminating in the "rapid collapse and dissolution of Jewish communities" and their resulting dislocation.[24]

Prior to the Jews' attrition in Syria, they were largely integrated with their neighbors; Jews lived on the same streets as Muslims and were not confined to ghettos. Members of the Jewish community practiced a range of crafts, which coincided with those of Muslims and Christians. In the eighteenth century, members of all three faiths could join guilds representing their trades.[25] Zenner elucidates how Aleppo's community "traces its history to the beginnings of the Jewish people."[26] Under the auspices of Muslim states, prior to the nineteenth century, Jews were qualified as *dhimmī*, "tolerated subjects who had to maintain a low profile but who had the rights to life, property, and freedom of living under their own religious law."[27] Most of Syria's Jews accepted the "privileges of foreign citizenship and to live in the Ottoman Empire under the protection of European states."[28] Many of these Jews were of Spanish origin, though Arabic was the community's principal language. Along with European Jews settling in the region, Jews from other areas in the Middle East, including Iran, also made Syria their home.

Yet, notwithstanding this heritage of Jewish integration in Syria, by 1875, as economic conditions under the Ottoman government took a dismal turn, Jewish livelihoods were adversely affected. Historian Yaron Harel underscores that as the Ottoman Empire was unable to repay its outstanding debts, the economic crisis that persisted in Damascus led to the diminishment of the city's Jewish financial elite, and ultimately to the disintegration of the Jewish community as a whole.[29] Harel further elaborates that the "harsh economic situation, the loss of foreign protection, the crumbling communal institutions and the weakening of social solidarity left the Jewish community almost completely exposed to the arbitrary treatment of Ottoman government officials."[30] Moreover, in this context of financial insecurity, accusations pertaining to the blood libel—that Syrian Jews utilized local Christian children's blood for ritual purposes—resurfaced in Damascus.[31]

In the early twentieth century, as Zionism began to take root and was perceived as a real threat to the Arab nationalist agenda, tensions continued to escalate between Syria's Jews and the country's Muslim and Christian communities.[32] Stillman claims that based on religious, socioeconomic, and political factors in the modern era, the Jewish exodus can be attributed to "forces of both push and pull."[33] In Damascus, there were Jews who responded to anti-Zionist and even anti-Jewish sentiments in the Christian and Arab nationalist press by organizing anti-Zionist demonstrations. However, irrespective of Jewish community members' attempts to exhibit solidarity with their fellow Syrians, public displays of their camaraderie and fidelity to Arab nationalism proved largely unsuccessful.[34]

The rise of Arab nationalism and the growing influence of Zionism, along with other concurrent factors, thereby became two precarious developments that "resulted in a new configuration of ethnic relations in Syria."[35] As Zenner explains, "Christians and members of 'heretical' or 'secretive' sects, such as Druzes and Alawis, could identify with a secular nationalist movement. After 1920, however, it became increasingly difficult for Jews to join the Arab nationalist movements, because the Arab nationalists regarded the Zionist movement—which sought to establish a Jewish homeland in Palestine—as an obstacle to be overcome. Despite disclaimers by their official leaders, Syrian Jews emigrated from Syria to [Israel]."[36] Given Arab nationalist leaders' early antagonism to Zionism, the watershed moment of Israel's establishment in 1948—the Nakba, or the ethnic cleansing of over seven hundred thousand Palestinians from present-day Israel—forever altered the situation of Syria's Jewish community. Zenner notes that in Qamishli, Jewish residents "were only permitted to travel within the town, and they had to report to the Jewish quarter at night." They relied on charity from abroad, and "there were charges that some Muslim individuals loitered about the Jewish quarter in a threatening manner. . . . Military intelligence personnel were said to enter Jewish stores . . . and help themselves to merchandise."[37]

The climate that Zenner glosses here is paramount to the world that Barakāt pictures in his novel—and how the Baʿath Party's restrictions and the lurking *mukhābarāt*, or secret service, contribute to an uneasiness in the text. In the story, Jews along with other minorities are closely monitored, and thus hostilities toward these communities are only intensified by the military regime. Barakāt's narrative heavily critiques the Baʿath Party following the 1966 coup d'état, and the ways in which a new and more oppressive conception of Syrian identity was adopted and enforced through the Military Committee's ascendancy. Even for Jews who did not adhere to Zionism's nationalist project and who saw themselves as fellow Arabs, the internal repression promoted by the Baʿath Party exacerbated tensions and the Jews' feelings of alienation.[38]

This historical juncture was marked by an intra-Baʿathist struggle in February 1966, resulting in a bloody coup and the violent overthrow of leader Amin al-Hafiz. Al-Hafiz's reputation had been sullied by his connection to defense minister Kamel Amin Thābet, who was discovered in 1965 to be Eli Cohen, "an Israeli spy [who had been] transmitting military secrets to Tel Aviv."[39] Cohen was subsequently hanged.[40] After the coup, the cofounders of the Baʿath Party, Michel ʿAflaq and Salaḥ al-Dīn al-Bīṭār, fled the country, never to return.[41] While the regime that replaced these pioneers was "ostensibly governed by civilians, it was in reality controlled by the military officers who had engineered the putsch."[42] Therefore, despite the Baʿath's initial call for an end to class exploitation—for cultivating freedom and democratic thought—the radical regime following 1966 stymied these idealistic and socialist tenets.

The repressive nature of this neo-Baʿathist ideology is further elaborated through Wendy Pearlman's fieldwork in *We Crossed a Bridge and It Trembled*.[43] One of her interlocutors, Muḥammed, explains that even though the Baʿath Party "came along with an idea of pan-Arabism . . . this brought Syrians of different backgrounds together, but it did not honestly address the problem that Syria is multicultural and multiethnic."[44] ʿIssām, an accountant from rural Aleppo whom Pearlman also interviews in her work, similarly illuminates this discrepancy, asserting that

> there used to be coexistence, but under security pressure and judicial control. It wasn't real coexistence. You couldn't even say to someone, "You're Kurdish or you're Sunni or Shiite." It was forbidden; you'd be fined or punished. We weren't educated about the different people in the country, so there wasn't real integration. Arabs didn't know about Kurdish culture. Arabs and Kurds knew nothing about Turkmens. We'd hear that there were people called Syriacs and Assyrians, but who are they and how do they live? We didn't know. The Druze? You know that they live in Syria, but what is their culture and what do they want? We were all just groups of strangers. A country of closed communities, held together by force.[45]

These revealing interviews, chronicling Syria's constraints under the Baʿathist regime, provide insight into the party's intolerance of diversity and the ways in which authoritarian rule promoted forms of silencing. Even though the country had been home to various multiethnic backgrounds for centuries, according to these recollections, it became an unspoken taboo—essentially forbidden—to acknowledge cultural and religious difference.

The suppression and lack of knowledge about minority groups, as well as the Baʿath's dogmatism, are particularly relevant for understanding how this stifling political environment led to loss. Barakāt's writing thoughtfully addresses and denounces the harsh climate described by this history and characterized by Muḥammad and ʿIssām. He gives voice to marginalized communities, the people who would be deemed the most foreign and unknown to the average Syrian and displays what Stef Craps posits in *Postcolonial Witnessing*, showing that "memories of different traumatic histories overlap, intertwine, and mutually influence each other."[46] In spite of these historical entanglements that Barakāt spotlights, however, considering the atmosphere of repression in the post–1967 War period, as well as the inherent limitations of documenting this lamentable account, we can also appraise the silences, divergences, and "misreadings" that typify the novel's disconcerting effect.

MINORITY IDENTITIES AND LANGUAGES IN THE NOVEL

In *Mādhā ʿan al-sayyida?* Barakāt employs dialogic exchanges to portray myriad views on Syrian identity and what it means to belong to Syria's national ethos. Specifically, the Kurdish protagonist's recognition of the country's political turmoil and his valiant attempts to know Qamishli's Jews serve as a lens through which Barakāt's own Arabic readers can come to understand Syria's history. Hence, in more than one respect, the novelist invites his readers to engage with, and gain an appreciation for, voices that remain peripheral to Syria's dominant culture.

The author's interest in unearthing multiple perspectives within his narrative is exemplified by an early conversation that Kīhāt has with his father, Awsī, and their neighbor Kātiyā. As they discuss the Egyptian-Syrian singer Farīd al-Aṭrash, Kīhāt asks his father, "Why does al-Aṭrash say that in Syria there exists a brotherhood between the crescent and the cross?"[47] Kātiyā interjects, explaining that in their country Muslims and Christians are brothers and sisters. Kīhāt asks him, "mādhā ʿan al-sītt Rāḥīl?" (What about Rachel?), referring to the Jewish meat seller in their neighborhood. "ʾAlaysat Rāḥīl sūriyyatan?" (Isn't Rachel Syrian?). The boy's father says, "kul al-sūriyyīn, sūriyyūn" (all Syrians are Syrian). Kīhāt, interpreting this as an empty remark, briskly rejoins that "kul al-sūriyyīn bilā sūriyya" (all Syrians [are] without Syria).[48] Kīhāt means that if one is unable to honor and identify all Syrians as such, the country is lost for everyone; the very essence of Syria ceases to exist.

Notwithstanding his father's noble attempts at consolation, the sixteen-year-old Kīhāt has come to perceive the inherent inequalities and hypocrisies within Syria's national and political spheres. This realization is confirmed when Kātiyā declares that it was the Jews who killed Jesus, thereby suggesting that unlike Muslims and Christians, who have experienced their own share of interreligious strife, Jews are in a marginalized category of their own.[49] Distinct from the other religious groups, they cannot be incorporated into al-Aṭrash's musical conception of Syrian brotherhood and fraternity.

While this dialogue indubitably references ethnic and religious affiliations and a particular logic of exclusion, another conspicuous aspect is that the conversation is seemingly bilingual. Though it appears solely in Arabic, Kātiyā alerts the reader to her own lack of understanding—Kīhāt has posed his original question about al-Aṭrash's music in Kurdish. In response to Kātiyā's request, Kīhāt translates his initial inquiry into Arabic. Although this repetition appears identically in the text, we are asked to imagine that this work is operating in multiple registers, and therefore polyphonically. That is, in thinking with Mikhail Bakhtin's analysis of the "plurality of independent and unmerged voices" found in novels, we can observe how diverse forms of utterance comprise the nation and are also not fully legible to everyone and all at once.[50]

Gilles Deleuze and Félix Guattari's discussion on minor literature is pertinent here. Explaining the ways in which minority identity can be fashioned, they propose that a "minor literature doesn't come from a minor language; it is rather that which a minority constructs within a major language," challenging the hegemonic culture and its centers of power through a mode of "deterritorialization."[51] Yet, despite Deleuze and Guattari's focus on the destabilizing effect that minor literatures may have on the dominant language, it is notable how minor tongues are subverted through such a framework. Barakāt significantly "monologizes" Syria's polyphonic culture—or uses Arabic in his illumination of Qamishli's linguistic difference in order to comment on the ways in which minor languages may be stifled but, strikingly, still endure within the prevailing discourse. Thus, even in the strictly Arabic text, language becomes a pivotal means of delineating identity and distinction.

Kātiyā, Kīhāt, and Awsī's dialogue soon takes a harrowing turn. Awsī says he has heard that "Jews are being killed in the country."[52] Deeply disturbed by this news, Kīhāt inquires, "Where are they being killed, in Qamishli?"[53] While his father cannot confirm the location, Kātiyā questions whether these events were reported on the radio. Awsī says he has not heard any related announcements on the radio, and Kīhāt draws his own conclusion, declaring that while "the radio does not lie, we lie over the radio."[54] Kīhāt here emphasizes the prevalence of misinformation in everyday discourse—or how the propagation of lies has become commonplace in Syria. Kīhāt's evaluation reveals how distortions of the truth are mobilized to silence dissent and bolster the legitimacy of the military powers.[55] Despite the ephemeral and inconclusive quality of the characters' exchange, their interaction illustrates how the reliability of narratives—and our ability to distinguish fact from fiction—are destabilized within the text.

Along with the unnerving mention of Jews being killed in Syria, the topic of the community's insecurity is similarly invoked during a conversation that Kīhāt has with his classmate Raḥīm. Raḥīm asks Kīhāt if their neighbors "will be punished by the state because of their Jewish background."[56] Raḥīm thus unveils his apprehension, demonstrating how "violence is present and implicated in the ordinary rather than the two being mutually exclusive."[57] Although officers from the military regime do not appear during this scene, the discomforting presence of the *mukhābarāt* continues to haunt the narrative.

As if evading his friend's troubling question entirely, Kīhāt redirects their conversation, inquiring again about the identity of Syrian Jews, and whether they are Arabs. Raḥīm exclaims in surprise, "yahūdūn ʿarab?" (Are Jews Arabs?). Exasperated that his friend cannot recognize such an obvious fact, Raḥīm continues, "ʾanaḥnu akrādūn ʿarab?" (Are we Kurdish Arabs?).[58] In other words, Raḥīm draws a parallel between the Jews' status in Syria and their own, effectively echoing Kīhāt's initial question.

After this, Kīhāt's inquiries become repetitious. He proposes again to Raḥīm, "ʾalaysū sūriyyīn?" (Are they not Syrian?). "Nʿam. Mithlanā" (Yes. Like us), Raḥīm answers.[59] Kīhāt, still unsatisfied, asks about their *jinsiyya,* their nationality and status as citizens. Raḥīm acknowledges his friend's preoccupation, and certifies that the Jews' *jinsiyya* is *maktūma,* or hidden—just like the Kurds.' While the boys' discourse becomes increasingly tiresome to the reader, their interaction presents how Kīhāt is again striving to pursue greater understanding and arrive at some irrefutable truth, "putting into question" that which he aims to resolve, or determine, about his Jewish neighbors.[60]

However, despite his attempts to appropriate knowledge in the novel, Kīhāt is represented as a decidedly inept reader. Just as Shoshana Felman describes how the abstruse portions in the prose of Henry James's novels create a "reading effect," one can similarly notice how in Kīhāt's "constant efforts at *deciphering* the goings-on," his "adventure turns out to be, essentially, a *reading-adventure*, a quest for the definitive, literal or proper meaning of words and of events."[61] As a result, through Kīhāt's shortcomings as an interpreter, Barakāt's work "reflects upon its own dramatization" of the search for meaning.[62] By elucidating his protagonist's pursuit for grasping what it signifies to be both Jewish and Syrian—which is never fully achieved—Barakāt cleverly instructs his readers on how elements of identity remain illegible, or unable to be decoded within the logic of his text.[63]

In particular, during a tense encounter in the novel, Kīhāt is aggressively questioned by an agent from the *mukhābarāt*, the *rāṣid*, or watchdog of the quarter, about his presence in the Jewish quarter. Although it is not explicitly stated why Kīhāt is subject to the agent's suspicions, one may conjecture that he is curious about the boy's potential ties to Israel and Jewish interests from abroad. After witnessing Kīhāt lingering outside Rāḥ īl and Līnā's doorway, the man asks Kīhāt if he lives in that house; Kīhāt responds that he does not. The man continues, "Do you have relatives here?"[64] The boy replies that he does not have family in this part of the neighborhood, and the man asks if he is Jewish. This too, Kīhāt admits, is not the case, and thus, based on the *mukhābarāt*'s prescriptive reasoning, the boy fails to provide a plausible explanation for being in this part of town. Given the strict sectarian climate of the Baʿathist state, Kīhāt's responses prove unsatisfactory. As Pearlman's interlocutors ʿIssām and Muḥammad highlight, intermingling among different groups is not customarily embraced in Syria. This unsettling dynamic helps reify the divisions that the regime enforces and that persist among the various communities, and therefore the dearth of knowledge that most Syrians have about the Other.

In responding to the man further, Kīhāt states that he is Kurdish. The man is bewildered, saying he is unaware of any Kurdish religion. Kīhāt attempts to clarify, "anā muslim" (I am Muslim).[65] Oddly, the man then asks in an even more confusing fashion, "muslim yahūdī, ʾam muslim ʿarabī"—is Kīhāt a Jewish Muslim or an Arab one.[66] The man's question is peculiar; is he cruelly mocking the boy, or simply befuddled? This perplexing conversation not only discloses the harsh and intimidating role of the *mukhābarāt*, but also accents the absurdity of their exchange. Rather than a religious identity, the man proposes Judaism as an alternative to the ethnic and linguistic marker of "Arab." This seemingly intentional misreading showcases Barakāt's incisive critique of the Baʿath Party's oppressive treatment, and further spotlights the circular and erroneous dialogues that destabilize the text—without any possibility for enhanced understanding or closure.

Notwithstanding Kīhāt's attempts to explain that he is a Kurdish Muslim, the man is insistent that the boy is a Kurdish Jew, suggesting strangely that "kulluhum yahūd," all of the Kurds, are Jewish.[67] Yet, in spite of the inanity of the man's conflation of identities in this scene, his imperceptive reading of Kīhāt also exhibits the *gaps, cryptic signifiers,* and "textual ambiguity" *that persist throughout.*[68] By observing this curious interaction, we can apprehend how "knowledge in the [text] . . . which must be *read*" is shrouded.[69] As the officer and Kīhāt struggle to communicate, they arrive at no decisive, collective understanding of what it means to be either a Kurd or a Jew. Hence, the tensions and uneasiness that reverberate in this dialogue underscore how the two characters are figuratively speaking a different language, demonstrating what cannot be realized directly and what is left unresolved in the novel. As Christa Schönfelder proposes about trauma narratives more generally, in attempting to relate a traumatic account, Barakāt portrays "that which resists ordinary processes of . . . narrating . . . representation and comprehension."[70]

In addition to Barakāt's focus on the difficulty of negotiating and defining minority identity, the author also references multilingual and multivocal disparity, foregrounding the loss of minority languages in the Arab world. For Barakāt, language becomes an essential attribute of both belonging and exclusion. "Foreign" accents are regularly identified and commented upon, and Kīhāt and his brother Mūsā are notably treated as outsiders quite indiscriminately.[71] At one point in the text, Kīhāt is questioned by another character, Nibhān, who is also frequently and inexplicably found loitering in the Jewish quarter. We are informed that this mysterious figure speaks with a Bedouin accent and always addresses Kīhāt with hostility. In this scene, Nibhān inquires whether the protagonist is indeed speaking Arabic: "ʾahadhihi lugha ʿarabiyya?" (Is this language Arabic?), he glibly asks, remarking on Kīhāt's unintelligible elocution of the majority language.[72]

While references to variances in language or accents are only alluded to and not represented formally within the text, Barakāt nonetheless meditates on how minorities operate within the dominant language, but yet are unceasingly reminded of their peripheral status. Bakhtin's understanding of language can be applied to reflect upon the ways in which literature serves as a powerful means of recovering memory and "worldmaking."[73] As Caryl Emerson contends, according to Bakhtin, "each language embodies its own specific worldview, its own system of values. And this means that every speaking subject speaks something of a foreign language to everyone else. . . . Life in language is in fact dependent upon the preservation of a gap. Two speakers must not, and never do, completely understand each other; they must remain only partially satisfied with each other's replies, because the continuation of dialogue is in large part dependent on neither party knowing exactly what the other means."[74] Emerson's reading discloses the failures and shortcomings of translation and the limits of legibility, which are prevalent themes in Barakāt's novel. The gaps and indeterminacies of language between characters contribute to the work's "linguistic silences" and what the text "leaves open," highlighting the ways in which attaining knowledge about the Other is sought, but never adequately achieved, in Syria's repressive political climate.[75]

As evidence of the story's linguistic discrepancies, Kīhāt's own name, Kurdish for "Who came," is unfamiliar to the other Syrian characters, and likely to Barakāt's Arabic readers as well.[76] Thus, the author's choice of names for his protagonist serves as a linguistic notation for marking difference. With this in mind, although the novel is composed in the majority language, the text still asserts an alternative political affiliation and collective identity.[77] Ethno-linguistic and religious variances continue to play a prominent role within the narrative through Barakāt's references to individuals speaking or writing in Kurdish, Armenian, and Hebrew. Thus, while the story explores notions of legibility quite broadly, Barakāt's invocations of diverse means of communicating function as a way to both heed and bridge distinction. As another apt example, linguistic differentiation is clearly depicted through Kīhāt's attempts to express his love for Rāḥīl's daughter, Līnā. When considering how to best articulate and reveal his inner feelings, he resolves to compose his letter in Hebrew—a language that he figures would be most familiar for and even cherished by Līnā. For this task, he solicits the help of his Jewish classmates Samīr and Naʿīm, requesting that they write "I love you" in Hebrew.[78]

Shortly after Kīhāt asks Samīr and Naʿīm for their assistance, he reflects on the ways in which Hebrew is highly politicized. While he chooses to have the declaration of his love written in what he perceives to be the language most sacred for the girl whom he adores, he also acknowledges the ways in which this choice is a form of "trespass."[79] The complexities and politics of uttering a language other than one's own are hereby predicated quite transparently, as Kīhāt negotiates becoming closer to Līnā through a foreign language—and markedly, one that has been subject to his personal suspicions and reproach.[80]

Kīhāt's Armenian friend Boghos suggests that Kīhāt appeal to Līnā in Kurdish instead.[81] Boghos thus signals the importance of language as a signifier of personal affinity and identity. Similarly, when Boghos begins speaking about his imminent relocation to Armenia, he proclaims that he will only know if Qamishli misses him if the town expresses her longing in Armenian.[82] As with the earlier references to Hebrew and Kurdish writing, Boghos's response exemplifies the ways in which the variant minority communities struggle to achieve genuine communication both with one another and with the state. Therefore, in spite of the dialogic exchanges that Barakāt illuminates and the multiethnic identities that he forges, his readers are also continuously reminded of language's limitations—and what cannot be fully grasped through polyphonic discourse.

As Barakāt shows, the Baʿath regime's denunciation, suppression, and misrepresentation of difference have instigated the need for not only the Jewish exodus, but for all of Syria's minorities to seek more welcoming homes. While the magnitude of speaking or writing in one's own language should not be underestimated, there is also a level of misapprehension among the groups—a manner in which another's language cannot be easily uttered or reproduced. Hence, regardless of cross-cultural relations and solidarities, there are inevitable restraints on one's communication with, and understanding of, the ethnic, religious, and linguistic other.

Therefore, despite the naïve and utopic vision that Boghos and Kīhāt conjure, in which Syria's multilingual identity can be dignified and upheld through the preservation of minority tongues, the novel's somber culmination thwarts such an idea. Barakāt unveils a Syria that is ultimately left in a shambles. In the novel's concluding scenes, Kīhāt travels to Rāḥīl's home in order to deliver his Hebrew missive to Līnā, intending to confess his love to the young Jewish girl. However, upon his arrival, he discovers that without any forewarning, Rāḥīl and her daughter are gone. After likely being smuggled out of the country, the two Jewish characters have forever vanished from Kīhāt's world, and he is left outside their doorway, unheard and heartbroken.[83]

In utter despair, a weeping Kīhāt dramatically shreds his love note and chews the pieces like gum, then buries the pieces, grieving his loss.[84] Kīhāt's sorrow, however, extends beyond his relationship with the meat seller and her daughter. In the final lines of the novel, the boy hums the word "Sūriyya" and then proceeds to break the word apart syllable by syllable, softly mumbling, "Sū Rī Yā." Through the literal brokenness of the text, Barakāt represents how, with the loss of the Jewish community, the country has also fragmented into pieces. As Kīhāt inhales deeply, he begins to cry.[85]

Through an account of minority discourses and experiences, and from the perspective of a sixteen-year-old Syrian Kurd, Barakāt implores us to combat our amnesia about Syria's past. He invites us to wonder about one individual in order to grieve for an entire community—to continue asking ourselves, "mādhā ʿan al-sayyida al-yahūdiyya rāḥīl?"—what about Rachel, the Jewish lady?

Kīhāt's inability to draw satisfying conclusions about the loss of Jewish life in a Syrian city mirrors how Barakāt's narrative fails to provide clear expository answers to the questions being raised. From the story's anticlimactic end, we may surmise that Rāḥīl and Līnā have forever disappeared from Qamishli after emigrating. In spite of Kīhāt's inquiries about what it means to be Jewish in Syria and what will happen to his beloved Jewish neighbors, the culminating moments reintroduce these questions without offering a conclusive answer, thereby depriving the reader of a satisfactory release. With little plot aside from glimpses into Kīhāt's repetitious dialogic exchanges and daily life—and with an unsettled denouement punctuated by Rāḥīl and Līnā's abrupt departure—any hopes of relieving the building anxieties within the text are foreclosed.

As readers, we are left in stillness to give testimony to the boy's tears as he mourns a world that was once complete and whole. While the novel does not meditate nostalgically or elegiacally, instead offering a lens into ordinary life for Qamishli's rich community, this scene is nevertheless one of ineffable sadness. The vibrant multiethnic and multicultural groups had survived until the mid-twentieth century in Syria, until authoritarian forces and political pressures eventually tore the country apart. Kīhāt's loss of adolescent love allows us to reflect on the more widespread loss of Jewish life in Syria. Barakāt therefore beseeches us to understand and bear witness to the catastrophic history that began in Qamishli under Baʿathist rule, and that, tragically, persists today.

Notes

1. Qamishli is considered a relatively new community in Syria, built primarily under the French Mandate. According to historian Walter Zenner, the "area is highly sensitive," given that it sits close to the borders of both Iraq and Turkey (*Global Community*, 57).

2. Miller, *Narrative and Its Discontents*, 3.

3. Gana, *Signifying Loss*, 158.

4. Cvetkovich, *Archive of Feelings*, 7.

5. Zenner, *Global Community*, 56–57.

6. Zenner, *Global Community*, 57.

7. Zenner, *Global Community*, 36.

8. Stillman, *Jews of Arab Lands*, xxiii.

9. Rothberg, *Multidirectional Memory*, 2.

10. Fakhreddine, "Salīm Barakāt's Poetry," 147.

11. Barakāt is an author of Kurdish background. His fascination with language, and his foray into complicating his Arabic prose, can be read as a reflection of his position as an outsider in the language in which he writes—composing an intricate narrative in his nonnative tongue.

12. Felman, *Literature and Psychoanalysis*, 155.

13. Barakāt, *Mādhā ʿan al-sayyida*, 14–16.

14. Zenner describes this as a common practice in twentieth-century Syria, during which Muslims visited the homes of Jewish residents on Saturday, the Jewish Sabbath, in order to turn lights on and off (*Global Community*, 59).

15. Barakāt, *Mādhā ʿan al-sayyida*, 402. Translations are my own.

16. Barakāt, *Mādhā ʿan al-sayyida*, 402.

17. Cvetkovich, *Archive of Feelings*, 22.

18. Barakāt, *Mādhā ʿan al-sayyida*, 74.

19. Caruth, *Unclaimed Experience*, 5.

20. Adami, *Trauma Studies and Literature*, 7.

21. Schönfelder, *Wounds and Words*, 31. Here she is paraphrasing Caruth, *Trauma*, 153–55, and Caruth, *Unclaimed Experience*, 115.

22. Barakāt, *Mādhā ʿan al-sayyida*, 7–9.

23. During the early years of Islamic civilization, Jews apparently preferred the Umayyad Empire to the Byzantines, and even held positions in the royal court of Muʿāwiya. Carr and Maʾoz, "Syria," 388–97.

24. Stillman, *Jews in Arab Lands*, xxiii.

25. According to Zenner, Jewish butchers were the only contingent that "formed a religiously exclusive guild," based on their strict dietary laws (*Global Community*, 43).

26. Zenner, *Global Community*, 22.

27. Zenner, *Global Community*, 22.

28. Zenner, *Global Community*, 24.

29. Harel, *Zionism in Damascus*, 1.

30. Harel, *Zionism in Damascus*, 7.

31. Harel, *Zionism in Damascus*, 8. For a notorious example of a blood libel case, see Florence, *Blood Libel*.

32. Harel, *Zionism in Damascus*, 167.

33. Stillman, *Jews of Arab Lands*, xxi.

34. Stillman, *Jews of Arab Lands*, 88–89.

35. Zenner, *Global Community*, 49.

36. Zenner, *Global Community*, 49.

37. Zenner, *Global Community*, 57–58.

38. Notably, as Harel spotlights in *Zionism in Damascus*, Damascene Jews, such as Eliahu Sasson, saw themselves as integrated into Syria's national sphere. In response to a demonstrator's accusatory words about the Jewish community "accepting orders from the heads of the Zionist movement in Jerusalem," Sasson declared that "verily, as Syrians, we are brothers and, as Jews, cousins," emphasizing the links that tie the different religious communities together within the country (169).

39. McHugo, *Syria*, 147.

40. McHugo, *Syria*, 147.

41. "The word '*baʿath*' means rebirth or resurrection, and this renewal of Arab-ness was Michel ʿAflaq's aim. It meant the end of lesser loyalties that contradicted this unity, especially sectarian and regional ones" (McHugo, *Syria*, 118).

42. Bunton and Cleveland, *History of the Modern Middle East*, 425.

43. This authoritarian outlook can be identified as an attribute of the Baʿathist regime in other parts of the Arab world as well. For example, in Egypt and Morocco, the Copt and Amazigh communities, respectively, have similarly been targeted.

44. Pearlman, *We Crossed a Bridge*, 65.

45. Pearlman, *We Crossed a Bridge*, 66–67. I have rendered Muḥammad and ʿIssām's names with diacritics here, even though Pearlman does not use them in her account.

46. Craps, *Postcolonial Witnessing*, 6.

47. The celebrated Syrian singer and actor Farīd al-Aṭrash performed "Nashīd al-fidāʿ" (Hymn of redemption) following the

Palestinian Naksa, or setback, of the 1967 War. Al-Aṭrash's performance of this song may provide additional context for why he excludes Jews from the national fabric of Syrian society, and the ways in which Jews in Arab lands were conflated with Israelis following the 1967 War.

48. Barakāt, *Mādhā ʿan al-sayyida*, 100–102.

49. Barakāt, *Mādhā ʿan al-sayyida*, 101.

50. Bakhtin, *Problems of Dostoevsky's Poetics*, 6.

51. Deleuze and Guattari, *Kafka*, 16.

52. Barakāt, *Mādhā ʿan al-sayyida*, 103.

53. Barakāt, *Mādhā ʿan al-sayyida*, 103.

54. Barakāt, *Mādhā ʿan al-sayyida*, 103.

55. Wedeen, *Authoritarian Apprehensions*, 14.

56. Barakāt, *Mādhā ʿan al-sayyida*, 57.

57. Hermez, "War Is Going to Ignite," 327. Here I am invoking Wedeen's discussion on contemporary Syria in her book *Authoritarian Apprehensions*, and how she deftly utilizes "apprehension" as a "synonym for *arrest* or *capture* . . . [and also] 'to understand or perceive.' And it [additionally] connotes ongoing anxieties" (17). Wedeen suggests that these three meanings are all applicable for appreciating the "complicated ideological relations central to the maintenance of authoritarian power" (17).

58. Barakāt, *Mādhā ʿan al-sayyida*, 57.

59. Barakāt, *Mādhā ʿan al-sayyida*, 63.

60. Miller, *Narrative and Its Discontents*, 4.

61. Felman, *Literature and Psychoanalysis*, 126, 153.

62. Felman, *Literature and Psychoanalysis*, 155.

63. Felman, *Literature and Psychoanalysis*, 143.

64. Barakāt, *Mādhā ʿan al-sayyida*, 38.

65. Barakāt, *Mādhā ʿan al-sayyida*, 39.

66. Barakāt, *Mādhā ʿan al-sayyida*, 39.

67. Barakāt, *Mādhā ʿan al-sayyida*, 40.

68. Felman, *Literature and Psychoanalysis*, 119.

69. Felman, *Literature and Psychoanalysis*, 157.

70. Schönfelder, *Wounds and Words*, 30.

71. Mūsā is also questioned about his background at school, given his strange accent. He is subsequently asked if he is an Arab, to which he responds that he is Kurdish. This reply is met with even more suspicion, as he is then accused of loving both the Americans and Zionism (Barakāt, *Mādhā ʿan al-sayyida*, 408).

72. Barakāt, *Mādhā ʿan al-sayyida*, 461.

73. Erll, *Memory in Culture*, 144.

74. Bakhtin, *Problems of Dostoevsky's Poetics*, xxxii.

75. Felman, *Literature and Psychoanalysis*, 119.

76. This phrase was uttered by Kīhāt's father, Awsī, after a knock was heard on the door during the boy's birth. The interrogative nature of Kīhāt's name may also serve a symbolic purpose, showcasing the uncertainty, or precarity, of his status in the country.

77. Deleuze and Guattari, *Kafka*, 16–17.

78. Barakāt, *Mādhā ʿan al-sayyida*, 431.

79. Although speaking of a different context, Lital Levy's book *Poetic Trespass* is a useful reference for understanding the linguistic and sociopolitical divides that typify Arab/Jewish writing and identity politics.

80. Barakāt, *Mādhā ʿan al-sayyida*, 432–43.

81. Barakāt, *Mādhā ʿan al-sayyida*, 523.

82. Barakāt, *Mādhā ʿan al-sayyida*, 529.

83. The smuggling of Jews is only alluded to in the novel, although Barakāt does make direct reference to the historical figure Judy Carr (*Mādhā ʿan al-sayyida*, 330), a Canadian woman who was influential in smuggling thousands of Jews out of Syria as part of a secret operation in the late twentieth century.

84. Barakāt, *Mādhā ʿan al-sayyida*, 561.

85. Barakāt, *Mādhā ʿan al-sayyida*, 562.

Bibliography

Adami, Valentina. *Trauma Studies and Literature: Martin Amis's "Time's Arrow" as Trauma Fiction*. Frankfurt: Peter Lang, 2008.

Bakhtin, Mikhail. *Problems of Dostoevsky's Poetics*. Translated by R. W. Rotsel. Ann Arbor: Ardis, 1973.

Barakāt, Salīm. *Mādhā ʿan al-sayyida al-yahūdiyya rāḥīl?* Beirut: Arabic Institute for Research and Publishing, 2019.

Bunton, Martin, and William Cleveland. *A History of the Modern Middle East*. 6th ed. New York: Westview Press, 2016.

Carr, Judy, and Moshe Ma'oz. "Syria." In *Encyclopedia Judaica*, edited by Fred Skolnik and Michael Berenbaum, 2nd ed., 19:388–97. Detroit: Macmillan Reference USA, 2007.

Caruth, Cathy. *Trauma: Explorations in Memory*. Baltimore: Johns Hopkins University Press, 1995.

———. *Unclaimed Experience: Trauma Narrative, and History*. Baltimore: Johns Hopkins University Press, 1996.

Craps, Stef. *Postcolonial Witnessing: Trauma out of Bounds*. New York: Palgrave Macmillan, 2015.

Cvetkovich, Ann. *An Archive of Feeling: Trauma, Sexuality, and Lesbian Public Cultures*. Durham: Duke University Press, 2003.

Deleuze, Gilles, and Félix Guattari. *Kafka: Toward a Minor Literature*. Minneapolis: University of Minnesota Press, 2008.

Erll, Astrid. *Memory in Culture*. Translated by Sara Young. Basingstoke: Palgrave Macmillan Memory Studies, 2011.

Fakhreddine, Huda. "Salīm Barakāt's Poetry as Linguistic Conquest: '. . . the Shot That Kills You, May You Recover.'" *Middle Eastern Literatures* 21, nos. 2–3 (2018): 134–53.

Felman, Shoshana. *Literature and Psychoanalysis: The Question of Reading; Otherwise*. Baltimore: Johns Hopkins University Press, 1982.

Florence, Ronald. *Blood Libel: The Damascus Affair of 1840*. New York: Other Press, 2006.

Gana, Nouri. *Signifying Loss: Toward a Poetics of Narrative Mourning*. Bucknell: Bucknell University Press, 2011.

Harel, Yaron. *Zionism in Damascus: Ideology and Activity in the Jewish Community at the Beginning of the Twentieth Century*. Translated by D. Gershon Lewental. London: I. B. Tauris, 2015.

Hermez, Sami. "'The War Is Going to Ignite': On the Anticipation of Violence in Lebanon." *PoLAR* 35, no. 2 (2012): 327–44.

Levy, Lital. *Poetic Trespass: Writing Between Hebrew and Arabic in Israel and Palestine*. Princeton: Princeton University Press, 2014.

McHugo, John. *Syria: A History of the Last Hundred Years*. New York: New Press, 2015.

Miller, N. A. *Narrative and Its Discontents: Problems of Closure in the Traditional Novel*. Princeton: Princeton University Press, 1981.

Pearlman, Wendy. *We Crossed a Bridge and It Trembled: Voices from Syria*. New York: Custom House, 2018.

Rothberg, Michael. *Multidirectional Memory: Remembering the Holocaust in the Age of Decolonization*. Stanford: Stanford University Press, 2009.

Schönfelder, Christa. *Wounds and Words: Childhood and Family Trauma in Romantic and Postmodern Fiction*. Bielefeld: Transcript Verlag, 2013.

Stillman, Norman. *The Jews of Arab Lands in Modern Times*. Philadelphia: Jewish Publication Society, 1991.

Wedeen, Lisa. *Authoritarian Apprehensions: Ideology, Judgement, and Mourning in Syria*. Chicago: University of Chicago Press, 2019.

Zenner, Walter P. *A Global Community: The Jews from Aleppo, Syria*. Detroit: Wayne State University Press, 2000.

CHAPTER 7

Documenting and Debating Turkey's Loss

İLKER HEPKANER

Two documentary features in the mid-2010s broke new ground in representations of the history, memory, and contemporary lives of Jews in Turkey. Rita Ender's *Las Ultimas Palavras* (The last words; 2015) and Enver Arcak's *Hermana* (2016) departed from previous examples of documentary features, such as *Trees Cry for Rain: A Sephardic Journey* (1989) and *Si Je t'oublie Istanbul* (If I forget thee Istanbul; 1990), which showcased Turkey's Jewish heritage and community to foreign audiences while relegating the historical and political processes that shaped the life trajectories of the films' subjects to the margins of their visual narratives. In contrast, both recent documentaries center communal and public debates on the diverse losses Turkey's Jewish community has endured in the twentieth century. A close reading of these documentaries, contextualized by interviews with the filmmakers, readings of their other work, and an analysis of the films' circulation in Turkey and abroad, reveals a new chapter in the debates about the Jewish community's past, present, and future in Turkey.

THE LONG TWENTIETH CENTURY OF THE JEWISH COMMUNITY IN TURKEY AND THE AMBIGUOUS PRESENT

Turkey's Jewish community has witnessed multiple losses throughout the twentieth century. Following the collapse of the multiethnic, multilingual, and multireligious Ottoman Empire, the newly founded Turkish state implemented a number of Turkification policies in order to create a Sunni-Turkish majority. Geared toward the non-Muslim minorities, these policies aimed to render the Sunni-Turks not only the majority of the population but also, and more importantly, the most dominant group in the economic, political, and cultural realms. As a result, the Jewish community experienced a number of changes in their legal rights, communal organization, and linguistic makeup. In 1926, the Chief Rabbinate of Turkey renounced most of the legal and cultural rights granted to Jews by the 1923 Treaty of Lausanne.[1] Anti-Jewish attacks across the country (most notably the Thrace events in 1934 and the September 6–7, 1955, attacks on non-Muslim businesses in Istanbul)[2] as well as the Wealth Tax in 1942, which taxed non-Muslims disproportionately vis-à-vis Muslims, further crippled the non-Muslim tradespeople's role in the economy, and accelerated the emigration from smaller cities to Istanbul and Izmir, or to Europe, North America, and Israel.[3] Government-supported campaigns encouraged, if not forced, Jews who spoke Judeo-Spanish, French (an impact of Alliance schools across the Ottoman Empire), Greek, Kurdish, and Arabic in their daily lives to adopt Turkish as their primary language in public.[4] In the 1970s, Jews continued emigrating out of Turkey, this time mostly to Israel, sometimes due to political turmoil in Turkey and sometimes following a global migration pattern that followed Israel's victory in the 1967 Arab-Israeli War.[5] The twentieth-century Jewish migration to Israel from Turkey and Arab countries had some commonalities, especially in reasons, but their timetable and impact on the remaining community differed. By the time the 1992 Quincentennial Celebrations of the Ottoman Welcome, one of the biggest cultural outputs of the Jewish community of Turkey, were being planned at the end of the 1980s, the community had already lost a majority of its members, along with their multilingual makeup and their important role in the country's economy and innovation over the first seventy years of the republic. This is why the 1992 Quincentennial Celebrations have been incessantly criticized for their cultural content, political goals, and impact on the Jewish memory.[6] Currently, most of Turkey's Jews live in Istanbul, with a sizable community of more than one thousand in Izmir and smaller ones (in the double digits) in Bursa, Ankara, Adana, and Antakya. The total number of Jews is sixteen thousand, although the numbers are always debated. These numbers point to an ever-shrinking community, and the loss is twofold: while the Jewish community is losing its members to emigration, Turkish society is losing one of its foundational communities because the Turkish state has never treated them as equals to Sunni Turks, the primary population group designated by the republican elite as the model citizens of the new republic after the fall of the multiethnic and multireligious Ottoman Empire.

The politics and practices of memory have witnessed a change in the last twenty years across the nation in Turkey. The end of the 1990s saw a memory boom focused on questioning the legacy of the republican era. After coming to power in 2002, the Political Islamist Adalet ve Kalkınma Partisi (Justice and Development Party) has also rewritten the cultural codes in the country, bringing a considerable change to how republican history is discussed in the public domain. After the Gezi Park resistance in 2013, the urban educated class has also been confronting its own lack of critical engagement with the country's history, especially the history of the twentieth century. A critical approach to modern history has been adopted in various pockets of Turkish society, and the Jewish community is no stranger to this shift. With the support of civil society foundations, funded by international and domestic donors, various retellings of the twentieth-century history of Turkey's minority communities have found opportunities to circulate in the cultural sphere of the country. This is where Rita Ender's *Las Ultimas Palavras* and Enver Arcak's *Hermana* enter the scene, showing audiences how the Jewish community and Muslim majority are now publicly debating history and the loss of Jewish life in Turkey.

Two Filmmakers and Their Supporters

A human rights lawyer, journalist, and documentary filmmaker, Rita Ender is probably one of the best equipped among the young people in the Jewish community to undertake the task of bringing the broader debates into a documentary with utmost care, and this is exactly what she does in *Las Ultimas Palavras*. Ender's previous documentary asked crucial questions about the issue of representation among religious minorities in Turkey. With her sister Karin, Ender collected answers from Armenian, Greek Orthodox, Jewish, and Assyrian citizens of Turkey to the following questions: "How are you represented? Do you think the [religious] community you belong to represents you? How well does the Armenian / Greek Orthodox / Jewish / Assyrian community represent an Armenian / Greek

Orthodox / Jewish / Assyrian individual? Are you happy with the system, or would you rather have a different one?"

Rita Ender's engagement with memory and minority communities' issues is not limited to her documentaries. Between 2012 and 2014, Ender interviewed multiple professionals and artisans who still practice professions that are on the verge of extinction. She published the interviews first in *Agos*, an Armenian newspaper based in Istanbul, and later as a volume entitled *Kolay Gelsin* from İletişim, one of the most prestigious publishing houses in Turkey. In this series of interviews, Ender asked intriguing questions to a corsetier, a hatmaker, a clock repairman, a blacksmith, a typewriter repairman, and so on. In addition, she also interviewed those who, even if given the chance, would never give up their profession of doctor, teacher, and architect. "Kolay Gelsin is a phrase one says to anyone at work in Turkey, and it literally means "Let [your work] come easy [to you]." By saying the phrase, the person who witnesses the labor acknowledges and almost sanctifies it. "Kolay Gelsin" is also a wish for the continuation of labor. The interviews and the book collectively record these professions on the verge of extinction, but in a way they also wish for their continuation. Ender penned two more books of interviews. *İsmiyle Yaşamak* (To live with one's name) is about the religious minorities' challenges of living with a non-Muslim/Turkish name in Turkish society, and *Aile Yadigarları* (Family heirlooms) is about how Jewish families pass on family history via objects inherited across generations.

Ender's second documentary about the condition of Judeo-Spanish in Turkey, *Las Ultimas Palavras* was supported by Sivil Düşün, an EU program, as it was to be the latest addition to Ender's work that draws on ordinary people's real lives. According to Richard Youngs and Müjge Küçükkeleş, Sivil Düşün (Think civil) is a program specifically designed for supporting individuals and platforms that are not institutionalized like civil society organizations or their networks: "Sivil Düşün funds individual activists, associations, foundations, networks, loosely organized platforms, unions, and city councils. The European Union has expressly oriented the initiative toward small, quick, and short-term grants because the unpredictable and fraught political situation increasingly militates against large, high profile, and multi-annual grants."[7] The European Union's support for *Las Ultimas Palavras* given to Rita Ender, an individual, is important in deciphering the tone of the documentary. The fact that Ender did not produce the documentary as part of a civil rights organization or a state institution probably provided her the artistic and creative autonomy necessary to discuss an often politicized topic like Jewish memory in Turkey. As is the case with the Quincentennial Celebrations in the late 1980s and early 1990s, the state funds Jews' memory practices only when they serve its foreign policy goals.[8] One of the important aspects of the documentary is its inclusion of many debating voices, which also sets *Las Ultimas Palavras* apart from previous documentaries or other cultural products that deal with Jewish memory in Turkey. While *Las Ultimas Palavras* focused more on the communal debates, another documentary a year later followed in its footsteps but took the Jewish memory debate to the "wider public."

When Ender made *Las Ultimas Palavras*, she was already an established, popular figure in the Jewish and other religious minority communities as a lawyer, journalist, and filmmaker. The director of *Hermana*, Enver Arcak, on the other hand, was an art history and archeology graduate embarking on his first documentary project. Arcak is a member of the "wider public"—meaning he is not Jewish—and his interest in the Jewish memory of Ankara, the city he was born in, derived first and foremost from his efforts to understand his native city's untold histories.[9] In this sense, Ender's film is a communal affair, with messages geared to both the Jewish community and wider society, but Arcak's film is an act of recording Ankara's Jewish memory, and an invitation to the wider public to confront the republican history. In addition to this invitation, Arcak's film also produced an archive on the subject matter.[10]

Arcak's efforts in narrating Jewish memory were supported by multiple civic and academic institutions. As he was visually constructing his narrative, he used the archives of the History Foundation of Turkey, Koç University's Ankara Studies Research Center, Salt Research Center, and the Quincentennial Foundation Museum of Turkish Jews archives. The project was supported by the Dr. Mehmet Bozdoğan Fund of Salt Research Center, a prestigious academic research center that supports projects on architecture, social and economic history, and contemporary memory. It is understandable that Ender, as an established storyteller of the Jewish community, relied on her own network within the community and needed only funding for a memory retelling project, while Arcak, a budding documentary director outside the Jewish community, had to rely on the support of multiple foundations in realizing his narrative and proving it was academically sound. Despite drawing on similar issues of loss, their directors' different backgrounds and support systems are not the only ways the two documentaries differ.

Recounting the Loss

Both documentaries have interlacing topics, use similar narrative devices, and focus on the loss suffered by both the Jewish community and Turkish society, although their approaches and foci differ somewhat. *Las Ultimas Palavras* is about Jews across the country who are either losing or revitalizing Judeo-Spanish. Its geographical focus is wide—the whole country. *Hermana*'s geographical focus is narrower: it narrates the history of Ankara's Jews by incorporating interviews of Jewish people who lived there. The documentary blends memory narratives with academic expertise provided by an Ottoman historian and an archeologist, and enriches the narrative with shots of historical documents and old pictures. While *Las Ultimas Palavras* is structured around testimonies of Jewish youths and commentary by the filmmaker, *Hermana* takes a more academic route by blending academic opinions with interviewee testimonies.

Both documentaries center loss in their narratives, and in each case it is a loss that both the Jewish community and Turkish society as a whole suffer. However, which loss they prioritize differs. *Las Ultimas Palavras* centers the Jewish community's loss of language as it starts with a declaration of death for the language of Judeo-Spanish. "Dear island habitants, the Judeo-Spanish who lived on the island passed away. The funeral will be held at Büyükada Synagogue tomorrow at 12pm. Our sympathy to Sephardic families and relatives." A holiday spot for Istanbul's elite, Büyükada is where most of the Jewish community of the city comes together in summer. In a way, for two and a half months Büyükada becomes the center of Jewish life in Istanbul. Therefore, it is very fitting that Ender starts her documentary about the death of Judeo-Spanish in this place of continuing communal importance.

Hermana centers Turkish society's loss in its visual narrative. For example, right at the start, multiple interviewees who used to live in Ankara describe the Jewish neighborhood from memory. Their descriptions of a lively community are juxtaposed with shots of the neighborhood's current dilapidated state, which show rundown houses and common spaces such as the fountain. The dilapidation of the space evoked by memory is a confrontational moment, inviting an audience from the "wider public" to interrogate the reasons behind the situation depicted on screen.

Despite the difference in priority of the loss, both documentaries build on oral accounts of Jewish community members. *Las Ultimas Palavras* consists of interviews with young Jewish people in Turkey who express their opinions and feelings about the loss of Judeo-Spanish, a language they did not learn from their parents but had heard here and there within the family and the community. Ender's commentary, inserted between clusters of interviews, contextualizes the documentary's narrative. The loss described in the film is not an absolute or finished affair. In fact, the interviewees first mention the Judeo-Spanish words and idioms they know despite being unable to understand full conversations or construct complete sentences orally or in writing in this supposedly dying language. Ender's commentary rightfully states that these unforgotten words and idioms are not random. As the list of the unforgotten words and idioms goes on, the interviewees also explain *why* they know (or remember) them: the last remaining words are about emotions, such as curses or warning exclamations; they are about community, since most of them are adjectives for human characteristics; and they pertain to culinary traditions, because food is shared across generations, and Judeo-Spanish is primarily the language of their parents and grandparents.

Ender's commentary lays out the circumstances of the loss very clearly. The "Citizen, Speak Turkish!" campaign of 1928, the subsequent Turkification policies, and anti-Jewish and anti-non-Muslim attacks in urban centers all contributed to the abandonment of Judeo-Spanish in favor of Turkish. The new Republic wanted to coin new citizens based on the Sunni Turks and anyone outside this identification were either killed by genocide, as was the case for Armenians; exchanged, as was the case for most of the Greek Orthodox; or forced to leave or to adapt to the new Turkish identification, as was the case for remaining Armenians, Greek Orthodox, Alawis, and, of course, Jews. One of the ways to force Jews to be "like" Sunni Turks was to force them to speak Turkish, and as a language already in decline due to the influence of the Alliance schools, Judeo-Spanish was hit the hardest since Jews were no longer allowed to speak their language freely in the street. While *Las Ultimas Palavras* focuses on the erosion of Judeo-Spanish usage, the loss of the language is not lamented at the same rate and intensity by everyone in the community. The language may be dying for some, but the others are fighting to keep it alive. Some community members consider the death of the language a natural process. "Just like we learned Spanish, a language that was not what our ancestors were speaking when they moved to Spain, we also forget it when we come here [the Ottoman Empire]," says one of the interviewees. Another interviewee pushes back on the idea that Judeo-Spanish is dead, and states that "calling it dead is burying it alive." She gives an example from her own experience, and proves that at least on an individual level, the language is alive.

At the New York premiere of the documentary, literary scholar Dalia Kandiyoti said that despite declaring the death of the Judeo-Spanish, in a paradoxical way the film also contributed to the revitalization of the language. In fact, despite the pessimistic tone in the film, the documentary is not oblivious to the efforts to preserve the language. One of the snippets included in the film is in fact from a cooking workshop held in Judeo-Spanish at the Dia Internasyonal del Ladino / Judeo-Espanyol, the International Ladino / Judeo-Spanish Day celebrations in Turkey, which has been celebrated—including by Turkey's younger generations—for the last few years.

The conservation of Judeo-Spanish has been an important topic since the 1970s, when a vast number of Judeo-Spanish speakers emigrated out of Turkey. This is why, according to İzzet Bana, a household name in the cultural life of the Jewish community in Turkey, it is no coincidence that when amateur Jewish theater-makers first staged *Kula 930*, a musical with numerous Judeo-Spanish songs, in 1978 for the first time, it kick-started the conservation efforts of Judeo-Spanish in the country. The play also facilitated the foundation of Los Paşaros Sefaradis, a band that would gain fame performing Judeo-Spanish songs internationally.[11] Los Paşaros Sefaradis has played concerts in North America, Europe, and Israel, either on their own, as part of the Jewish heritage practices of Turkey, or in the company of others. For example, they sang with the Turkish pop music diva Sezen Aksu in the Türkiye Şarkıları (Songs of Turkey) concert series, which brought musicians of religious and ethnic minorities together on the stage in Turkey in 2002, despite much protest in the mainstream political and cultural realms.[12] The concert series also went on a European tour in support of Turkey's then-budding EU membership bid.[13] In addition to Los Paşaros Sefaradis, Esteryakas d'Estambol (Stars of Istanbul), a choir that İzzet Bana founded in 2004 to teach Judeo-Spanish to the younger generations, with the support of Jewish community leaders, keeps Judeo-Spanish alive.[14]

The interviewees in *Las Ultimas Palavras* confirm the effectiveness of music in preserving the language, too. Some interviewees explain how they remember some words from Judeo-Spanish songs. For example, one of the interviewees says he connected with Judeo-Spanish through his father's singing with friends. Apparently he memorized the lyrics to the songs without understanding their meaning at first. However, the moment he methodically learnt the meanings of the lyrics, he says, "the meaning slipped from [his] hands." He became unable to sing the songs "correctly." Despite this setback, he plays the guitar in the documentary and sings "Avraham Avinu" in Judeo-Spanish. Jewish amateur theater is also instrumental in keeping the language alive.[15] Hence, although Judeo-Spanish may have been pushed out of the public sphere by the state's monolingual policies and emigration, the language made its way back to the community via culture, music, and theater. *Las Ultimas Palavras* is another iteration of this cyclical feed, adding a documentary to the cultural products that increase the visibility of the language.

Very few of *Hermana*'s interviewees who narrate the Jewish memory of Ankara were based in the Turkish capital at the time of the film's production, pointing to a more permanent, absolute loss. Most of them are based in Israeli cities, where Jews from Turkey prefer to live the most, such as Ramat Gan, Rishon LeZion, and Tel Aviv. The reason behind this dispersion is explained in the documentary by the interviewees. When Istanbul's importance in trade increased, a lot of Jews moved out of Ankara to join their trade partners in Istanbul. When the Turkification policies negatively impacted the Jewish community, some of them moved to Israel. Without articulating it in so many words, the testimony and the visuals come together and ask an important question to the wider audience: "What happened to the Jewish community in Ankara?"

The answer is emigration, sometimes to other cities in Turkey but mostly to Israel. Nonetheless, some interviewees want to assure the audience that they never considered their lives in Ankara undesirable. One emphasizes that the Jewish neighborhood "was not a ghetto." He adds: "There were no walls like this, but we lived marvelously with our very specific Muslim brothers. But there were mostly Hebrews, there were Jews." The target audience for this comment is larger than the wider public, since their knowledge of ghettos is limited to cultural representations of European history, not historical facts. In the Ottoman Empire, and then modern Turkey, Jews did live in their own neighborhoods, and they did experience some problems with their Muslim and Christian neighbors. But their neighborhoods never went through the ghettoization seen in Europe. Among the interviewees, there is a resistance to seeing (and narrating) the Jewish life in Turkey from a Eurocentric point of view. By repeating that their neighborhood was not a ghetto, they make sure that their history is not seen as European history. It was nevertheless a modern one, with devastating attacks, sometimes organized or protected by the state, on Jewish communities across the country.

It is important to analyze the methods employed by directors as well. While *Las Ultimas Palavras* relies on its director for the historical commentary, *Hermana* uses a number of methods in order to provide a historically complex and compelling narrative about the loss of Ankara's Jewish community. In addition to historical documents, newspaper clips, and pictures shown in the documentary, the audience listens to the recording of the testimony of Ilya Araf, recorded for the 1000 Witnesses to History Project, completed in 2004. Although Mr. Araf died in 2007, thanks to this recording he becomes a part of a documentary made in 2016. In this way, *Hermana* recycles previously recorded material, an effective technique of narrative-making on a subject like *loss*, which is often exacerbated by the lack of systematic recording of witness testimonies or archiving.

Arcak's documentary reflects an anxiety around historical accuracy, maybe because of his own training at college or the larger aspects of the project, which aims to establish an archive for Jews of Ankara. Although the documentary is about loss and memory, Arcak twice uses academic expertise as a confirmation of facts told in oral history form. Archeologist Julian Bennett's testimony confirms the existence of Jews in Anatolia long before their migration out of the Iberian Peninsula and into the Ottoman Empire in the sixteenth century. Bennett dates Babylonian Jews' resettlement in Anatolia back to the fourth to second century BCE and deduces that Jews have lived in Ankara at least since the second century BCE. Although no one in the documentary makes this explicitly clear, this historical narrative places Jewish habitants in Anatolia long before the Muslim Turkish tribes, who arrived after the eleventh century CE.

The second academic confirmation comes from Ottoman historian Professor Özer Ergenç. Although Ergenç's testimony is included in the film to bring scholarly depth to the oral history snippets, when Ergenç reproduces the Ottoman rescue narratives, which have been much criticized and often debunked, his testimony in fact hurts the validity of the documentary's quest for academic authority. However, the filmmaker did not rely only on academics for accuracy. As mentioned above, he also used extensive archives in constructing his narrative, such as the History Foundation of Turkey, Koc University's Ankara Studies Research Center, Salt Research Center, and the Quincentennial Foundation Museum of Jews in Turkey archives, and the project was supported by Dr. Mehmet Bozdoğan Fund of Salt Research Center. Arcak's film therefore collects multiple stamps of approval from academic authorities and makes an almost historically sound argument about the memory of Ankara Jews. The documentary's close relationship with historiography is not limited to its narrative. Arcak stated that the collection of documents for the visual archive he is creating around the project is ongoing. How well the project will eventually function as an archive for further research will only be revealed when new projects utilize what Arcak has created through *Hermana* and make additional or new arguments about the Jews of Ankara and elsewhere.

The accuracy or politicization of academic knowledge aside, this historical narrative, supported by an archaeologist, should serve as a reflective moment for the wider public, reminding them that Jews lived in Anatolia long before the Muslim Turks who form the majority of the country today. This reflective moment becomes more poignant with the interviewees narrating how Ankara's Jewish community became smaller and smaller throughout the twentieth century. The touching story of the community's erosion, from approximately six hundred members in 1965 to approximately fifty in the late 2010s, is juxtaposed with stories that remind the audience of the richness that Jews contributed to the social and economic life of Ankara. As former Ankara inhabitants tell their family histories regarding the jobs that their fathers or relatives did and give examples of innovation and technology brought to Ankara by Jewish tradesmen, they prove two arguments to the audience: Jews in Ankara were not foreigners or colorful aspects of life in the city, rather they were a fundamental element of society, as well as the standard bearers of innovation and technological development.

DEBATING CONTEMPORARY MEANINGS OF HISTORY

Both documentaries also foreground other issues connected to the history of loss. Their contribution to contemporary debates among members of the Jewish community and the wider public casts both films as venues for a lively debate about contemporary life in Turkey. For example, *Las Ultimas Palavras* speaks to more than just language preservation within the Jewish community in Turkey. In fact, it is possible to read the documentary as representing the shifting debate about Jewish memory and loss on a wide range of topics. For instance, the declaration of the death of Judeo-Spanish is proclaimed in Büyükada, but the documentation of the loss is not limited to Istanbul. In fact, the documentary incorporates opinions of Jewish youths in Izmir and Bursa, respectively the third- and fourth-largest cities of Turkey, reminding the audience that there are still Jews living outside Istanbul. This reflects a shift in the heritage practices of the Jewish community's other cultural actors and institutions as well. The 1992 Quincentennial Celebrations focused on Jews in Istanbul: its events were mostly held in Istanbul, the Jewish Museum, which was to cement the efforts of the celebrations, was designated to be in Istanbul, and the bulk of the funds to restore Jewish heritage sites were allocated for those in Istanbul.[16] However, in the last ten years the Jewish histories of places other than Istanbul are also surfacing, shattering what I call the "Istanbul-centric" understanding of the Jewish twentieth-century history of Turkey.[17] For example, the updated content of the Quincentennial Foundation Museum of Jews in Turkey details where else Jews lived across the country through an interactive map. In Izmir, seven synagogues are now being restored thanks to an international initiative led by the Mordechai Kriaty Foundation.[18] This bottom-up documentary, realized thanks to the efforts of an activist and filmmaker from the Jewish community, contributes to the diversification of debates and geographies of Turkey's Jewish life's losses, past and present.

Las Ultimas Palavras is about words, forgotten or kept, and is based on interviews. However, physical space still plays an important role in the film in bringing out contemporary debates. Each interview takes place in a different space, and their backdrops diversify the documentary's narrative about the contemporary lives of Jews in Turkey. Some of the interviewees talk in their homes and offices, while others are in recognizable institutions, such as the Quincentennial Foundation Museum of Jews of Turkey or the Ulus Private Jewish School. The representation of space is especially important for the film's audience of the "wider public," which is what the Jewish community calls the Muslim majority in Turkey. Interiors of the homes and offices, presenting almost no difference from a Muslim person's home or office, contradict the anti-Semitic imagery circulating in the Turkish mainstream media, which fictionalizes evil Jewish people plotting against Turkish society and the state.[19] The normalcy of these spaces shows Muslims who have no Jewish friends or colleagues that the popular representation of Jewish people's houses and offices is absolutely false.

Some backdrops are not neutral, as they bring additional meaning to the words of the interviewees. For example, one of the interviewees speaks from the hall of the Ulus Private Jewish School, a space dominated by a larger-than-life portrait of Mustafa Kemal Atatürk, the first president of the Turkish Republic. Atatürk imagery in Turkey is omnipresent and takes up different meanings according to the political context. In this instance, the portrait's dominance can be read in two ways: as a sign that the Ulus Private Jewish School is no different from any other public or private school in the country, a necessary point against the aforementioned mainstream anti-Semitic depictions of interiors; or as the continued allegiance of the Jewish community to Atatürk and the republic he often embodies in the visual political language of the country.

On the other hand, one interviewee's backdrop reflects the varying attitudes toward the political debates regarding the minorities' lives in Turkey. This interview is conducted in front of a whiteboard bearing a detailed drawing of Hrant Dink, the Armenian journalist who was killed by ultranationalists protected by the state. His assassination, despite his plea to the police for protection, the good treatment of his assassin by the state officials, and the injustices Dink's family has faced in the justice system have unfortunately turned Dink's imagery into a symbol of the state's crushing power over the oppressed, and especially over minorities. Dink's image reminds the audience of the Ottoman and Turkish governments' violence-ridden scorecard regarding minorities, which has the Armenian Genocide, the 1923 Greek-Turkish population exchange, massacres of Alawites, the September 6–7 events, repression of Kurds, and so on. In a documentary about a minority community's dying language, Dink's portrait is more than a sketch on the wall, it is an act of remembrance, a symbol of a cautionary tale, and a face of resistance. The backdrops used in the documentary reflect various aspects of the community's relationship with the symbols of state repression, resistance, and assimilation.

In *Hermana*'s visual narrative, the confrontation with republican history with political repercussions is very strong, especially in the beginning. The geographical dispersion of the interviewees and the subject matter of the documentary reproduce the shift discussed above for *Las Ultimas Palavras* in dealing with the Jewish memory of Turkey. *Hermana,* just like *Las Ultimas Palavras,* rejects an Istanbul-centric remembrance of Jewish memory in Turkey. The importance of the rejection of Istanbul-centrism is especially important for the "wider public," which needs to relearn republican history and abandon the narrative of Istanbul losing its cosmopolitan, imperial diversity due to Turkification policies. In fact, the entire country was affected by these policies, resulting in the current Muslim majority. Arcak mentioned in an interview that a lot of people who watched the film were "shocked" to hear about Ankara's Jewish past, and sometimes they expressed their nostalgic take on the days told through the documentary's narrative.[20]

Although *Las Ultimas Palavras* brings more contemporary debates to the silver screen than *Hermana,* the second documentary has an advantage in terms of its reach to wider audiences. Following their release in Turkey, both documentaries have been shown in Europe and North America, along with their filmmakers' attendance to postscreening discussions. I have had the chance to watch two screenings of *Las Ultimas Palavras,* both in New York, and one of Arcak's postscreening discussions is on YouTube. In the discussions after *Las Ultimas Palavras,* I realized that a lot of members who wanted to ask a question or make a comment started talking about their own connection to Judeo-Spanish. Ender's film invoked an urge to tell one's own story, which was always very similar to the interviewee's testimonies in the film. By sharing their own stories, audience members were enriching the film's message to the audiences. However, their current availability is not equal. *Hermana,* along with the documentaries Arcak produced after it, is available on BluTV, a streaming platform based in Turkey. *Hermana* is within the reach of a click to its main target audience—the urban educated who have been questioning the history taught at schools in the last twenty years, while *Las Ultimas Palavras* does not have the same online presence, even behind a paywall. Thanks to *Hermana*'s availability on BluTV, and the visual archive project that was created, *Hermana*'s mission may have a longer shelf life than *Las Ultimas Palavras*.

The two documentaries I analyze in this essay heralded a new moment in communal and public discussions regarding Jewish memory in Turkey. However, sometimes the narrativization of memory tells more about the present than the past, more about society as a whole than a single community. These two documentaries narrate stories of loss, either about a language or an entire community, but they may also function as vessels to discuss contemporary problems.

Las Ultimas Palavras is about the possibility of being multilingual individuals and communities and the political implications of such existence, which goes against the mainstream nationalist outlook. It asks the Jewish community whether it is only the language that must be saved from the nationalist demands of the Turkish state, or can it do something more? In the last decade, Turkey has become a country that hosts more than three million Syrian refugees as well as more than one million Iraqi, Afghani, and Iranian refugees. Can the painful memories of Jews about their loss of Judeo-Spanish encourage the wider public to reconsider their—mostly negative—attitude toward their Arabic-, Farsi-, and Pashtoo-speaking new neighbors? What if the monolingual wider public in fact advocated for their multilingual neighbors to learn, live, and create in their own languages?

In the case of *Hermana,* can the project's research and archiving structure be a model for other cities and communities? Or, with *Hermana*'s reach increased via streaming platforms, can documentaries with political and social messages contribute to the changing attitudes of Turkish audiences toward matters of history and memory? With the decline of mainstream media under the heavy censorship of the government, and the tightening grip of the government over freedom of expression in social media, could documentaries be the next stop for resilient and resisting voices to express themselves?

These two documentaries do more than inform their audiences about loss. They reconfigure it, and for attentive audiences they may offer solutions for not repeating the mistakes of history. These documentaries were produced meticulously, hence they have great potential as starting points for more debates than those already underway in Turkey.

Notes

1. Bali, *Cumhuriyet Yıllarında Türkiye Yahudileri Bir Türkleştirme Serüveni*, 34–102.

2. Bali, *1934 Trakya Olayları*; Bali, *Devlet'in Örnek Yurttaşları*, 56–73.

3. I abstain from calling these events "pogroms" following Ella Shohat's criticism of Eurocentric takes on Jewish histories in the Muslim-majority countries. Calling anti-Jewish attacks "pogroms" flattens the complex history of Jewish-Muslim relations in the region and categorizes them as an addition to the European history of anti-Semitism. Shohat, *On the Arab-Jew*.

4. Bali, *Cumhuriyet Yıllarında Türkiye Yahudileri Bir Türkleştirme Serüveni*, 102–96.

5. Toktaş, "Turkey's Jews," 505–19.

6. Baer, *Sultanic Saviors*; Brink-Danan, *Jewish Life*.

7. Youngs and Küçükkeleş, "New Directions."

8. Bali, *Devlet'in Örnek Yurttaşları*.

9. Hermana film Q&A with director Enver Arcak.

10. "Hermana—'Jews of Ankara'—Sephardic Heritage International (SHIN) DC," accessed January 4, 2021, https://shindc.org/exhibitions/hermana/.

11. Güllü and Esen, "Ulus Özel."

12. Eyüboğlu, "Niye Gülüyorsun?"

13. Çolak, "Sezen Aksu'dan AB'ye Konser."

14. Güllü and Esen, "Ulus Özel"; "Estreyikas d'Estanbol." I explore the role of Jewish theater in Judeo-Spanish preservation in my article "Rosy, White, and Clean."

15. Hepkaner, "Rosy, White, and Clean."

16. Mallet, *La Turquie*.

17. In Turkish Naim Güleryüz published books on Jews of Edirne and Gaziantep, and Sara Pardo on Jews of Izmir. Even American university presses are taking note of this geographical diversification of Jewish history in Turkey, as Stanford University Press recently published Dana Danon's *The Jews of Ottoman Izmir*, which covers Jewish history in Izmir from the end of nineteenth century to the foundation of the republic in 1923.

18. "The Izmir Project, the Hidden Secrets of the Ancient Synagogues of Izmir," ESefarad, accessed January 3, 2021, https://esefarad.com/?p=33291; "The Izmir Project," AEJM, accessed January 3, 2021, https://www.aejm.org/members/the-izmir-project/.

19. Korucu, "Bir Propaganda."

20. "Hermana film Q&A with director Enver Arcak."

Bibliography

Aktar, Ayhan. *Varlık Vergisi ve "Türkleştirme" Politikaları*. Istanbul: İletişim, 2002.

Baer, Marc David. *Sultanic Saviors and Tolerant Turks: Writing Ottoman Jewish History, Denying the Armenian Genocide*. Bloomington: Indiana University Press, 2020.

Bali, Rıfat N. *1934 Trakya Olayları*. Istanbul: Kitabevi, 2012.

———. *Cumhuriyet Yıllarında Türkiye Yahudileri: Aliya; Bir Toplu Göçün Öyküsü, 1946–1949*. Istanbul: İletişim, 2003.

———. *Cumhuriyet Yıllarında Türkiye Yahudileri: Devlet'in Örnek Yurttaşları, 1950–2003*. 1. baskı. Istanbul: Kitabevi, 2009.

———. "Los Pasharos Sefaradis." In *Encyclopedia of Jews in the Islamic World*. Leiden: Brill, 2010. https://referenceworks.brillonline.com/entries/encyclopedia-of-jews-in-the-islamic-world/los-pasharos-sefaradis-SIM_0014020.

———. "Toplumsal Bellek ve Varlık Vergisi." In *Türkiye'nin toplumsal hafızası: Hatırladıklarıyla ve unuttuklarıyla*, edited by Esra Özyürek. Istanbul: İletişim, 2006.

Bali, Rıfat N., and Laurent-Olivier Mallet, eds. *Turkish Jews in Contemporary Turkey*. Istanbul: Libra Kitap, 2015.

Brink-Danan, Marcy. *Jewish Life in Twenty-First-Century Turkey: The Other Side of Tolerance*. Bloomington: Indiana University Press, 2011.

Çolak, Saliha. "Sezen Aksu'dan AB'ye Konser." *Milliyet*, September 10, 2002.

Danon, Dana. *The Jews of Ottoman Izmir: A Modern History*. Stanford: Stanford University Press, 2020.

"Estreyikas d'Estanbol | Judart Görsel Sanatlar Topluluğu." Accessed January 4, 2021. https://www.judart.com/estanbol.html.

Eyüboğlu, Ali. "Niye Gülüyorsun? Bölücü Müsün?" *Milliyet*, September 22, 2002.

Güllü, Fırat, and Uluç Esen. "Ulus Özel Musevi İlk. Okulu Tiyatro Çalıştırıcısı İzzet Bana ile Söyleşi." Mimesis Sahne Sanatları Portali, March 18, 2010. Accessed January 23, 2022. http://www.mimesis-dergi.org/2010/03/ulus-ozel-musevi-ilkogretim-okulu-tiyatro-calistiricisi-izzet-bana-ile-soylesi/.

Hepkaner, İlker. "'Rosy, White, and Clean Pages of History': Jojo Eskenazi's 'Moiz Plays' and the Politics of Contemporary Jewish Theatre in Turkey." *Comparative Drama* 52, nos. 3–4 (2018): 323–47. https://doi.org/doi:10.1353/cdr.2018.0014.

———. "Where Is a Minority's Popular Culture Archived? An Answer from the Jewish Community of Turkey." *Journal of Popular Culture* 53, no. 6 (2020): 1358–72.

Hermana film Q&A with director Enver Arcak, moderated by Susan Barocas. YouTube, May 14, 2020. Accessed January 23, 2022. https://www.youtube.com/watch?v=8EgZLDQRzUk.

"Hermana—'Jews of Ankara'—Sephardic Heritage International (SHIN) DC." Accessed January 4, 2021. https://shindc.org/exhibitions/hermana/.

Korucu, Serdar. "Bir Propaganda Dizisi Olarak Payitaht Abdülhamid." -Avlaremoz, October 30, 2017. Accessed January 23, 2022. https://www.avlaremoz.com/2017/10/30/bir-propaganda-dizisi-olarak-payitaht-abdulhamid/.

Mallet, Laurent Olivier. *La Turquie, les turcs et les juifs: Histoire, représentations, discours et stratégies*. Istanbul: Isis, 2008.

Shohat, Ella. *On the Arab-Jew, Palestine, and Other Displacements: Selected Writings*. London: Pluto Press, 2017.

———. "Rupture and Return: Zionist Discourse and the Study of Arab-Jews." In *Taboo Memories, Diasporic Voices*, 330–58. Durham: Duke University Press, 2006.

Toktaş, Şule. "Turkey's Jews and Their Immigration to Israel." *Middle Eastern Studies* 42, no. 3 (May 1, 2006): 505–19. https://doi.org/10.1080/00263200500521479.

Youngs, Richard, and Müjge Küçükkeleş. "New Directions for European Assistance in Turkey." İstanbul Policy Center, March 2017. https://ipc.sabanciuniv.edu/Content/Images/Document/new-directions-d3a570/new-directions-d3a570.pdf.

CHAPTER 8

Exile in a Contemporary Artistic Project in Morocco

Jewish Memories in Form and Concrete Territories

NADIA SABRI

The urge to explore Casablanca's Museum of Moroccan Judaism (MMJ), its history, and the micro- and macro-histories in the objects that make up its collection served as the inspiration for the collaborative art exhibit *Exiles: A Dialogue with the Museum of Moroccan Judaism in Casablanca*.[1] The first time I visited the MMJ in the summer of 2015, I was immediately struck by the strange feeling that I was not in a museum in the traditional sense of the word. The way the building displayed its viewing and reading materials under aquarium glass, including its collection of ethnographic objects and their labels, evoked fragments of stories told together. The collection called to mind specific Moroccan dates and places, cultural narratives, and stories of everyday objects to emphasize, as Sophie Wagenhofer has indicated in her study on the MMJ, the sameness of Jews and Muslims instead of stressing the differences.[2] The building itself was rather subtle about its identity as a museum. In contrast to the usual cavalcade of signage, logos, banners, and other advertising artifacts that typically identify such spaces, the MMJ, tucked away from the Casablanca city center, was nearly anonymous. It could be reached only by a series of wrong turns and retraced steps in the Oasis residential neighborhood. A single sign labeled "Museum," which does not reveal its identity, serves to indicate the entrance.[3] The front door

FIG. 8.1 The main door of the Museum of Moroccan Judaism in Casablanca, located in the Oasis neighborhood. Photo © M'hamed Kilito.

was not marked in any way, and only the presence of a police officer and the Moroccan flag hinted at the institution within the villa (fig. 8.1). The museum acts as a mirror space, a heterotopia of my artistic quest. All manner of artists have filled this stencil space with absence-presence according to their own perspectives, bringing their own stories into dialogue with the physical and symbolic narratives of the MMJ.

Casablanca's MMJ is a private ethnographic museum established in 1997, set up in a building that once held an orphanage for Jewish children. The villa was built after World War II and was overhauled by the architect Aimé Kakon in 1995–96.[4] Though it took a collective effort, the MMJ is nevertheless unquestionably the work of Simon Lévy (1934–2011), an anthropologist and a founder of the foundation of Jewish-Moroccan cultural heritage, who led the MMJ until his death in 2011.

Both present and unpresent, visible and invisible, the MMJ lies in a halfway space. It is an unreadable space despite the didactic nature of the building and its collections. Since the beginning, my approach has been informed by the image of the building and my first impression of it. During my first scouting expedition to the MMJ in 2015 with the artist Mustapha Akrim, both of us expressed interest in this uncanny ambivalence between visibility and invisibility. We thought it would prove a fruitful point to highlight in our curatorial and artistic approaches.

THE ARTISTIC PROJECT

Ranging from "symbolic architecture" to the haphazard collections of objects assembled from what has survived in collective memory, artists Mustapha Akrim, Ulrike Weiss, Josep Ginestar, Myriam Tangi, and Zineb Andress Arraki have forged paths of inquiry into opening and closing, erasure and tracing, as well as fragmentation and dispersal (figs. 8.2 and 8.3). These mirror-artistic investigations (by which is meant the artistic procedure, a mirror of the reality of dispersion as manifested through the techniques used, such as collage and molding, and also by the meaning of the materials used in these works, like wax, concrete, and even soap) take place in a space long charged with history, particularly the collective departure of almost the entire Moroccan Jewish community in the last quarter of the twentieth century. This mirroring is also reflected in the display of the exhibition on the principle of presence-absence, dispersion of the showcases and the confines of the exhibition halls, creating a feeling of questing in the visitor. The mirror effect created by the works and the scenography is thus built around the experience of exile. The MMJ is laden not only with its own history but also with the visible/invisible history of a community

FIG. 8.2 Mustapha Akrim, *Now, in Exile*, 2016. On the walls and display windows of the permanent exhibition of the Museum of Moroccan Judaism. Photo © M'hamed Kilito.

FIG. 8.3 *Safarad IV*, exhibit of Josep Ginestar in display windows between two menorahs in the Museum of Moroccan Judaism. Photo © M'hamed Kilito.

subject to disappearance. The space is both open and closed off, and the museum becomes a nonplace, a heterotopia in the Foucauldian sense.[5] The artworks on display here were created out of a preparatory time of wandering, two years in which the inaugural exhibition of Rabat's Bab Rouah National Gallery went on tour in a variety of Moroccan art galleries. It was displayed in the Portuguese city of El Jadida, in Tétouan (at the Cervantès Gallery for the National Institute of Fine Arts' "Gallery Night"), and in Casablanca (at the Cervantès Cultural Center), before specific works were added to the collection for its arrival at the MMJ.

This artistic project, which centers on both lost and reignited memories, will be influential in how *Exiles* evolves and takes shape. The project will serve as an engaged, multidisciplinary platform that examines the various consequences of exile, carrying forward the momentum of the ideas and human action that began in 2015. This platform was created out of a variety of collaborations and meetings with artists, writers, researchers, and cultural agents from diverse backgrounds. The exhibition that happened in the MMJ in 2016–17 constituted an important way station in the development of the entire project, as my artistic approach has traversed several different methodologies of investigation and memory-jogging.

The memories involved are part of the contemporary history of Morocco, and they have complex ramifications for a larger, evolving history. In fact, the impact of Morocco's Jewish history is still deeply relevant to the social and political environment not only of Morocco, but also of the Middle East as a whole, since the majority of emigrations and exiles were made to Israel, imbricating this mass movement in the geopolitics of the Israel-Palestine conflict. However much my project may be anchored in historical context, it participates in an evolving introspection as much as it investigates discursive forms of loss. It also explores a more profound kind of tactile history, one in which reawakened memories are made manifest in handicrafts, the use of materials, and the outward appearance of the work. They can even emerge in the investigation of a spatial subconscious between the reference frame of wandering and the paradoxical one of anchoring, an investigation marked by a "convulsive semantics," which is reflected in the mirror effect I explained above.

BETWEEN VISIBILITY AND INVISIBILITY: AN EXAMINATION OF THE GAPS IN THE METAPHOR MUSEUM

In his portfolio, Aimé Kakon explains the role he played as architect in the remodeling of the MMJ, particularly concerning the choice to preserve the stone wall that traversed the villa, the original building, when it was an orphanage.[6] Kakon explains that the wall was maintained in memory of the orphaned children who had lived there. Further, the photographic archives that Kakon consulted prior to beginning the project influenced the role he played as architect, establishing within him a sort of "architectural bias."

The orphanage provides a second history that intersects physically and symbolically with the museum building. The stone wall takes on the significance of a caesura, or an anteroom, or even a tabula rasa upon which the delicate works of Ulrike Weiss (such as tracings and reproductions in gauze of the face of the famous Jewess of Debdou, known as the "Mona Lisa of Debdou") would later find resonance. As with any entry into a space dedicated to official memory (the history of Moroccan Judaism as told by the museum) and to other adjunct memories (the memory of place and of collected objects across Moroccan Jewish geography), adding a contemporary art exhibit to the MMJ was not a trivial matter.

Via sequential steps, this experience has shown how the museum can create its own stories (however limited), as well as how it can write its own narratives in juxtaposition to works of art and objects of diverse histories and uses. This exhibition in the MMJ has necessitated following several approaches: understanding and approaching a space that is the result of a history (that of an orphanage) and integrating an ethnographic collection that is full of microhistory. Therefore, for me, the choice was not to implant the artistic works in and with the collection in a logical relationship of causality or similarity, but to infiltrate the interstices of the plural narratives, both visible and invisible, that the museum offers its visitors. The visit of our temporary exhibition became, as a result, a tool that reveals, like a photographic process, writings of exile and loss that the collection of the museum was offering inadvertently. Globally, my approach to this project has effectively been to imbue the MMJ with a presence that highlights points of tension and underlines certain absences through form, the language of the tactile, and the significance of space.

The history of the building that houses the MMJ reinforces the metaphorical principle of "placehood." A project completed by Celia Bengio in 1948, the building was first an orphanage, dedicated to the memory of her late husband, Murdock Bengio. This same building was repurposed in the seventies as an orthodox Jewish school, or yeshiva. In 1995, it was remodeled to house the future MMJ, and Kakon was placed in charge.

On the subject of remodeling the orphanage into a museum, Kakon writes,

> When I visited the sites before demolition, I studied the photographic archives and felt a sense of overwhelming compassion. . . . I do not know what has become of them [the orphans] today. . . . I decided to preserve, restore, and elongate a long stone wall that bifurcated the building in two, and to install bay windows that would make this caesura noticeable from end to end and from side to side. I also chose to preserve four exterior walls, an enclosure forever enshrined, a slice of the life these children lived, a place from which emanated such hope and such nebulous expectation.[7]

A reference to Jerusalem's Wailing Wall is easily detected in Kakon's words. I, however, consider the wall a more global point of reference: a caesura, or a physical wound that marks the building alongside of the memory of these children and all of the interlocking memories beyond. The wall, evidently, is a physical marker of the entire history of Moroccan Jews' mass emigration and the loss that ensued. But one wall may hide another, and the emigration of the Jews of Morocco calls to mind other mass migrations in other lands, notably that of the Palestinians impacted by geographical disputes and mass exile. The contributions of artist Mustapha Akrim will bring a historical reminder to the museum through references to the poetry of Mahmoud Darwish, the well-known Palestinian poet, that underline exile as a universal experience. The MMJ's initial wall thus becomes an allegory for other walls (literal or symbolic) erected as caesuras or breaks.

Another standout element of Kakon's architectural contribution lies in the treatment of aquarium-glass displays, in turn reinforcing the notion of reading into the psyche of the place. They are concave in shape, leading the visitor to physically bend over, and these public-facing, airtight cases also appear to be surfaces without depth, mirrors that show the visitor their own reflection as much as they show objects under glass. This double vision follows naturally from the fact that a range of memories and geographies of loss are displayed. The architecture makes an effort to respect all of these elements, taking the form of a minimal, humble contribution: "Respect for this memory and its many associated memories, guided my process. . . . Sometimes architecture is best practiced with a degree of humility."[8]

All these factors influence my approach to the museum's space, as well as the ways in which artists present their work. I will travel a meandering circuit, akin to the path that winds through the museum's garden. The architect's use of granulated, raw stone in the garden creates a path around the entire building, calling to mind a ricocheting, leaping trip through a cavalcade of memories. One needs only touch the stone to be reminded of this borrowing.

FROM ARCHIVE TO ARCHIVE: HANGING THREAD

Ulrike Weiss's artistic approach mixes narration, memory, and handcrafted materials. Her practice centers on the visual archives that she has amassed during her research on Jewish Moroccan craftspeople and their handcrafting methods, namely weaving and metallurgy. Once she selects them, Weiss manipulates these visual documents with precise techniques: collage, clippings, enlargements, cropping, and drawings overlaid with stitching on the surface of the work. Weiss uses the archives as materials in an artistic process that reactivates memory through form. These visual archives clearly have the value of historical documents, and they are inherently scientific. In this sense, Weiss treats the visual archives she works with using techniques that erase their first, generalist reading to foreground details and postures. In her work, Weiss takes on the procedures of the archivist and the researcher, not to give historical truths but to underline the intimate history of the photographs and the mysterious characters they represent. Nevertheless, the artist opts for a formal treatment—decoupage, recycling, and the process of enlarging fragments and filling them in with drawings or sometimes paintings of her own. These artistic techniques clearly call to mind the approach of the archivist/researcher who uses archives as material for discursive historical projects: investigations, readings, selections, and cuts, all focusing on specific archival elements in favor of others.

The bodily movement of the artist as it interacts with visual archives, however, is also an investigation and a bodily reactivation of deep-seated memory: handicrafts that condense a visceral, corporeal memory. Ancestral handiwork sits at the intersection of cultures and beliefs that are much wider in scope than narrow prisms of identity (fig. 8.4). In her article "Judaic Threads in the West African Tapestry: No More Forever?,"[9] which discusses Jewish handicrafts and West African textiles, Labelle Prussin shows how practices of handiwork were widespread and interconnected across the Trans-Saharan commercial route. Beyond the commercial exchange of lives and materials, narratives and stories were circulated throughout the African continent by way of the work and artistry of migrant Jewish craftspeople. With this in mind, I will continue to examine Weiss's take on these visual archives, which include photographs of craftswomen at work with their needles and the jewel-patterned *khalalah* (fibula) of the Jewess of Debdou, "classic" iconography of of Jewish woman from eastern Morocco who wears, as an odd adornment, a molded triangular fibula. This fibula, in its capacity as jewelry, appears in a 1916 postcard depicting a Moroccan Jewish woman, copies of which are easily accessible on the internet today. One can make out the stamped words "Occupying forces of Oriental Morocco" in

FIG. 8.4 Ulrike Weiss, untitled, 2016. Photograph, drawing, 50 × 80 cm. Photo © Ulrike Weiss.

one of these photographs. Note how the direct reference to the Jews of Oriental Morocco enjoins a reference to the handmade crafts that characterized their community. The document offers us a new historical layer: the perspective of the Occidental military-ethnological photograph that bears the image. It is easy to imagine the context in which the costumes and poses of these Jewish Berber women were frozen by the Western gaze in "Orientalizing" positions (see fig. 8.5).

FIG. 8.5 Ulrike Weiss, Jewish woman of Debdou, a postcard from the colonial period. The detail of the right hand and the clothing above it were exploited in the photographic montage of the preceding work. Photo © Ulrike Weiss.

Even as Weiss reactivates memories of weaving and tapestry-making with craft-making and movement that she adds to her collages and photomontages, she is particularly captivated by a specific metallurgical motif: the motif of the fibula (and hence the triangle), which calls to mind the tradition of "metaphor writing" and its narrative forms. Weiss's technique overlays reproduced images with tracings made on gauze and paper.

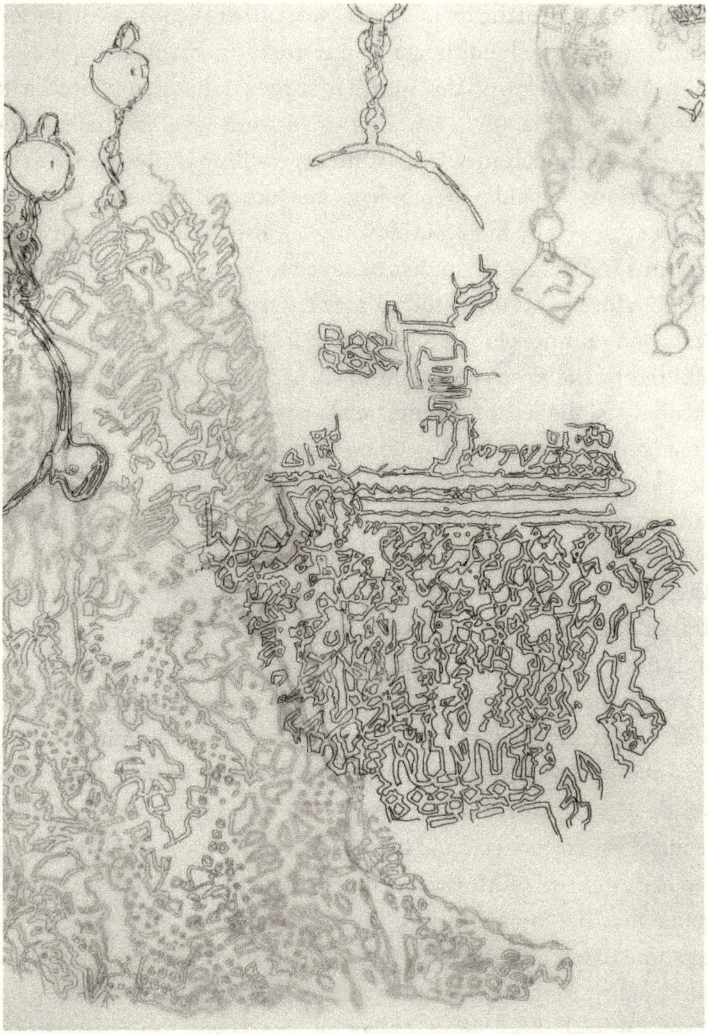

FIG. 8.6 Ulrike Weiss, untitled, 2016. Chinese ink, photographic montage, 70 × 100 cm. Photo © Ulrike Weiss.

This layering of drawings on transparent supports, which could in effect be called "a variation on the theme of the fibula," stacks shapes that interact with the light in the exhibit room and increase or reduce in visibility, all according to the spectator's angle of view. Some of these drawings abandon the fibula's triangular form for swarms of motival elements until the form is entirely erased (fig. 8.6).

The fibula is one of the metallurgical works that Weiss uses in her formal research as well. It is the ultimate geometric form, one that expresses the geometric symbolism of the number three, transformed into a two-dimensional triangle. This takes us to another level in the reading of memory: the examination of beliefs and superstitions imbued in the shapes and inscriptions of handcrafted objects in Morocco. The jewel as a decorative object, especially in rural traditions, is also a receptacle for magical inscriptions and shapes in amulets believed to guard chiefly against the evil eye. In her aforementioned study, Prussin describes the generative power of letters and numbers in the Sefer Yetzirah (Book of Creation),[10] a power transmitted by the forms and techniques used in handcrafting. According to such beliefs, the use of geometric shapes (circles, triangles, spirals) in handmade objects, and the visualizing of these shapes, unleashes an arcane power. Hence the popular tradition of amulets wherein magical practices combine numbers and letters (still recognized in Morocco) ritually protects against the evil eye and other aspects of magic and sorcery.[11]

The mystical power of shapes is believed to transform the substance itself. By depicting these geometric shapes in tracings and gauze, Weiss reminds us of the inherent, occult power traditionally attributed to handicrafts as creators and transformers of the world, all through the power of their memories and the form of their narratives. Francis Ramirez and Christian Rolot also emphasize superstitions and magic in their book *Tapis et tissages du Maroc* (Moroccan tapestries and weaving),[12] which touches on the magical beliefs that go hand in hand with the process of weaving tapestries in certain parts of Morocco, emphasizing the processes of dying and color-making. The tools involved, like the spindle, serve as protective amulets in some cases, and the job of weaving was imbued by weavers with a magical quality. Motifs associated with weaving, like the number five, the *Khemssa,* the seal of Solomon, or the number seven, are expressions of a powerful belief in magic.[13]

In her artistic process, Weiss reactivates a collective memory through the ornamental motif and the artisanal gesture. What is reactivated is, in Pierre Bourdieu's terminology, a kind of sociocultural habitus that belongs not only to the Jewish-Moroccan community, but also to the community of Jewish and Muslim craftspeople.[14] In essence, this memory is the symbolic territory of the contemporary artist, wherein they can displace ancestral traditions from their original context in favor of a new environment, thus allowing the memory to evolve. This is the archeology of memory, which the artist approaches by way of forms and perception.[15]

In "Le Narrateur: Réflexions à propos de l'œuvre de Nicolas Leskov" (The Storyteller: Reflections on the Work of Nikolai Leskov), Walter Benjamin offers a reflection on storytelling as an art and the transmission of memories therein.[16] The art of storytelling is first and foremost the art of communicating and preserving memories. Benjamin reminds us that this transmission was once heavily associated with the work of sailors and merchants, who have always been conveyors of narratives and memories. He also highlights another category of purveyors of memory: craftspeople. The craft industry is therefore defined by the philosopher as the essence of storytelling. Indeed, Benjamin describes storytelling as a loom. Much like the weaver, the storyteller evokes their muse, akin to the manipulation of the loom: "The storyteller's muse is an indefatigable, divine woman who ties the thread that ultimately pulls together a collection of stories. Each story is tied to the next, as all of the great storytellers, and especially Eastern writers, have enjoyed demonstrating."[17] Weiss's work on the visual archives is, at this point, a collection of narrations through the procedures of adding and erasing details and creating a collage of different parts. Like a narrator, she adapts the ingredients of her story to a format and level of meaning that are foregrounded at the expense of others. Weiss serves as a weaver of narratives and histories contained in the photographic images that she works with.

OBJECTS OF EXILE: A CONCRETE STORY

With an entirely different approach, the artist Mustapha Akrim has explored the realities of exile by working with concrete, evoking the metamorphosis that objects of exile undergo in their process of petrification. Jewels, frames, keys, and even purses are cast in concrete to represent the fossilized reality of exile, and their encasement in stone underlines the profound psychological transformations that accompany it.

In "al-ān fī al-manfā, naʿam fī al-bayt" (Now in exile, even at home), drawn from the poem "Manfā" (Exile) by Mahmoud Darwish, Akrim tackles the paradox of exile from the perspective of the Palestinian poet: the plight of living in two opposite situations at the same time, both in exile

FIG. 8.7 Mustapha Akrim, *Now, in Exile*, 2016. Installation, concrete, variable dimensions. Exhibit *Exiles*, Galerie Nationale Bab Rouah, Rabat. Photo © M'hamed Kilito.

and at home. As a whole, he approaches exile as a paradox space, which situates us within it and outside it all at once.

This poetic fragment, however, is not a simple quote or epigraph to the artist's work, as it plays an integral role therein (fig. 8.7). Through both the title and content of the work, the poem of exile is molded into concrete: mineral material that Akrim chooses for molding various objects into his sculpture-installation. Akrim's research on form has led him to work with unchanging symbols of exile as universal elements of the exile experience. The symbolism is clearly present: the key, the photo frame, the jewel, the purse, all are "classic" objects in the nomenclature of exile. In a way, then, these are *objets-valise* (suitcase objects) that compress and preserve personal stories of exile and of ancestry.

Whether as a state of being or as the result of the metamorphosis of petrification, exile transforms the exiled person into an organic form whose inner being is fossilized into a shape that evolves and transforms. Akrim's concrete-molding technique is interesting when viewed this way. The material that forms the cast, the memory object, communicates through the formal language of transformation, in this case a brutal metamorphosis. The material itself does not speak; instead, it makes the act of metamorphosis speak to the memory object, to whose contours it molds. Through the semantics of its shape and the permanent transformation made possible by its fluidity, the concrete reveals the details and folds on these objects, transformed by time, giving them new forms through the degradation of the original material. We presented these objects in several exhibitions between 2016 and 2018, and each time they were denatured by time and various manipulations. Before each presentation, Akrim carried out the process of restoring and repairing the object, like an archeologist who supplements a discovery with exogenous material.

Raw concrete calls to mind the unadorned reality of objects and the great human fragility that this rawness carries within it. Molding concrete (a living material) around the sculpture objects demands a precise and sparing technique because these objects are extremely fragile. They are, after all, intimate things that live in the folds of memory. Once the molding process is complete, there is the question of how these objects will be displayed in an exhibition space. Akrim has experimented with two modes of presentation: wall-mounting (at Rabat's Bab Rouah National Gallery) and dispersion (at the MMJ). The objects and the shelves that hold them are scattered sparsely on various walls throughout the gallery. However, the casts are not displayed in the showcases with the other objects in the collection. Instead, the artist chose to affix concrete shelves in the hallways between one exhibition room and the next, on the borderlines that separate rooms. Situated on the edges of walls, the objects of exile form an extratextual space outside the narratives of the collection and the space of the MMJ.

These additions are anachronisms that tell stories of exile in opposition to the stories of settlement and daily life to which the MMJ's collections speak. Alongside such artistic engagements, readings about the physical form, molding, texture, and the grain on the material's surface provide other points of access to these many stories of exile. As an object form, exile becomes a mise-en-abyme of itself, an infinite cycle. In choosing this mode of presentation, Akrim creates a parallelism between objects cast in concrete that trace the temporality of the imprint and the molding of Darwish's poetry, creating a story within a story. From the exile of Moroccan Jews to the exile of Palestinians, to even the exiles of the world, timelines and geographies intermingle in writings and stories that meet in the raw material of larger history.

One can engage directly here with Darwish's poetry and the opposition between "home" and "exile" in its interlocking layers. This layering of two opposing realities is very important in that Darwish highlights the ambiguity, even the impossibility, of defining the state of being included, instead opting to consider the quest as a place of belonging. Between exile poetry and nationalist fervor, Darwish invests fully in the idea of "journey," which is to say the quest that leads to the self: "Now, in Exile, even at Home." Darwish is most explicit about this in his poem "House":

> The path leading to the house is still more beautiful than the house itself, because the dream lives more beautifully and more clearly in the reality that gave rise to the dream. The dream is now an orphan. I returned to say that the path leading to the house wins out over the house.
>
> My close relationship with the house flowered in exile, or in diaspora. Being exiled deepened my sense of what a home, what a homeland is, in contrast to exile. But now I can no longer define exile as the opposite of the hearth, nor as the opposite of the homeland. Now things are different, and homeland and exile are similar things.[18]

This is the cornerstone of the paradox that torments displaced people, as they are torn between feelings of exile and nationalist sentiment. In *Reflections on Exile,* Edward Said writes on this subject, "Nationalisms are about groups, but in a very acute sense exile is a solitude experienced outside the group. . . . How, then, does one surmount the loneliness of exile without falling into the encompassing and thumping language of national pride, collective sentiments, group passions?"[19] For Darwish, the answer to Said's question is the quest. Somewhere between wandering and a jingoistic anchorage to one's homeland, Darwish constructs the quest as an in-between point or a state of movement, a product of following one's own internal geographic journey.

This is a physical experience and an internal, mystical one, wherein opposites contradict each other in a state of "nonplacement" and exile. It is a model that escapes the notion of being lost and forgetting: a fertile paradigm and a state of continual metamorphosis, propelled by overwhelming momentum toward two contradictory ideas: memory and the future.

Our artistic approach in the project *Exiles* and the exhibition in the MMJ was to begin from a common metaphorical ground and to develop clear narratives from there. Each production was born out of an artist's perception of the museum and its collections, as well as the way in which they resonate with a history that has yet to be written. These visual narratives, both formally and spatially distanced, hold within them a process of historicization affected by the language of form, reminders of the handicraft gesture, and evocations of the inherently perceptible aspects of places and objects. These architectural and artistic interventions open a way of accessing "gaps in history," and they fill in these interstitial spaces differently than a museum dedicated to "official" collective memory would. The micronarratives condensed in each shape and artistic reference effectively create a distance from the narrative of history to which MMJ is devoted. As Hayden White writes in his work on narrative stories and historicization, the act of historicization must be spatialized (or localized) in another space.[20] Official history is distanced when the narrator renders themselves invisible so that the narrative can tell itself through its own formal mechanisms.

In our communal approach, both thoughtful and intuitive, this distancing and narrativizing is accomplished in the intimate sphere of the museum, which is to say within its walls, under its glass, and at the edges and borders of its rooms. These stories have been woven by artists out of ethnographic fragments and perceptions of space, as if they were totemic objects that held their own narratives. The artworks have underlined their own expressivity alongside their evocative and memorializing power, through both their formal mechanisms and the techniques applied to objects and spaces. These perceptible stories are brought forth by way of fragmentation, enlargement, collage, molding, quoting, allusion, and perspective adjusting. This even extends to the cutting of a whole into fragments, then reassembled and restitched so as to amplify their power to evoke and reminisce.

The exhibition *Exiles: A Dialogue with the Museum of Moroccan Judaism* has served as an important waystation for the project *Exiles: A Fertile Paradigm,* which debuted at Rabat's Bab Rouah National Gallery in 2016 and in the MMJ during the same period. The project continued its evolution in Brussels in 2018 with the exhibition *Memory-Sequential Movement in Darna:*

The Moroccan Flemish Cultural Center, and then again between 2018–19 with the exhibition *Of Links and Exiles* at the Boghossian Foundation's Villa Empain in Brussels.[21] This most recent exhibit focused on the need to rethink what holds together our contemporary society. Constantly changing perspectives have made this project possible as both a space for reflection and the creation of an artistic product that concerns the universal questions of loss and return to self that hover over the exile experience.

Notes

1. *Exiles*, Museum of Moroccan Judaism in Casablanca, November 22, 2016–January 31, 2017.
2. Wagenhofer, "Framing Jewish Identity," 293–94.
3. Aomar Boum similarly describes his experience in discovering the MMJ building in his work *Memories of Absence*.
4. Aimé Kakon (1939–2014) was an architect, ceramicist, sculptor, and Moroccan plastic artist. See his biography in *Aimé Kakon*.
5. Foucault, *Dits et écrits*, 1571.
6. Kakon, "[Untitled portfolio]."
7. Kakon, "[Untitled portfolio]," [4]. Translation mine.
8. Kakon, "[Untitled portfolio]," [4].
9. Prussin, "Judaic Threads."
10. *Sefer Yetsirah* (Hebrew: ספר יצירה, "Book of Creation" or "Book of Learning" or "Book of Expression") is a cosmogonical Jewish book written "by a third-century CE Jewish scholar in Palestine" (Prussin, "Judaic Threads," 333).
11. Prussin, "Judaic Threads," 333.
12. Ramirez and Rolot, *Tapis et tissages du Maroc*, 114–42.
13. Canonical literature offers plenty of examples that illustrate the power of weaving, notably in Homer's *Odyssey*, in regard to the character of Penelope and the transformational power of her weaving during the years of Odysseus's voyage.
14. Bourdieu, *Esquisse*.
15. See more on this subject in an article by Chetrit, "Identité judéo-marocaine."
16. Benjamin, "Le Narrateur."
17. Benjamin, "Le Narrateur."
18. Darwish, *Plus de roses*, 29.
19. Said, *Reflections on Exile*, 177.
20. White, *Content of the Form*; White, "Value of Narrativity."
21. See Sabri, *De liens et d'exils*, a collected catalogue of the work exhibited at the Boghossian Foundation's Villa Empain.

Bibliography

Aimé Kakon, architecte plasticien. Introduction by Mohamed Arkoun and André Azoulay. Casablanca: Archi Média éditions, 2011.

Benjamin, Walter. "Le Narrateur: Réflexions à propos de l'œuvre de Nicolas Leskov." In *Écrits français*, 251–300. Paris: Gallimard, 2003.

Boum, Aomar. *Memories of Absence: How Muslims Remember Jews in Morocco*. Stanford: Stanford University Press, 2013.

Bourdieu, Pierre. *Esquisse d'une théorie de la pratique: Précédé de trois études d'ethnologie kabyle*. Geneva: Droz, 1972.

Chetrit, Joseph. "L'Identité judéo-marocaine après la dispersion des communautés: Mémoire, culture et identité des juifs du Maroc en Israël." In *La Bienvenue et l'adieu: Migrants juifs et musulmans au Maghreb, XVe–XXe siècles. Actes du colloque d'Essaouira, migration, identité et modernité au Maghreb, 17–21 mars 2010*, edited by Frédéric Abécassis, Karima Dirèche, and Rita Aouad, 2:135–64. Casablanca: Centre Jacques-Berque, 2012.

Darwish, Mahmoud. "Manfā."

———. *Plus de roses*. Edited by Aziz Azrhai, Fouad Chardoudi, and Abdellah El

Haïtout. Paris: Espace Expression CDG, 2018.
Foucault, Michel. *Dits et écrits*. Vol. 2, *1976–1988*. Edited by Daniel Defert and François Ewald. [Paris]: Gallimard, 2001.
Kakon, Aimé. "[Untitled portfolio]." http://www.melca.info/kakon%20aime.pdf. Accessed April 5, 2022.
Prussin, Labelle. "Judaic Threads in the West African Tapestry: No More Forever?" *Art Bulletin* 88, no. 2 (2006): 328–53.
Ramirez, Francis, and Christian Rolot. *Tapis et tissages du Maroc: Une écriture du silence*. Courbevoie: ACR, 1995.
Sabri, Nadia, ed. *De liens et d'exils*. Brussels: CFC, 2018.
Said, Edward W. *Reflections on Exile and Other Essays*. Cambridge, MA: Harvard University Press, 2000.
Wagenhofer, Sophie, "Framing Jewish Identity in the Museum of Moroccan Judaism in Casablanca." In *Framing Jewish Culture: Boundaries and Representations*, edited by Simon Bronner, 293–311. Jewish Cultural Studies, vol. 4. London: Littman Library of Jewish Civilization.
White, Hayden. *The Content of the Form: Narrative Discourse and Historical Representation*. Baltimore: Johns Hopkins University Press, 1990.
———. "The Value of Narrativity in the Representation of Reality." *Critical Inquiry* 7, no. 1 (1908): 5–27.

CHAPTER 9

Narrating the Homeland from Exile

Iranian Jewish Writers Writing on Their Departure, Identity, and Longing

LIOR B. STERNFELD

MEMORY AND HISTORIOGRAPHY: PLACING IRANIAN JEWISH HISTORY IN THE IRANIAN NATIONAL STORY

Over the past decades, Jewish writers—once again—have become part of the Middle Eastern literary scene. Sometimes they have made cameos in new fiction as characters, direct or implied, narrators, and more. In Israeli literature, now past the generation of Eli Amir, Sami Mikhael, Jacqueline Kahanoff, Shimon Ballas, and Samir Naqqash, we see a new wave of fiction, poetry, nonfiction, and movies that locate Jews' place in the Middle East.[1] When it comes to Iran, however, relatively few Jewish authors write about it, even though Iran hosts the largest population of Jews outside of Israel. Whereas writers in Arab countries such as Egypt, Lebanon, Morocco, and Iraq contemplate aloud the relations with former Jewish communities now lost to emigration and exile, writers in Iran—Jewish and Persian—remain largely silent about Jews in the national context.[2] Nevertheless, novels and memoirs shape Iranian Jewish memories and convey notions about the past. Below, I explore narratives that have been overshadowed by popular literature and nonfiction. These literary works serve as personal archives of memories that help to present the complexity and diversity of a significant and thriving community that underwent a tremendous transformation over the course of the twentieth century. In fact, these works help us to see that the experiences of Jews in Iran represent not just *a* community but Iranian Jewish communities.

Iran's Jewish communities are some of the oldest in the world, dating back to the Babylonian exile. These communities knew periods of relative prosperity as well as periods of pressure, forced conversions, and social ostracism. Yet the many political, cultural, and social transformations of the early twentieth century led to their increased integration into general society, and this even gained them prominence in various fields.[3] Iranian Jews have always considered themselves natives of Iran, proud guardians of Iranian language and culture; and their presence in Iran is older than Islam itself. That Iran and Israel had close diplomatic relations until the 1979 Revolution helped to nurture different kinds of national belonging in story and practice.

Unlike the vast majority of Arab countries, which have significantly lower, if not wholly absent, Jewish populations, Iran still has a Jewish community. Made of about fifteen thousand people (a shadow of its former size of one hundred thousand people before 1979), this community's presence may be why non-Jewish Iranian novelists, thinkers, and other intellectuals do not lament the total loss of that ancient community. Iranian writers have myriad collective traumas to process from the past four decades: the 1979 Revolution, the Iran-Iraq War, the struggles of civil society, and the conflict with the West. Because of the active state of that conflict, we can also see that the intellectual trend of longing for Iran's "glorious cosmopolitan past" is not as developed as it is in other countries, such as Egypt, Morocco, and Iraq. This may explain the absence of religious minorities in this soul-searching.

Literature—fiction and nonfiction alike—shapes the public imagination when it focuses on or takes place in regions that are not well known because of limited knowledge or because linguistic and cultural barriers limit the dissemination of that knowledge. Memoir, in particular, is a constructive genre in the sense that it tells a personal story, but may also illustrate a general situation, especially when we lack direct knowledge of the past or present. Therefore, the private case may represent the experience of the broader community (unless the authors themselves use their voices to render their own experiences exceptional). Below we will look at memoirs and fiction to consider their impact. Because of their truth claims, memoirs provide a lens affording glimpses into the past (or pasts) of certain groups, political parties, movements, classes, or clubs. Memoirs by nature, however, tell a much more circumscribed story than historical research. The perspective of a memoir is usually limited to the author's own experience, despite its best intentions. Memoirs and fiction overlap in how they reflect authentic representation. When it comes to stories about the Middle East, however, the scarcity of popular or nonacademic texts and other cultural products, language barriers, and elements of Orientalism results in memoirs removing filters and synthesizing these cultural markers as all the same. In the Iranian-Jewish case, time froze for most Jewish authors in the aftermath of the 1979 Revolution, in no small part due to the departure of most of the community to the United States, Israel, and Europe. As a result, we cannot really find fiction or memoirs that narrate Jewish experiences in Iran beyond 1988.[4] Ella Shohat examines the unique value of memoirs written in exile, in a language other than the author's native tongue, for an audience outside their homeland. The analytical framework Shohat suggests is helpful for the purposes of this project too.[5]

I am not a literary scholar. Thus, I approach this topic from my position as a historian, and inevitably I historicize these texts. A memoir, despite its truth claims and rootedness in reality, cannot escape the laws of circulation and global forces that shape the book market globally. For instance, novelists writing from within Iran, such as Simin Daneshvar, Mahmoud Dawlatabadi, Jalal Al-e Ahmad, or Iraj Pezeshkzad (or the poetry of Nima Yooshij or Forough Farrokhzad), are considered to be authentic voices of the modern Iranian experience even beyond their status as best-selling authors. Still, how they shape the public perception of Iran or the Iranian experience is, at best, only secondary to works such as Betty Mahmoodi's *Not Without My Daughter* or Azar Nafisi's *Reading Lolita in Tehran*, works with strong Western biases that often demonize Iran and dehumanize the Iranian experience. Despite being very much personal stories, these works are often considered to represent Iran as a whole. While the former group is known mainly to Iranian culture enthusiasts or students (for lack of better terms), the latter are celebrated as heroic voices. This is just a tiny sample, of course. Still, it is worth noting that one was adapted into a Hollywood blockbuster movie and nominated for the Pulitzer Prize upon publication. The other was on the *New York Times* best-seller list for more than one hundred weeks and has been translated into thirty-two languages.[6] The answer is rooted in the book's reception, original language, distribution, and marketing value. Because the general English-reading audience has limited resources at their disposal to "make sense" of Iran, the editorial choices of book publishers dictate how Iran (or other non-Western countries) is portrayed, depicted, and interpreted. This reality extends to the even trickier question of Jewish memory in Iran. With Iran being a hot topic in the news for the past four decades, constantly positioned at odds with Western values or even as a threat to the "free world," potential readers' natural curiosity may encourage publishers to add Iran-related titles. Those which are readily available tend to replicate those that already succeeded: works that offer simple binaries of good and evil, black and white. In the Iranian-Jewish case, we can add another dimension to the US-Iran tensions: Iran-Israel relations and the Israeli efforts to portray Iran as a global danger. Such efforts are often supported by literature that presents Iran as an anomaly in the world.

Creating a Jewish memory of Iran through memoirs poses even more challenges. It is an emotionally charged project. For example, how can writers respect the circumstances of Jews who remained in Iran? How should authors treat Jewish sites in the face of the ever-changing political circumstances in Iran? Moreover, what are we to make of the fact that texts are often written from outside Iran? More specifically, these authors are immigrants, refugees, or second-generation Jews living in Israel or the United States (seldom in Europe). Thus, their stories are told within a context of social assimilation, within current societies, and in the light of the struggle with the authors' Iranian past. How can the authors reconcile broken traditions with the work to overcome stigma and existing notions of the Jewish existence in Muslim countries? For example, writers may deal with new conditions in their now-homelands, as their immigration may have drastically altered their social status or level of comfort (not just materially, but also their sense of belonging). They may have changed views about the 1979 Revolution, something that they cannot contemplate aloud in Israel or the United States, where the revolution is considered to be the incarnation of evil. Women authors surely have struggled with the Iranian and the Iranian-Jewish patriarchy (e.g., childhood arranged marriage, lack of rights in family matters). Finally, the ways in which they established relations within their new society—American or Israeli—also have profound effects. Their pride in Iranian culture conflicts with its inferior status, conveyed via Western stereotypes and ridicule in Israel, and one can note community formation in places like Los Angeles or Long Island. A careful reading of multiple texts can portray a nuanced picture of the Iranian-Jewish communities in the twentieth and twenty-first centuries.

Several of these memoirs became so influential that they created a monolithic image of the Jewish experience in Muslim societies. In his seminal book *The Dispersion of Egyptian Jewry*, Joel Beinin critically analyzed the role and impact of Bat Ye'or's books *Le Juif en Egypte* (1971) and *The Dhimmi: Jews and Christians Under Islam* (1985). These volumes played a role in the foundation of the neolachrymose narrative,[7] which typically sees no path for Jewish integration into Muslim societies. The neolachrymose school creates a selective timeline of Muslim-Jewish history emphasizing rivalry between the two communities. It highlights the discriminatory laws and regulations against Jews (and Christians) without providing any context and clarifying that these codes were only seldom enforced and never uniformly across the entire Muslim world.

Furthermore, this historiographical school aspires to blur the differences between many societies and countries (for example, the fate of Jews in Iran is inevitably similar to the fate of Jews in Egypt and Iraq and most Muslim societies) and to fabricate the idea that Jewish existence anywhere in the Muslim world was unbearable. In his essay, Daniel Schroeter added that Bat Ye'or's book was promoted by the Israeli Foreign Ministry to counter the image of a tolerant Islam and to cement the use of the term "Islamic anti-Semitism."[8] Another crucial point: the book was published originally in French before it was translated into Hebrew, English, Russian, and German. It thus became a "reliable" source on Jewish-Muslim relations and history only by virtue of its wide circulation.

Let us provide a brief historical context for the reading and discussion of the pieces below. At the turn of the century, the Jewish population in Iran overwhelmingly lived on the margins of society. They were mostly impoverished and rural but slightly more educated than the general population. In 1941, during World War II, the American Jewish Joint Distribution Committee (JDC) started to operate in Iran, mostly to help the many Polish and eastern European Jewish refugees who found shelter in the country. Upon arrival, JDC officials mapped the Jewish communities and found that there were around one hundred thousand Jews living in the country. About 10 percent of them belonged to the country's elites (industrialists, bankers), 10 percent were among the relatively new urban middle class, and 80 percent were on the social and geographical periphery of Iran. In 1977, the JDC once again surveyed the Jewish communities and found that still there were one hundred thousand Jews living in Iran, and 10 percent still remained in the top of the country's elite despite the fact that it looked significantly different than in 1941.[9]

The most surprising fact is that by the late 1970s 80 percent of the Jewish population counted themselves among the country's middle and upper-middle class, while an additional 10 percent remained impoverished and lower class. This transformation is in many ways unparalleled in the life of any minority community in the span of less than four decades.[10] With that in mind, there were two major waves of Jewish immigration out of Iran. Between 1948 and 1951 some twenty thousand Jews left, primarily to Israel. These immigrants were the poorest and neediest of all Iranian Jews, those for whom immigration to Israel could better their situation or provide them with religious redemption in the form of Zionism. The second wave occurred immediately after the Iranian Revolution, between 1979 and 1989, when some fifty thousand Jews left Iran because of several factors, including political and economic instability. In fact, this wave of emigration included many of the upper-middle-class Iranians who would leave Iran temporarily, at least. Most important for the Jewish community, however, was the execution of one of the prominent leaders of the Iranian Jewish establishment, Hajj Habib Elghanian, and the subsequent fear of a rise in anti-Jewish violence. This time the majority of Iranian Jewish immigrants left for the United States, and only about a third of them chose to relocate to Israel. This wave of Iranian Jews primarily moved to the Los Angeles area, and they helped establish the largest Iranian diasporic community outside Iran, estimated at around six hundred thousand in 2020; about fifty thousand of its members are Iranian Jews.[11] These new immigrants to Southern California reflected the socioeconomic transformation that the Iranian Jewish community had undergone in the 1960s and 1970s. They were more affluent, placed higher on the social ladder, and more *Iranian* than the generations of the 1940s and 1950s. Therefore, they chose to relocate to the United States along with the other Iranians of the same socioeconomic classes, regardless of religious affiliation or identity. Hakakian and Saper, who were respectively eighteen and twenty-seven years old at the time, also moved with their families to the United States. This background information is crucial, considering the means through which this cultural context might condition the representation of Iran and its "the Jewish story" in the second half of the twentieth century.

I want to look at three major texts written in different styles by different authors with varying circumstances of life. Despite these differences, though, these authors and their works complement one another in providing a historical understanding of Jewish pasts in Iran, especially in the twentieth century.[12] The first is Dorit Rabinyan's *Persian Brides* (1998), which was originally published in Hebrew in 1995 under the title *Simtat ha-Shekediyot be-Omerijan*; the second is Roya Hakakian's *Journey from the Land of No: A Girlhood Caught in Revolutionary Iran* (2004); and the third is Jacqueline Saper's *From Miniskirt to Hijab: A Girl in Revolutionary Iran* (2019). The three books, when read together, present the many aspects of Jewish life in Iran in the twentieth century.

Rabinyan's *Persian Brides* is the only fictional work of the three, and the novel's plot periodization is unclear. There is one clue that it takes place in the period of Reza Shah Pahlavi (1925–41), suggested at the beginning of the novel when the narrator tells the reader about an "ambassadorial procession held in honor of the king, Reza Shah Pahlavi."[13] Another clue is a description of a portrait on the wall, which suggests that it takes place early during the Mohammad Reza Pahlavi period (1941–79). At the end of the eighth chapter, we learn that "through the curtain of colored wooden beads that hung in the kitchen doorway, Nazie [the orphaned eleven-year-old would-be bride] could see the face of the queen of Persia."[14] The original Hebrew edition tells us that the queen was Soraya Esfandiari-Bakhtiyari, Mohammad Reza Pahlavi's second wife (1951–58).[15] The other two memoirs are set before, during, and immediately after the 1979 Revolution (Hakakian's story ends in 1984, and Saper's goes to 1987). Hakakian is slightly younger than Saper, and they belonged to Tehran's middle and upper-middle classes, respectively. Through these narratives, we can trace the changes that Iranian Jews underwent in the tumultuous twentieth century, shifting from high social status and acceptance to conditions that led to the departure of the majority of Iranian Jews, namely the Islamic turn of the 1979 Revolution. The memoirs discussed here both show Jewish life in crisis because of the revolution, and Hakakian and Saper convey the feeling of profound loss of the Iran of their childhood. Rabinyan's narrative, because it is fiction and based in a much earlier period, helps frame Jewish life in Iran before this major transformation.

Before delving into the texts themselves, I want to comment on the process of creating public memory in the context of Jewish culture, the Middle East, and literature. About half of the Jewish population of Israeli society has roots in the Muslim world (Mizrahi Jews). For many years, any attempt by these Jews to reconnect with their Arab past and culture was belittled and ridiculed by the dominant Ashkenazi culture.[16] This cultural mold led to widespread ignorance on the part of the general public (including second- and third-generation Mizrahi Jews) regarding Arab and Middle Eastern societies, Jewish histories of the region, and their culture—both high and popular. In recent years, however, several cultural projects have emerged that sponsor the translation of modern Arabic literature and poetry into Hebrew, and a group of young Mizrahi poets—most notably Ars Poetica—have presented the opportunity to discuss the specific Jewish Mizrahi and Arab identity. As a result, there is a fascination in Israel with Jewish-Arab identity, its culture, its past, its relations with Muslim neighbors, and the cultural and spiritual loss experienced by the Jews *as well as* the societies that they once called their own. As a result, this network of engagements became a cultural phenomenon in American Jewish circles, as seen in stories in various Jewish outlets such as the *Forward*, the *Jewish Review of Books*, and *Tablet*. Such stories have even made it into the pages of the *New Yorker*, the *New York Times*, and the *Los Angeles Review of Books*, for example.[17] Additionally, the prominent Israeli intellectual and translator Orly Noy almost single-handedly introduced some of the masterpieces of modern Iranian literature to Hebrew readers.[18] But in both bodies of work there is an enormous void of knowledge concerning the Jewish experience. This is most pronounced in the Iranian context for a variety of reasons, most notably the time that has passed since the vacating of the Arab world compared with Iran, and the subsequent animosity between Iran and Israel. While multiple memoirs and fiction by Jewish authors have been written in or translated into Hebrew in recent years, they all present the same frame narrative of overt Orientalism, captivity in Iran, a yearning to leave, and a final redemption in Israel or the United States. The politics of translation also play out in the availability of these works in Hebrew (or the lack thereof, depending on how much they conform to or depart from the accepted narratives). Hakakian's *Journey from the Land of No* was translated and published in Israel only in 2022 (full disclosure: I initiated this translation, edited it, and wrote the postscript), despite being published in English in 2004, winning prestigious awards, receiving rave reviews and international recognition, and assuming arguable relevance for the Israeli audience.[19] One of the reasons, I suspect, is that the narrative presents Iran and the Jewish communities with their multitude of complexities, and does not rest behind the metaphorical veil.

ON THE EVE OF A RAPID TRANSFORMATION: *PERSIAN BRIDES*

Rabinyan's *Persian Brides* was first published by a leading publishing house in Israel (Am Oved) when she was only twenty-two years old. The book immediately became a bestseller and won multiple awards, including the Israeli Emerging Novelist Award in 1994 and the Jewish Quarterly-Wingate Prize in 1999. Rabinyan's parents were Iranian-born, but she was born in Israel in 1972. In an interview, she said that she "tried to live two days in her grandmother's stories."[20] The story takes place in the fictional village of Omerijan, Iran. The protagonists are fifteen-year-old Flora, who is pregnant and about to become *kuchik madar* (a little mother), and her eleven-year-old orphaned cousin, Nazie, who lives in endless expectation of marrying her cousin Mousa and becoming a *kuchik madar* herself. They all live in a multigenerational household, which was—and still is—very common in rural Iran, especially in the first half of the century. Rabinyan's use of language is immaculate, her imagistic language triggering sensory responses in the reader through evocative passages. For instance, the narrative draws attention to a variety of smells at the same time: sweat and dirt, the honey smell in Flora's hair, fruits, and piss in the street. The family house is small, and their poverty is implied, but it does not become something that defines the Ratoryan household.

Omerijan is a village with people and demons, and demons are more influential than humans in establishing order. The local culture devotes much time to rituals intended to appease them. Rabinyan writes, "They instructed Flora to pass her first water of the day, the thickest and strongest tea-colored pee, on a hen's egg that had been laid at dawn, then break the pissed-on egg under a blossoming tree. In the evening she was to burn crackling espand seeds on a censer, fill her innards with their smoke, and plead with the moon to remove the curse that it had laid on her."[21] Every tragedy thrown at the villagers is seen as a sign from demons, including the stillborn delivery of Flora's brothers—Miriam Hanoum's children. And so, "when Miriam Hanoum found the third baby lying life-less, with cat hair in his ear, she uttered a long howl, and all the village cats rubbed their paws on their noses with satisfaction. Miriam Hanoum and her husband returned from the cemetery determined to do all that was necessary to placate the angry god of the cats."[22]

Rabinyan's vibrant characterizations give further life to the mnemonic space provided in her narrative. There is the hardworking butcher and his family; Shahin, the sleazy merchant who impregnated Flora and was then found married again to a Baha'i snake-oil seller at the bazaar of Babol Sar;[23] Mamou the cursed whore, and more. The entire story is written in picturesque language, almost in the style of magical realism. Even when the occurrences are soul-crushing, the rhythm of the narration remains uninterrupted (for example when Flora is raped near the opium pit, on the coffeehouse floor).[24] Typically, such characterization of protagonists, descriptions of the hammam and the chador-covered women, special attention directed toward this aesthetic of noise and smells, an implicit sexuality woven throughout the story: all of this would often provoke thoughts of Orientalist clichés. That said, I argue that the careful positioning of Rabinyan in an Iranian village during a period in which Iran was overwhelmingly a rural, illiterate, impoverished society gives another layer of historicism to this novel. It is worth contemplating, though, whether the reader who is not immersed in Iranian or Jewish-Iranian history can see the historical value of this novel beyond the metaphors, or even place the Orientalist imagery in the right context when reading the book.

In fact, these qualities make this novel an Iranian novel more than it is a Jewish one. While some of the characters are marked as Jews, and we see Jewish-Iranian traditions (kashrut, trade practices, getting the help of the Jewish mullah, the Jewish religious figure of the village) in the background, the story is very much Iranian-centric. This quality makes the narrative stand out in the genre of Jewish literature. It places Jews, Armenians, Baha'is, Zoroastrians, and Muslims as nominally equal members, if not of the Iranian society in the 1920s to 1950s then at least in the story itself. Arguably, the characterization of Iranian society of the 1940s as a pluralistic one stands in sharp contrast to the way we have come to perceive Iranian society during the period of the Islamic Republic, despite the immense ethnic and linguistic diversity of the country. The centrality of pluralism in the story can serve, at the same time, as a lament over the loss of a more tolerant "old society," contrary to the reality that Iranian society in the 1940s was far less tolerant toward Jews and minorities than in the 1970s. It yearns for the fluid boundaries of each community and its shared spaces in ways that are no longer possible in Iran and could never exist in Israel.

Rabinyan makes no attempt to cast the Jews as more oppressed or marginalized than they were, and the reader, perhaps even unconsciously, gets the feeling and understanding that the dire situation of the Ratoryan family and the people of Omerjan was not unique to them. One of the scenes that perhaps makes the best case for an Iranian-centric story is where Nazie seeks permission to marry Moussa, her Jewish would-be husband, despite not having gotten her first period. In her hour of need, she goes to see the soft-spoken mullah Jaʿafar at the mosque. The mullah has kind eyes and a huge nose. Shared spaces of worship and pilgrimage come to mind while reading this scene. Both Jews and Muslims frequent many shrines and tombs for their holy virtues, as Mostafa Hussein shows in chapter 3. I believe that Rabinyan's distance from Iran allows this literary magic to happen. As Rabinyan herself said, she wanted to go back to her grandmother's life in Iran. The fact that she was writing about an old era and different life, when most Jews lived in poverty and destitution, allowed her to create a reflection of Jewish life in Iran of a couple of generations before her time.

LIVING THE IRANIAN DREAM: *JOURNEY FROM THE LAND OF NO*

In the 1950s and especially the 1960s, the Jewish communities of Iran experienced unprecedented upward social mobility. At this point, many of the Jews had lived in cities and about half of the Jewish population lived in the capital. They were educated thanks to school networks like the Alliance Israélite Universelle, Obshchestvo Remeslenava Truda (Association for the Promotion of Skilled Trades), and other community-owned schools becoming more visible, even within cities.[25] Subsequently, they slowly abandoned the old *mahalleh* (Jewish neighborhood) in favor of newer and more affluent neighborhoods. Hakakian's *Journey from the Land of No* allows us to follow the trajectory of such communities. This memoir provides a glimpse into the urban life of the majority of the Jewish community through a private lens. Unlike *Persian Brides*, Hakakian's story is very Jewish and rooted in the Jewish-Iranian experience of the 1970s. By this I mean that it is more Iranian and projects a new type of practicing of Jewish life. Hakakian celebrates the unparalleled Jewish-Iranian success in the 1970s, illuminates this unique experience in a way that has not been told before, and mourns the community's decline from the 1980s onward. It is a record not only of the Jewish community in Iran, but of the irreversible transformation of Iranian society after the establishment of the Islamic Republic.

The first chapters draw the road map for this cultural development. The second chapter narrates the quintessentially Iranian experience of the 1970s urban middle class. The chapter is ornamented with excerpts from Samad Behrangi's most controversial book, *Mahi-ye siyah-e kuchulu* (The little black fish), a children's book published in 1968. It tells the story of a little fish that defies the rules of its society and eventually achieves liberation.[26] Behrangi's work instantly received the status of a revolutionary book, one that inspired a generation of Iranians, and a decade later it would be a central part of the Iranian Revolution. Behrangi himself was seen as part of the anti-Pahlavi opposition movement, and his drowning in the Aras River in the fall of 1968 was erroneously believed to be the work of the Sazman-e ettela'at va amniyat-e keshvar (Intelligence and Security Organization of the Country; SAVAK), the notorious intelligence service during the reign of Mohammad Reza Shah. Hakakian's brother, Albert, it appears, was present in the circles that would embrace Behrangi as a model intellectual.

Hakakian's family were avid readers of *Tofigh*, a satirical magazine, named after its establisher and having no direct relation to Jewish-Iranian culture, to which Albert also contributed, as well as their father, using the pseudonym Roya Hakakian. Hakakian presents her family in a way that is not defined by their Jewishness, but rather by cultural and socioeconomic class. For instance, their home was near the Pahlavi Foundation office in the "Alley of the Distinguished." Their being part of Iranian society and the urban middle class comes across in every line of the text. They express their appreciation "for living at a time and in a city where a Jew could mingle with others so freely that he was mistaken for a Muslim" (28).[27] The most outstanding detail, however, is the acknowledgment of the existence of SAVAK and its horrors. This is offered not as an anecdote in passing, nor from a spectator, nor as something that "happens to them" (i.e., as an outsider, or loyal to the Shah). Instead, it is something frightening that has significant consequences for their lives as Iranians.

Hakakian's depiction of Jewish holidays also draws a vivid picture of Jewish culture within Iranian society. Passover, a recurring theme in the story, seems to carry a special meaning in modern Jewish-Iranian Jewish life. It is a holiday that comes up in many stories. Maybe it is the story of Passover that gets new and relevant interpretation in every generation, but in *Journey from the Land of No* it is the central Jewish holiday. Despite this almost universal significance, the Passover chapter also reveals gaps or tensions between the Iranian story and the Jewish one. In the way the memory unfolds, one can sense that the special status of that specific night, of that specific holiday, comes also as a moment of finality: it is an attempt to cherish, mourn, and rejoice during this near-terminal moment before everything changes. It is the last opportunity to celebrate the life that they built for themselves, perhaps the culmination of a twenty-seven-hundred-year-long process. Hakakian introduces Uncle Ardi, who "had shed the 'ghetto' speech, Persian peppered with Hebrew" (50). But Uncle Ardi is more than just a character. He embodies the hopes, fears, experiences, pains, and successes of Iranian Jews in that decade:

> [He] had made a safe passage to the other side, even shed the ghetto jobs; he wasn't a butcher or a salesman, but an insurance man. He was so assimilated, so certain of his prospects in Iran, that he even insured Muslims. . . . What Uncle Ardi had really shed was fear, the fear of claiming his share of the good life like any other middle-class citizen. But he did not call it fear. Instead, he said, "I know how to live." And the place where he knew best to live, where he belonged, was Iran. Everything about him was Iranian, even his name: Ardi, short for Ardeshir, the king of an ancient Persian empire. He was so settled that he was even willing to invest in vanity, to buy depreciating goods—like a BMW. No other car would have matched his optimism, the exuberant claim he laid to Tehran. Tehran and no other city. And never more confidently than in 1977. (51)

The description of the Passover seder at the Hakakian household in 1977 represents the interwoven threads of religious and national belonging:

> Naturally it caused an uproar at the Seder when Father asked Uncle Ardi to read the Ha-Lachma. Everyone burst into laughter, even

> before he began. He obeyed and read, but not without a touch of subversion, a bit of mischief:
>
> "'This is the bread of affliction'—some affliction!—'that our forefathers ate in the land of Egypt. This year we are slaves.' May this slavery never end! 'This year here and next year at home in Israel.' Pardon me for not packing!"
>
> . . . The family dreamed of the land of milk and honey but wanted to wake up in Tehran. . . . After reciting the Ha-Lachma, Uncle Ardi asked, "So, Hakakian, are your bags packed or is the flight to Jerusalem postponed for another year?"
>
> Father smiled and waved him away, assuming his question had been meant in jest. But Uncle Ardi, without the slightest hint at humor, pressed on: "Really, Hakakian, why say it? Why not leave it at 'Love thy neighbor like thyself!' and call off the rest?" (51–57)

As the story line progresses and gets closer to revolutionary events, Hakakian reveals the dilemma that Iranian Jews faced, not necessarily as Jews, but as Iranians of the middle class who had benefitted from some of the Pahlavi policies. These policies helped Jews feel equally Iranian and Jewish, not more or less. The occasional arrest of relatives at the hands of SAVAK, the return of *The Little Black Fish* with its direct connection to the revolutionary events, the ritual of shouting from the rooftops, and the heart-wrenching dilemma of whether the young Hakakian should utter the *Allahu Akbar* chants along with her Muslim neighbors (112–13).

Hakakian's point of view as a teenage girl is fascinating in how it captures the developments within her family and community, namely the revolutionary pressure in the streets, in schools, and in her own home. She offers a depiction of a nightly ride with her parents in the car in the midst of an argument, and her thoughts wander to the crowd protesting outside: "Not to those screaming strangers in the car, but to the streets, to their rapturous cascade that beckoned me with undeniable clarity, I belonged. To the revolution I belonged. To the rage that unlike me had broken free. It would guide me as no one else could, raise me as no one else knew how. And to be its daughter, I would emulate it in any way I could" (124). The chaotic times of the revolution did not pass over the Jews, of course. No decision could have been made lightly. Wondering if she should shout from the rooftop was one thing, but seeing the graffiti that read, "Johouds Get Lost" caught the narrator and her family unprepared. "Johoud" is a word that Hakakian's "father buried before he left the village" (134), before the ultimate assimilation of Iranian Jews into society, and markedly in the village, into the great city of Tehran, where it now appeared as well. But this is not the end of the story. Hakakian continues to narrate her time in Iran throughout the revolution and the establishment of the Islamic Republic, as well as to the beginning of the war with Iraq, or the Sacred Defense, as it is called in Iran, up until the eventual departure of the family to the United States.

AN INSIDER/OUTSIDER'S VIEW: *FROM MINISKIRT TO HIJAB*

Jaqueline Saper was born in Tehran in 1961. Her Iranian father met her English mother in Birmingham, England, when he was there as a student of chemical engineering. She spent her childhood living in Tehran in an upper-middle-class family, and during the summers she would go to England to visit her mother's family. Her father taught at two universities in Tehran, worked with Habib Elghanian, a prominent leader of the Jewish community, and also worked as a businessman and philanthropist. Elghanian would also become the first Jewish victim to be executed by the revolutionary courts. He had a framed photograph with the Shah.

Saper describes the cultural assimilation of her family in similar ways to those of Hakakian. They were proud Iranians, emotionally invested in the country, culture, and society. Through her Muslim maids, she learned about the grievances of the poorer Iranians against the Pahlavi regime. Saper provides a sober understanding of what had been going on in Iran in her childhood years. When she talks about the twenty-five hundredth anniversary of the Iranian monarchy, for example, she recognizes the injustice, even if—as a child—she articulated it differently. "Why were the foreigners having all the fun? Why were only a few Iranians invited? Why didn't they spend some of this money on the poor people?" Saper asks.[28]

Saper's family cherished the Pahlavi project, which aspired to the separation of state and religion and the transformation of women's status in Iran. And here, too, we learn of the Passover seder night in 1977. Not far from the Hakakians' house, Saper's cousin Kami jokes in response to the "next year in Jerusalem," emphasizing that "we already lived in the best place on earth and had great lives. We had no reason to go anywhere. In full agreement and with no reason to doubt Kami's words, we all burst out laughing."[29]

Slightly older than Hakakian during the Revolution era, Saper was well aware of public sentiment. She heard the students quietly speaking about their disgust toward the Shah, and her family had a run-in with SAVAK (her father warned her never to get involved in anything political due to their presence). She took notes of the ways that the Shah deserved this resentment, including by creating an imperial calendar that took Iran overnight from the year 1355 (Hijri Shamsi) to 2535, much to the dismay of large segments of the population. She was amused by President Carter's infamous toast on the New Year's Eve in 1978 that "Iran, because of the great leadership of the Shah, is an island of stability in one of the most troubled areas of the world."[30] She grew up hearing stories from her family in London about living under the threat of the blitz and nightly attacks, and she could not imagine anything like it from her comfortable life in Tehran. Later in the memoir, she discovered what it felt like when Iran was under similar attack during the Iran-Iraq war, noting the subsequent loss of peace and stability.

At the height of the revolution, returning from a visit to England that had been prolonged due to the intensification of the anti-Shah demonstrations, Saper met Ebi, a medical student and the son of family friends, and fell in love with him immediately. From her account, we see the rooftop shouting ritual as a pivotal moment: the question of whether they should stay or go. She talks about women wearing the hijab during the revolution, not as a symbol of religiosity but as an act of subversion against imposed secularization. Saper writes, "Until this period of revolutionary fervor, I had rarely seen women or girls wearing thick large headscarves that covered part of their faces. Traditional women had been content with wearing the chador, but now covering heads and wearing loose clothing had become an expression of rebellion."[31] In the same vein, when we get to the immediate aftermath of the revolution, she talks about the March 8 protest against the first attempt of Khomeini to impose the wearing of the hijab.[32] Notably, Saper joined this protest. For her, the day ended with attacks of an angry mob against the protesters. This subplot is tremendously important, because it shows that Jewish individuals took to the streets along with their non-Jewish compatriots in every major event.

It should be noted, though, that based on multiple accounts and narratives of that day, thousands of men joined the protest wearing hijabs to mock the new suggested requirement. Many women who would otherwise wear it removed their hijabs to stand in solidarity. Saper also makes a problematic observation regarding the Baha'is: "But now, the Baha'i faith was not recognized as an official religion, and its members continued to be harassed and persecuted."[33] While there is no doubt that the situation of the Baha'is in Iran deteriorated rapidly following the revolution, it should be clearly stated that the Baha'i faith was never recognized as a religious minority or protected group. Throughout most of the Pahlavi period, the Baha'i community prospered. On a few occasions, however, when the monarch needed to appease the clergy for ad hoc work, the government would run anti-Baha'i campaigns.

The following year, Saper and Ebi get married in a Jewish wedding in the newly formed Islamic Republic, after which they move to Shiraz. They have their first child shortly before the start of the Iran-Iraq War, and Ebi is sent to the front line to treat wounded soldiers for a month every year. Saper's narrative adds a lot to what we know about the Jewish experience in the aftermath of the revolution, such as the ambiguity regarding Iranian Jews' ability to leave the country. Saper says that every Iranian needed an exit visa, and in the bureaucratic chaos some got it while others did not. She adds that "there were no laws that were passed on this issue, but it was unofficially close to impossible for Jews to leave Iran as a family unit."[34] This was true for most Iranians regardless of their faith, but likely stricter for religious minorities.

Saper's narrative shows the rise in anti-Jewish bias in the general public or the legitimacy to express these views more freely in the Islamic Republic. That said, Saper and her family continued to lead relatively comfortable lives, interrupted periodically by the reminder that in some cases they are second-class citizens. They lived in spacious housing, provided by the hospital staff where Ebi worked, and they had a close community (of mostly Muslims) around them. But after their oldest child, Leora, went to first grade, she was forced to wear the hijab, and her parents had concerns about her education and future, thus prompting their decision to leave Iran. They were able to obtain the exit visa through a senior government acquaintance of Ebi, something that became available thanks to their status, class, and Ebi's military service. In their last night in Tehran, as they were saying their goodbyes, they experienced another bombing, just as Saper's mother's family had during World War II in London. The next day they boarded the flight and left Iran permanently.

CONCLUSION

The three works examined here reflect the complexity of an eventful century in Iran. Through reading them, one can see how the revolution transformed the country and Jewish life, as both Hakakian and Saper (who left Iran a few years after the revolution, in 1984 and 1987 respectively) present an overall balanced account of what had transpired.

The diversity of Jewish existence must not be ignored, especially when a representation of one experience becomes the hegemonic voice. In these texts, we see Jewish life in relative poverty, in a rural setting, against the backdrop of the emerging nationalism and subsiding religiosity; we then visit with a Jewish family, for whom the story as told by Rabinyan could have been very familiar. But at the time of our visit, they had made it into the Tehrani middle class. Last, we acquainted ourselves with a third family that allowed us to see the different experiences and almost different experiential dialects of the Jews from Isfahan, Tehran's upper middle class, and then Shiraz. We, as readers, should celebrate and embrace the many manifestations of Jewish life in Iran. We can only understand the loss and belonging (and the questions of cultural and national identity) when we understand the modern history, roots, and circumstances that allowed Jews to build this multifaceted relationship with the land, culture, and society of Iran. Loss and mourning can be expressed by Iranian Jews both in Iran and of the diaspora because the trauma that led to their grand departure was experienced by Iranians regardless of their faith. This chapter focuses on Jewish representation of this complex relationship, but similar sentiments could have been dictated among Muslims, Christians, or Iranians of any other faith or ethnic background.

The circumstances that led to the 1979 Revolution are clearly presented in Hakakian's and Saper's narratives, the appeal to the majority of Iranians is explained, and I would add that it is explained with empathy. Both memoirs are written from a very specific Jewish-Iranian angle but also reveal multitudes about Iranian society in general. The pain of leaving one's homeland is felt, but the accounts complicate commonly held narratives of rigidly defined, antagonistic relationships between Iranians of different religious beliefs. These texts present nuanced narratives that should be added to the communal memory and therefore to our scholarly analysis of this turbulent period.

Notes

1. Amir, Mikhael, Kahanoff, Balas, and Nakash are Arab-born novelists whose writings depict Jewish life in Iraq and Egypt around 1948 and their experiences after migrating to Israel.

2. For a useful survey of related works, see El Guabli, "Breaking Ranks."

3. For an in-depth analysis of the social, cultural, and political developments of the Jews of Iran in the twentieth century, see Sternfeld, *Between Iran and Zion*.

4. Saper's memoir, *From Miniskirt to Hijab*, goes all the way to the author's departure in 1987. Hārūn Yashāyāee published his own memoir, *Guzārish-i Yak Davarān*, in 2019. It is the only text written from within Iran that goes into the Islamic Republic period.

5. Shohat, "Lost Homelands, Imaginary Returns," 109–39.

6. For *Not Without My Daughter*'s Pulitzer nomination, see Montemurri, "*Not Without My Daughter*"; see Margret Atwood's rave review of *Reading Lolita in Tehran* ("Book Lover's Tale").

7. Beinin, *Dispersion of Egyptian Jewry*, 14–19.

8. Schroeter, "'Islamic Anti-Semitism,'" 1178–81.

9. See Farah's study of Jewish education in Iran as indicative of Jewish social mobility in the country: "School Is the Link"; see also Sternfeld, *Between Iran and Zion*, chap. 4.

10. Sternfeld, *Between Iran and Zion*, 63–91.

11. Hennessy-Fiske and Abdollah, "Community Torn by Tragedy."

12. Rahimieh, "Flights from History"; Shohat, "Lost Homelands, Imaginary Returns."

13. Rabinyan, *Persian Brides*, 11.

14. Rabinyan, *Persian Brides*, 89.

15. Rabinyan, *Simtat ha-Shekediyot be-Omerijan*, 76.

16. See, for example, the following texts: Khazzoom, *Shifting Ethnic Boundaries*; Shohat, "Sephardim in Israel"; Shenhav, *Arab Jews*.

17. Tsabari, "Mizrahi Artists Are Here"; Ramakrishna, "Ars Poetica"; Olidort, "Language We Inherit Is Not One"; "Young Mizrahi Israelis' Open Letter." Notably, the Van Leer Institute in Jerusalem started recently a series of translations of Arabic literature called "Maktub." The editorial team and translators are both Arabic and Hebrew speakers. See Chetrit, *Intra-Jewish Conflict in Israel*.

18. Examples of Noy's translations include Noy, *Yamim meshunim hem eleh, yafati*; Daulatābādī, *Sheḳi ʿat ha-ḳolonel*; Pazeshkzad, *Dodi napoleon*; Cheheltan, *Tehran, rehov ha-mahapekha*.

19. *Journey from the Land of No* is being translated into Hebrew by an independent publisher, KTAV, owned by Moshe Menasheof, an Iranian Jew who migrated to Israel.

20. Rabinyan, "Hotze Yisrael im Kobi Meidan."

21. Rabinyan, *Persian Brides*, 15.

22. Rabinyan, *Persian Brides*, 33.

23. Rabinyan, *Persian Brides*, 198.

24. Rabinyan, *Persian Brides*, 172.

25. Obshchestvo Remeslenava Truda was a Jewish network of education and vocational training that started in Russia and had branches in many Jewish communities worldwide; see Farah, "School Is the Link."

26. Milani, *Eminent Persians*, 838–39.

27. Subsequent parenthetical page references in this section are to Hakakian, *Journey from the Land of No*.

28. Saper, *From Miniskirt to Hijab*, 22.

29. Saper, *From Miniskirt to Hijab*, 28.

30. Saper, *From Miniskirt to Hijab*, 36.

31. Saper, *From Miniskirt to Hijab*, 72.

32. Saper, *From Miniskirt to Hijab*, 84. See Afary, *Sexual Politics in Modern Iran*; Mottahedeh, *Whisper Tapes*.

33. Saper, *From Miniskirt to Hijab*, 93. See a similar statement on p. 139. See more on the status and history of the Baha'is in Iran in Brookshaw and Fazel, *Baha'is of Iran*; Afshari, "Discourse and Practice."

34. Saper, *From Miniskirt to Hijab*, 133.

Bibliography

Afary, Janet. *Sexual Politics in Modern Iran*. Cambridge: Cambridge University Press, 2009.

Afshari, Reza. "The Discourse and Practice of Human Rights Violations of Iranian Baha'is in the Islamic Republic of Iran." In *The Baha'is of Iran: Socio-Historical Studies*, edited by Dominic Parviz Brookshaw and Seena Fazel, 232–77. London: Routledge, 2008.

Atwood, Margaret. "The Book Lover's Tale: A Review of *Reading Lolita in Tehran: A Memoir in Books*, by Azar Nafisi." *Literary Review of Canada*, September 2003. https://reviewcanada.ca/magazine/2003/09/the-book-lovers-tale/.

Beinin, Joel. *The Dispersion of Egyptian Jewry: Culture, Politics, and the Formation of a Modern Diaspora*. Berkeley: University of California Press, 1998.

Brookshaw, Dominic Parviz, and Seena Fazel, eds. *The Baha'is of Iran: Socio-Historical Studies*. London: Routledge, 2008.

Cheheltan, Amir Hassan. *Tehran, rehov ha-mahapekha*. Translated by Orly Noy. Tel Aviv: Yediot Ahronoth, 2016.

Chetrit, Sami Shalom. *Intra-Jewish Conflict in Israel: White Jews, Black Jews*. London: Routledge, 2010.

Daulatābādī, Maḥmūd. *Sheḳi'at ha-ḳolonel*. Translated by Orly Noy. Tel Aviv: Am Oved, 2012.

El Guabli, Brahim. "Breaking Ranks with National Unanimity: Novelistic and Cinematic Returns of Jewish-Muslim Intimacy in Morocco." In *Generations of Dissent: Intellectuals, Cultural Production, and the State in the Middle East and North Africa*, edited by Alexa Firat and R. Shareah Taleghani, 159–88. Syracuse: Syracuse University Press, 2020. https://www.doi.org/10.2307/j.ctvz9383k.

Farah, Daniella L. "'The School Is the Link Between the Jewish Community and the Surrounding Milieu': Education and the Jews of Iran from the Mid-1940s to the Late 1960s." *Middle Eastern Studies* 57, no. 5 (2021): 793–809. https://www.doi.org/10.1080/00263206.2021.1892646.

Hakakian, Roya. *Journey from the Land of No: A Girlhood Caught in Revolutionary Iran*. New York: Three Rivers Press, 2004.

Hennessy-Fiske, Molly, and Tami Abdollah. "Community Torn by Tragedy; Bianca Khalili's Death Divides the Westside's Persian Jewish Enclave. Police Deem It Suicide, but Some Don't Agree." *Los Angeles Times*, September 15, 2008.

Khazzoom, Aziza. *Shifting Ethnic Boundaries and Inequality in Israel: Or, How the Polish Peddler Became a German Intellectual*. Stanford: Stanford University Press, 2008.

Littman, Gisèle. *The Dhimmi: Jews and Christians under Islam*. London: Associated University Presses, 1985.

Mahmoodi, Betty. *Not Without My Daughter*. London: Corgi, 1989.

Milani, Abbas. *Eminent Persians: The Men and Women Who Made Modern Iran, 1941–1979*. 2 vols. Syracuse: Syracuse University Press, 2008.

Mirakhor, Leah. "After the Revolution to the War on Terror: Iranian Jewish American Literature in the United States." *Studies in American Jewish Literature* 35, no. 1 (2016): 52–76.

Montemurri, Patricia. "*Not Without My Daughter* All Grown up in Michigan." *Detroit Free Press*, March 19, 2016. https://www.freep.com/story/life/2016/03/19/not-without-my-daughter-michigan-mahtob-mahmoody/77563602/.

Mottahedeh, Negar. *Whisper Tapes: Kate Millett in Iran*. Stanford: Stanford Briefs, 2019.

Nafici, Azar. *Reading Lolita in Tehran*. New York: Random House, 2004.

Noy, Orly, ed. and trans. *Yamim meshunim hem eleh, yafati: Kovetz me-hashira ha-modernit be-iran*. Tel Aviv: Ktav, 2018.

Olidort, Shoshana. "The Language We Inherit Is Not One: A Conversation with Almog Behar." *Los Angeles Review of Books*, May 1, 2017. https://lareviewofbooks.org/article/the-language-we-inherit-is-not-one-a-conversation-with-almog-behar/.

Pazeshkzad, Iraj. *Dodi napoleon*. Translated by Orly Noy. Tel Aviv: Am Oved, 2012.

Rabinyan, Dorit. "Hotze Yisrael im Kobi Meidan: Dorit Rabinyan." Aired June 26, 2014, on Kan Kids Hinochit. https://www.youtube.com/watch?v=z8r5awdF52M.

———. *Persian Brides*. Translated by Yael Lotan. New York: George Braziller, 1998.

———. *Simtat ha-Shekediyot be-Omerijan*. Tel Aviv: Am Oved, 1995.

Rahimieh, Nasrin. "Flights from History: Gina Barkhordar Nahai and Dalia Sofer's Fiction." In *The Jews of Iran: The History, Religion, and Culture of a Community in the Islamic World*, edited by Houman Sarshar, 203–19. London: I. B. Tauris, 2014.

Ramakrishna, Prashanth. "Ars Poetica: Poeticizing Mizrahi Inequality in Israel." *Believer Magazine*, March 16, 2017. https://believermag.com/logger/ars-poetica-poeticizing-mizrahi-inequality-in-israelby-prashanth-ramakrishna/.

Saper, Jacqueline. *From Miniskirt to Hijab: A Girl in Revolutionary Iran*. Lincoln, NE: Potomac Books, 2019.

Schroeter, Daniel J. "'Islamic Anti-Semitism' in Historical Discourse." *American Historical Review* 123, no. 4 (2018): 1172–89. https://www.doi.org/10.1093/ahr/rhy026.

Shenhav, Yehouda. *The Arab Jews: A Postcolonial Reading of Nationalism, Religion, and Ethnicity*. Stanford: Stanford University Press, 2006.

Shohat, Ella. "Lost Homelands, Imaginary Returns—The Exilic Literature of Iranian and Iraqi Jews." *Rozenberg Quarterly*, n.d. https://rozenbergquarterly.com/lost-homelands-imaginary-returns-the-exilic-literature-of-iranian-and-iraqi-jews/.

———. "Sephardim in Israel: Zionism from the Standpoint of Its Jewish Victims." *Social Text*, nos. 19–20 (1988): 1–35. https://www.doi.org/10.2307/466176.

Sternfeld, Lior B. *Between Iran and Zion: Jewish Histories of Twentieth-Century Iran*. Stanford: Stanford University Press, 2019.

Tsabari, Ayelet. "Mizrahi Artists Are Here to Incite a Culture War." *Forward*, March 16, 2016. https://forward.com/opinion/335653/mizrahi-artists-incite-culture-war-against-israeli-elite/.

Yashāyāyī, Hārūn. *Guzārish-i Yak Davarān*. Tehran: Nashr-i Māhrīs, 2019.

Ye᾽or, Bat. *Les Juifs en Egypt*. Geneva: Editions de l'Avenir, 1971.

"Young Mizrahi Israelis' Open Letter to Arab Peers." *+972 Magazine*, April 24, 2011. https://www.972mag.com/young-mizrahi-israelis-open-letter-to-arab-peers/.

CONTRIBUTORS

ABDELKADER AOUDJIT is an independent scholar of philosophy and literature based in Arlington, VA. He holds a PhD in philosophy from Georgetown University. He is the author of *The Algerian Novel and Colonial Discourse: Witnessing to a "Différend," Algerian Literature: A Reader's Guide and Anthology,* and *The Algerian Historical Novel: Linking the Past to the Present and Future.*

BRAHIM EL GUABLI is Associate Professor of Arabic Studies and Comparative Literature at Williams College. He is the author of *Moroccan Other-Archives: History and Citizenship After State Violence.* He is currently completing a second book, to be entitled "Desert Imaginations: Saharanism and Its Discontents." His journal articles have appeared in *LA Review of Books, PMLA, Interventions,* and *History in Africa,* among others. He is coeditor of the two volumes of *Lamalif: A Critical Anthology of Societal Debates in Morocco During the "Years of Lead" (1966–1988).* El Guabli is coeditor of *Tamazgha Studies Journal* and Georgetown University Press's Amazigh Studies Series.

İLKER HEPKANER is an editor of Velvele.net English. His research interests are cultural studies, historiography, heritage, and queer representation. His latest academic publication was an article in the *Journal of Popular Culture* titled "Where Is a Minority's Popular Culture Archived? An Answer from the Jewish Community of Turkey."

ISKANDAR AHMAD ABDALLA is a PhD candidate in Islamic Studies at Freie Universität, Berlin. His research interests are Islam and migration in Europe, queer theory, and history of film and cultural production in modern Egypt. His most recent publication is "The Visual Nation: Film, Soft Power, and Egypt as a Community of Spectators," in *Cinema in the Arab World: New Histories, New Approaches,* edited by Ifdal Elsaket, Daniel Biltereyst, and Philippe Meers.

LIOR B. STERNFELD is William J. and Charlotte K. Duddy University Endowed Fellow in the Humanities and Associate Professor of History and

Jewish Studies at Penn State University. He is a historian of the modern Middle East and focuses on Iran, Iranian Jewish history, and Jewish histories of the Middle East. Among Sternfeld's publications are *Between Iran and Zion: Jewish Histories of Twentieth Century Iran* and *Jews of Iran: A Photographic Chronicle* (coauthored with Hassan Sarbakhshian and Parvaneh Vahidmanesh). Sternfeld's current research focuses on the Iranian Jewish diaspora in the United States and Israel.

LITAL LEVY is Associate Professor of Comparative Literature at Princeton University, where she teaches literature, critical theory, and intellectual history, with specializations in Hebrew, Arabic, Jewish studies and Middle Eastern studies. Her research encompasses literature and film from Israel/Palestine, the modern intellectual and cultural history of Arab Jews, the interface of Jewish literature and world literature, and comparative non-Western literary modernities. She is the author of the award-winning book *Poetic Trespass: Writing between Hebrew and Arabic in Israel/Palestine* and coeditor of *Unsettling Jewish Knowledge: Text, Contingency, Desire* as well as numerous scholarly articles.

MOSTAFA HUSSEIN is Assistant Professor in the Department of Judaic Studies at the University of Michigan, Ann Arbor. Hussein's research centers on the intellectual and cultural intersections between Jews and Arabs in modern Israel/Palestine and the Middle East. He is particularly interested in the influence of Arabo-Islamic culture on the development of Jewish thought in Palestine/Israel during the late nineteenth and mid-twentieth centuries. Additionally, he explores the evolving perceptions of Jews in Arabic-speaking countries throughout the Middle East from the late nineteenth through the late twentieth centuries.

NADIA SABRI is an academic and independent curator and president of the Moroccan section of AICA (International Association of Art Critics). Sabri has built projects around art and societal issues over the last fifteen years. She conceives artistic projects as a driving force combining research, demonstrative processes, and experiences. Sabri has written and directed several research projects and publications on contemporary art and its relationship to sociopolitical issues such as cities, exile, or even artist commitment. In 2015, she founded *Exiles, paradigm fertile,* a multidisciplinary platform for reflection and creation around the issue of exile as a creative and evolutionary paradigm.

SARAH IRVING is a lecturer in international history at Staffordshire University and a Leverhulme Early Career Fellow, researching a social history of the 1927 Palestine earthquake. She is the editor of *The Social and Cultural History of Palestine: Essays in Honour of Salim Tamari* and coeditor of *"The House of the Priest": A Palestinian Life (1885–1954)* (with Niqula Khoury, Charbel Nassif, and Karène Sanchez Summerer).

STEPHANIE KRAVER holds a PhD in Near Eastern Languages and Civilizations from the University of Chicago. She is a scholar of modern Arabic literature and Arabic and Hebrew poetry and poetics from the twentieth century to the present. Her research interests sit at the intersection of Palestinian/Israeli literature and film, constructions of memory after loss, anticolonial theory, and gender and sexuality studies. At the University of Chicago, she served as a doctoral fellow in the Pozen Center for Human Rights and an affiliated fellow in the Franke Institute for the Humanities. Her current manuscript, "Reading Past Difference: Mahmoud Darwish's and Dahlia Ravikovitch's Poetics," identifies how poetic verse creates imaginative and political possibilities beyond the limits of ethno-national borders and separatist ideologies.

INDEX

Page numbers in italics denote figures, and endnotes are indicated by "n" followed by the endnote number.

1948 War
in Egyptian television, 15, 93, 95
Jewish names and, 76
State of Israel, establishment of, 5, 6–7, 81, 113–14, 129–30, 141
Syrian emigration and, 136
1956 War, 71, 73, 81, 84
1967 War, 30, 32, 136, 139–43, 155
See also Kurdish-Arab-Jewish Memory
1979 Revolution, 191, 193, 195, 196, 203–4, 205–7

Abdalla, Ahmed, *Heliopolis*, 109
Abdalla, Iskandar Ahmad, chapter by, 18, 28, 93–112
ʿAbdelmegid, Ibrāhīm. See *Ṭuyūr al-ʿanbar* (Birds of ambergris) (ʿAbdelmegid)
Abraamidou, Maria, 127
Abraham Accords (2020), 17, 28, 45n7
adab al-muqāwamah (resistance literature), 80
Adalet ve Kalkınma Partisi (Justice and Development Party), 156
ʿAdl, Midḥat al-, 96, 97, 103
ʿAdl, Muhammad al-, 98
ʿAfia, ʿAmr. See *Ḥadd al-ghāwayah* (The edge of error) (ʿAfia)
ʿAflaq, Michel, 141
Agos (Armenian newspaper), 157
Agouim, Morocco, 33
Aït Moh, El Hassane, 34
Akrim, Mustapha, 172, 173, 183–88, *184*
Aksu, Sezen, 161
"al-ān fī al-manfā, naʿam fī al-bayt" (Now in exile, even at home) (Akrim), 183
Al-Daher (television series), 109
Alexandria, Egypt, 40, 69, 71, 72, 81–82
See also Arabic literature in Egypt
Algeria, 4, 6, 18, 49, 57–59, 66
See also Algerian literature
Algerian Association of Religious Scholars (AOMA), 64
Algerian literature
Décree Crémieux (1870), 55–56
Jewish indigeneity to Maghreb, 51–55
prospects for reconciliation, 65–66
stories of betrayal, 59–65
War of Independence (1954–62), 49, 57–59
World War II, 50, 56–57
writers' attitude toward Jews, 48–50
See also *specific works*
Algerian People's Party (PPA), 65
Alliance Israélite Universelle (AIU) (1860), 5, 38, 155, 200
Al-Nār wa-al-zaytūn (Fire and olives) (Farag), 80
Al-Yahūdī al-ḥālī (The handsome Jew) (Al-Muqri)
death and loss in, 121–30
as historical novel, 119, 120–21, 129–30
introduced, 113–14
postcolonial readings, 113–14, 128–29
southern Arabian historical context, 115–19
as Yemeni Novel, 119–21
Al-Yāhūdī al-ʿakhīr (The last Jew) (Nāṣir), 29–30
al-zaman al-gamīl (the "beautiful age"), 15, 28, 96–99
Amir, Eli, xi
Amrīkānlī: Amrī kān lī (The matter was mine) (Ibrāhīm), 71
Anā al-mansī (I am the forgotten) (Tazi), 34
ʿAnānī, Khāled al-, 69, 70
Ankara, Turkey, 158, 159, 162–64, 167
anti-Semitism
Egyptian television and, 94, 107, 108
following Décree Crémieux, 55–56, 59
"Islamic anti-Semitism," 194
Israeli support of OAS, 66
in narratives of separation, 1
World War II, 56–57, 58, 64–65
ʿAn yahūd miṣr (The Jews of Egypt) (film), 14–15, 109
Aoudjit, Abdelkader, chapter by, 18, 48–68

Aourid, Hassan, *Cintra*, 34
apocalyptic and messianic themes, 122–23
Arabic literature in Egypt
Arab-Israeli conflict, 80–81
interfaith marriage, 77–78
Jewish departure from Egypt, 81–84
literary representations of Jews, 70–74, 89n18
myth of religious homogeneity, 29
religion and politics, 84–89
renewed interest in Jewish heritage, 69–70
shared religious-cultural sphere, 75–77
space in cosmopolitan society, 74–75
struggle for power, 79–80
See also *specific works*
Araf, Ilya, 163
ʿArafa, Sharif, 109
Arcady, Alexandre, 49
Arcak, Enver. See *Hermana* (film)
architecture, 175–77
Archive of Feelings, An (Cvetkovich), 138
Arraki, Zineb Andress, 173
Ars Poetica (Mizrahi poets), 197
artisanship
in conveyance of memory, 183
in pre-1948 Syria, 139
superstitions imbued in, 182
as visual archive, 177–83, *179, 180, 181*
"withdrawal of tradition" following disasters, 126
Yemeni economic system and, 117
Ashkenazie, Eddie, xiii
Assmann, Jan, 100, 102
Aswānī, ʿAlāʾ al-, 71
Atatürk, Mustafa Kemal, 166
authoritarianism, 8, 36, 152n57
Awrāq ʿibrīyya (Hebrew papers) (Riyāḍ), 34, 43–44

Babylonian Jewry Heritage Center, xiv–xv
Badawi, M. M., 30
Bader, ʿAli, 12
Baghdad, Iraq, x–xi
Bahaʾi community, 206
Bahrain, 17, 45n7
Baier, Annette, 82
Bakhtin, Mikhail, 144
Ballas, Shimon, xi, 10
Bana, İzzet, 161
Bannā, Ḥasan al-, 106
Barakāt, Salīm. See *Mādhā ʿan al-sayyida al-yahūdiyya rāḥīl?* (What about Rachel, the Jewish lady?) (Barakāt)
Bashkin, Orit, 2, 11, 19
al-Batāwīn (Batawin), Baghdad, x–xi
Battle of Algiers (1957), 60
Bat Yeʾor, 194
Al-Bayt al-andalusī (The Andalusian house) (Laredj), 48, 50, 52, 53, 54, 66
Baʿath Party, 136, 141–43, 146, 151n41
"beautiful age" (*al-zaman al-gamīl*), 15, 28, 96–99
Behrangi, Samad, 201
Beinin, Joel, 194
Benghabrit, Kaddour, 64
Bengio, Celia, 176
Bengio, Murdock, 176
Ben-Gurion, David, 66
Benin, Joel, 94
Benjamin, Walter, 183
Bennett, Julian, 163
bilanguage *(bi-langue)*, 38
Bildungsroman genre, 136
Bīṭār, Salaḥ al-Dīn al-, 141
Booker, M. Keith, xi
Boudjedra, Rachid. See *La Dépossession* (The dispossession) (Boudjedra)
Boum, Aomar, 9, 11
Bourdieu, Pierre, 182
Bousbia, Safinez, 27
Brimath, Ben, 64
Bukhūr ʿadanī (Adeni incense) (Al-Muqri), 118
Buraq Wall, Jerusalem, 177

Cairo, Egypt, 72, 93, 98–99
Camp David Accords (1978–79), 78
Carapico, Sheila, 116
Carlos Rowe, John, 115
Carter, James, 205
Caruth, Cathy, 138–39
Casablanca, Morocco. See *Exiles: A Dialogue with the Museum of Moroccan Judaism* (exhibition)
Casanfa (Miliani), 34
Castel, Robert, 49
Cervantes Cultural Center, 174
Cervantes Gallery for the National Institute of Fine Arts, 174
Chakroun, Henri, 59
Chalabi, Poussy, 99
Chemouilli, Henri, 59

Chicago (Al-Aswānī), 71
Christianity
Christian reconquest of Spain, 53
Frankenstein in Baghdad and, x–xi
Jewish presence in Arabian Peninsula and, 117
Ottoman interventions and, 4
Spanish violence toward converts, 54
cinema. *See* film
Cintra (Aourid), 34
class, in new-consciousness genre, 84
Cohen, Eli, 141
collective memory. *See* memory
colonialism
French occupation, 4, 5, 55–56
grief and loss as allegory for, 115
Jewish-Muslim separation and, 3–4, 7–8
in Mazagan, Morocco, 43
postcolonial readings, 113–14, 128–29
War of Independence (Algeria), 49, 57–59
commercial tradition, 62, 63
concrete, 183–88, *184*
cosmopolitanism
defined, 89n4
Egyptian interest in Jewish heritage, 69–70
in Egyptian literature, 71
in Egyptian television, 103–5
interfaith marriage, 77–78, 89n39, 123
new-consciousness novel genre, 72, 84, 88
shared religious-cultural sphere, 75–77, 200
Zionism and, 80
See also multiculturalism
crafts. *See* artisanship
Craps, Stef, 142–43
cultural homogenization, xiii, 8, 36, 118, 192
Curiel, Henry, 104
Cvetkovich, Ann, 136, 138

Damascus Affair (Damascus Blood Libel) (1840), 4
Daraiseh, Isra, xi
Darwish, Mahmoud, 177, 183, 186
death and loss
in *Al-Yahūdī al-ḥālī* (The handsome Jew), 121–30
practices and discourses surrounding, 114–15
southern Arabian historical context, 115–19
in works of majority world writers, 115
Yemeni motifs, 119–21
De Certeau, Michel, 74
Decrée Crémieux (1870), 4, 5, 55–56
De Gaulle, Charles, 66
Deleuze, Gilles, 144
De Nesry, Carlos, 5
de-Orientalizing sociology, 37
"deterritorialization," 144
Dhimmī, The (Bat Ye'or), 194
Diarna (Geo-Museum of North African and Middle Eastern Jewish Life), xiii
Digital Heritage Mapping (nonprofit), xiii
Dink, Hrant, 166–67
Dispersion of Egyptian Jewry, The (Beinin), 194
disturbed burial, 126–28
documentary film
as mode of resistance, 168
loss articulated in, 26–28
Moroccan production, 13
On the Banks of the Tigris, 27
El Gusto (Taste), 27
Juifs marocains, destins contrariés, 13
Salāṭah baladī (An Egyptian salad), 14, 109
Si je t'oublie Istanbul (If I forget thee Istanbul), 154
They Were Promised the Sea, 13
Tinghir-Jerusalem, 13, 26–27
Trees Cry for Rain, 154
'An yahūd miṣr (The Jews of Egypt), 14–15
See also *Hermana* (film); *Las Ultimas Palavras* (The last words) (film)
Dreyfus affair (1894), 56
Drumond, Edouard, 56

economics, 62, 63, 79–80, 82–83, 117, 140
See also artisanship
Egypt
early Jewish emigration from, 52
Egypt-Yemen relations, 116
Jacques Hassoun's reminiscences of, 40, 41, 44
interest in Jewish heritage, 8–9, 69–70
The Jewish Quarter, Cairo, 98–99
new-consciousness novel, 72, 84, 88
prosperity under Khedive Isma'il, 4
theater and cinema, 14–15
twentieth-century Jewish departure, 81–84
See also Arabic literature in Egypt; Egyptian television
Egyptian television
the "beautiful age" *(al-zaman al-gamīl),* 15, 28, 96–99

cosmopolitanism, 103–5
figures of memory, 100–102
heroes and villains, 106–7
shifts in Jewish representation, 93–95, 108–9
Elayyan, Hani, x
Elghanian, Habib, 195, 204
El Guabli, Brahim
"age of loss," 20
on authoritarianism, 8
authors' approach and, 2
chapter by, 17–18, 25–47
mnemonic literature, 12–13
El Gusto (Taste) (film), 27
El Hassane, Aït Moh, 12
Eliyahu Hanavi synagogue, Egypt, xiii, 69
El Jadida, Morocco, 37, 40, 43
Elsaket, Ifdal, 102
Emerson, Caryl, 148
emigration
from 1954 to 1967, statistical data, 45n1
economic impacts, Egypt, 82
historical context, 1–8
from Iran, 195
Jerusalem's Wailing Wall and, 177
from Middle East to Maghreb, 52–53
from Morocco, 42
narratives of separation, 1–2
from Syria, 136
Turkification policies and, 155, 162
from Yemen, 6–7, 114, 117–18
See also loss as catalyst
Ender, Karin, 156
Ender, Rita, 156–57
See also *Las Ultimas Palavras* (The last words) (film)
"era of the witness," 28
Erdrich, Louise, 115
Ergenç, Özer, 164
Erinnerungsfiguren (figures of memory), 100–102
Eskander, Sa'd, xv
Esteryakas d'Estambol (Stars of Istanbul) (choir), 161–62
étranger professionnel (professional stranger), 38
Exiles: A Dialogue with the Museum of Moroccan Judaism (exhibition)
circulation of, 174–75
handicraft as visual archive, 177–83, *179*, *180*, *181*
mirror-artistic investigations, 173–74
Museum of Moroccan Judaism (MMJ), 171–72, *172*
objects of exile: a concrete story, 183–88, *184*
visibility and invisibility, 171–72, 175–77
Exiles: A Fertile Paradigm (exhibition), 187
Ezzedine Tazi, Muhammad, 12

Fakhreddine, Huda, 137
Farag, Alfred, 80
Felman, Shoshana, 137, 145
fibula motif, *180*, 180–82, *181*
figures of memory *(Erinnerungsfiguren)*, 100–102
film
Egyptian theater and, 14–15
loss depicted in documentary film, 26–28
Moroccan cinematic depictions of Jews, 13–14
See also documentary film; *and specific works*
Fī qalbī unthā 'ibriyya (There is a Hebrew woman in my heart) (Hamdi), 29
fluid identity *(identité fluide)*, 38
foreignness, 39
Foucault, Michel, 172, 174
France
colonial interventions, 3–6, 48, 55–56, 59
Vichy government policies, World War II, 56–57, 64–65
War of Independence (Algeria), 49, 57–59
See also Algerian literature
Frankenstein in Baghdad (Sa'dāwī), x–xi
Free Officers Revolution, 73
Freud, Sigmund, 10, 31, 38
"frientimate," the Jew as, 40–45
From Miniskirt to Hijab (Saper), 196, 204–7

Galerie Bab Rouah, 174, 185, 187
Gallicization, 5, 6, 59
gender, 72, 84, 87, 114, 123–25
geometric symbolism, 182
Gerber, Haim, 82
ghettos, 162–63
Ginestar, Josep, 173
Glissant, Édouard, 38
Goitein, Shlomo, 120–21
Guattari, Félix, 144

Hachkar, Kamal, 13, 26–27
Ḥadd al-ghawāyah (The edge of error) (ʿAfia)
holy sites, cross-religious veneration, 75–76
interfaith marriage, 78
introduced, 71
as new-consciousness novel, 72
representation of space, 74
Zionism in, 80–81, 85–87
Hadj, Messali, 64–65
Hafiz, Sabry, 31
Hafiz, Amin al-, 141
Hakakian, Roya, 195, 196, 197–98, 200–204
Halbwachs, Maurice, 100
Halevi, Leor, 114
Hamdi, Khawla, 29
handicrafts. *See* artisanship
Hanin, Roger, 49
Ḥārat al-Yahūd (The Jewish quarter) (soap opera)
the "beautiful age" *(al-zaman al-gamīl),* 15, 28, 96–98
cosmopolitanism, 103–5
figures of memory: Umm Kulthum, 100–102
heroes and villains, 106–7
The Jewish Quarter, Cairo, 98–99
public reception, 93–94
shifts in Jewish representation, 94–95, 107–9
Harel, Yaron, 140
Hariri, Ibrahim, 34–35
Hassan II, King of Morocco, 36
Hassoun, Jacques, 39, 40–43, 44
Hathaway, Jane, 116
Heliopolis (film), 109
Hepkaner, İlker, chapter by, 19, 154–70
Hermana (film)
circulation of, 167–68
historical accuracy, 163–64
loss of Ankara's Jewish community, 162–63
rejection of Istanbul-centrism, 167
support for, 158–59
heterotopias, 172, 174
High Atlas Mountains, Morocco, 33
historical novels, 119, 120–21, 129–30
history
debating meanings of, 165–68
historical accuracy, 163–64
historical amnesia, 32
historical context for separation, 1–8
"historical silence," 28
Iranian Jewish writers and, 194–96
"Istanbul-centric" understandings of, 165, 167
Kurdish-Arab-Jewish memory and, 139–43
lack of critical engagement with, 156
southern Arabian historical context, 115–19
spatializing historicization, 187
See also *Exiles: A Dialogue with the Museum of Moroccan Judaism* (exhibition); memory
History Foundation of Turkey, 158, 164
holy sites, cross-religious veneration of, 75–76
homogenization, cultural, xiii, 8, 36, 118, 192
Horn, Dara, xiii
"House" (Darwish), 186
ḥumaynī (Yemeni genre of poetry), 120, 130
Ḥurma (Al-Muqri), 118
Hussein, Mostafa
authors' approach and, 3
chapter by, 69–92
on engagement with Jewish spaces, 9

Ibrāhīm, Ṣunʿ Allāh, 71
Identité et Dialogue (Identity and Dialogue) association, 40
identité fluide (fluid identity), 38
identity
collective memory and, 102
cosmopolitanism and, 72, 73, 74–75, 105
Jewish indigeneity to Maghreb region, 51–55
Jewish loyalty to French and, 63–64
minority identities and language, 137, 143–50
See also nationalism
Ilā al-Amām (Forward!) (revolutionary organization), 8
"imagined communities," 71
impersonation of Jews, 82
Institut de Sociologie (Institute of Sociology), 37
intellectual projects, 37–45
interfaith marriage, 77–78, 89n39, 123
intergenerational memory, 26, 27
International Prize for Arabic Fiction, x, 113
intersectionality, 84
Iran
authors' approach and, 2
scholarship on Iranian and Iraqi Jews, 10
Syrian Jews from, 140

Iranian Jewish writers
creating public memory, 197–98
historical context, 194–96
Iranian-Jewish representation, 190–94, 207–8
Journey from the Land of No (Hakakian), 196, 197–98, 200–204
From Miniskirt to Hijab (Saper), 196, 204–7
Persian Brides (Rabinyan), 196, 198–200
Iranian Revolution (1979), 191, 193, 195, 196, 203–4, 205–7
Iraq
documentaries set in, 27
extant scholarship on, 10–11, 19
Iraqi Jewish Archive, xiii–xv
loss of Iraqi Jewish past, xi–xii
novels and novelists, x–xi, 12, 29–30
Irving, Sarah, chapter by, 18–19, 113–34
"Islamic anti-Semitism," 194
İsmiyle Yaşamak (To live with one's name) (Ender), 157
ISRAE, Elle . . . (ISRAE, she . . .) (Ouissaden), 35
Israel. *See* State of Israel
Israeli Emerging Novelist Award, 198
Israeli Foreign Ministry, 194
"Istanbul-centric" history, 165
"Iyya" (Ballas), 10

J'accuse (Zola), 56
James, Henry, 145
Jewish Joint Distribution Committee (JDC), 194–95
Jewish memory in Turkey
critical engagements with history, 156
debating meanings of history, 165–68
loss of Ankara's Jewish community, 162–63
loss of Judeo-Spanish language, 159–62
Turkification policies, 154–55, 160, 162
Jewish-Muslim relations
1967 War and, 30, 32, 136, 139–43
coexistence in Maghreb region, xi–xii, xv, 48, 53
Décree Crémieux and, 55–56
Egyptian interest in Jewish heritage, 69–70
historical context for separation, 1–8
interfaith marriage, 77–78, 89n39, 123
Jewish migration to Palestine, 117–18
Jewish presence in Arabian Peninsula, 116–17
Jewish presence in Iran, 191, 194–95
neolachrymose narratives, 194
prospects for reconciliation, 65–66
shared religious-cultural sphere, 75–77, 200
Turkification policies and, 155, 160, 162
War of Independence and, 49, 57–59
World War II and, 56–57, 64–65
See also Algerian literature; Arabic literature in Egypt; death and loss; Egyptian television; *Exiles: A Dialogue with the Museum of Moroccan Judaism* (exhibition); Iranian Jewish writers; Jewish memory in Turkey; Kurdish-Arab-Jewish Memory; loss as catalyst
Jewish Quarterly-Wingate Prize, 198
Jewish studies, 11–12
Jews
Algerian writers' attitude toward, 48–50
archaic depictions of, 85
conflation of Judaism and Zionism, 1, 2, 11, 86
as "frientimates," 40–45
as indigenous to Maghreb, 51–55
Jewish commercial tradition, 62, 63
moneylending, 82
North African Judaism, 6
on-screen reimaginings of, 94–95, 108–9
as professional strangers, 38–39
Turkification policies and, 155, 160, 162
See also Jewish-Muslim relations
Jews in Modern Egypt, The (Krämer), 81
Jmarhi, Mustapha, 43
Journey from the Land of No (Hakakian), 196, 197–98, 200–204
"Judaic Threads in the West African Tapestry" (Prussin), 178, 182
Juifs marocains, destins contrariés (film), 13
Jundi, Amru al-, 12

Kakon, Aimé, 172, 175, 176–77
Kamel, Nadia, 14, 109
Kandiyoti, Dalia, 161
Kateb, Yacine, 51, 52
Kattan, Naim, xi
Khatibi, Abdelkébir, 26, 37–45
Kincaid, Jamaica, 115
Koç University Ankara Studies Research Center, 158, 164
Kolay Gelsin (Ender), 157
Kosansky, Oren, 11
Krämer, Gudrun, 81

Kraver, Stephanie, chapter by, 19, 135–53
Küçükkeleş, Müjge, 157
Kula 930 (musical), 161
Kulthum, Umm, 96, 100–102
Kurdish-Arab-Jewish Memory
historical context, 139–43
literary language of trauma, 135–39
minority identities and language, 137, 143–50
Kuwait, 28

labor, 157
LaCapra, Dominick, 31, 32
La Communauté juive marocaine (conference; 1978), 40
La Dépossession (The dispossession) (Boudjedra)
Algerian portrayals of Jews, 48
Décree Crémieux and anti-Semitism, 55
FLN and War of Independence, 58
identity and ethnicity, 51, 53, 54
loss and nostalgia, 49
Muslim-Jewish solidarity, WWII, 50, 57, 65
Laghrari, Youness, 13
La Grotte éclatée (The exploded cave) (Mechakra), 51
Lāmī, Alā' al-, 28
language
Algerian national identity and, 50
authoritarianism and, 152n57
Gallicization, 5, 6, 59
loss of Judeo-Spanish language, 155, 159–62, 168
minority identities and, 137, 143–50
Moroccan terms evoking Jewishness, 32–33
nostalgia, etymology of, 97
Turkification policies, 155
Yemeni connotations, 119–20
L'Antijuif algérien (The Algerian anti-Jew) newspaper, 56
Laredj, Waciny, 48, 50, 52, 53, 54, 66
Laroui, Abdallah, 36
La Silhouette (The silhouette) newspaper, 56
Laskier, Michael, 5, 42
Las Ultimas Palavras (The last words) (film)
circulation of, 167–68
loss of Judeo-Spanish language, 159–62, 168
representations of space, 165–67
support for, 157–59
Lā tatrukūnī hunā waḥdī (Do not leave me here alone) (Al-Quddūs), 78
L'Autre juive (Sayegh), 10
Layoun, Mary, 127
Le Captif de Mabrouka (The captive of Mabrouka) (Ait Moh), 34
Le Dernier juif de Tamentit (The last Jew of Tamentit) (Zaoui), 48, 49, 50, 51–52, 53–55, 58
Le Foehn, ou, La Preuve par neuf (The Foen, or Casting out nines) (Mammeri), 48, 50, 59–61, 63
Le Foll-Luciani, Pierre-Jean, 64
Leiris, Raymond, 58
Le Juif en Egypte (Bat Ye'or), 194
Le Même livre (The same book) (Khatibi and Hassoun), 40
"Le Narrateur" (The storyteller) (Benjamin), 183
Le Scribe et son ombre (The scribe and his shadow) (Khatibi), 38–39
Levy, Lital
authors' approach and, 19
forward by, x–xvi
on loss in Ballas's "Iyya," 10
on space and identity, 74
Lévy, Simon, 162
literature
loss articulated in novels, 29–30
minor literature and minority identity, 144
mnemonic literature as subgenre, 32–37
new-consciousness novel, 72, 84, 88
representations of Iran, 190–94
reshaping of Arabic literary field, 30–32
translation, politics of, 197–98
in worldmaking, 147–48
See also Algerian literature; Arabic literature in Egypt; death and loss; Iranian Jewish writers; Kurdish-Arab-Jewish memory; loss as catalyst; *and specific works*
Liʿbet el-Set (The lady's puppet) (film), 83
lmllāh (the mellah' al-mallāḥ), 32
Los Paşaros Sefaradis (band), 161
loss
in Algerian literature, 49
as conceptual framework, 10–17
of cultural diversity, xiii, 8, 36, 118, 192
of Iraqi Jewish past, xi–xii
language loss and preservation, 159–62, 168
mnemonic literature and, 32–37
representations of death and, 121–30
trauma and memory, 136, 142–43

in works of majority world writers, 115
See also death and loss; Jewish memory in Turkey; Kurdish-Arab-Jewish Memory; loss as catalyst
loss as catalyst
Jew as "frientimate," 40–45
Jew as professional stranger, 38–39
Abdelkébir Khatibi's idea of "the Jew," 37–38
loss as generative force, 25–26, 44–45
loss in novels and film, 26–32
Moroccan mnemonic literature, 32–37
lqbūr n udāyn (the Jewish cemetery), 32

Mādhā ʿan al-sayyida al-yahūdiyya rāḥīl? (What about Rachel, the Jewish lady?) (Barakāt)
historical context, 139–43
literary language of trauma, 135–39
minority identities and language, 137, 143–50
Madhoun, Rabai al-, 12
Madīnī, Aḥmad al-, 43–44
Maghili, Mohamed ibn Abdelkarim al-, 54
Maghrebi Jewish communities
authors' approach, 2–3, 12, 16, 17–20
creation of public memory, 197–98
discourse and virtual resources, xii–xiv
emergent historiography, 1–2
expatriation of Iraqi Jewish archive, xiv–xv
Frankenstein in Baghdad (Saʿdāwī), x–xi
historical context for separation, 1–8
historical silence and remembrance, 8–9
Jews as indigenous to Maghreb, 51–55
loss as conceptual framework, 10–17
loss of Iraqi Jewish past, xi–xii
See also Algerian literature; Arabic literature in Egypt; death and loss; Egyptian television; *Exiles: A Dialogue with the Museum of Moroccan Judaism* (exhibition); Iranian Jewish writers; Jewish memory in Turkey; Kurdish-Arab-Jewish Memory; loss as catalyst
Maghreb pluriel (Plural Maghreb) (Khatibi), 39
magic, 182
Mahi-ye siyah-e kuchulu (The little black fish) (Behrangi), 201, 203
Mahmoodi, Betty, 192
Majnūn laylā al-yahūdiyya (The madman of Layla the Jewish woman) (Al-Rāshīdī'), 29
Mammeri, Mouloud, 48, 50, 59–61, 63
"Manfā" (Exile) (Darwish), 183
Marrakesh, Morocco, 33
Mawzaʾa Exile, 120
Mazagan, Morocco, 43
Mechakra, Yamina, 51
Megorashim (expelled), 53
memoirs
Iranian-Jewish representation and, 190–94
Journey from the Land of No (Hakakian), 196, 197–98, 200–204
From Miniskirt to Hijab (Saper), 196, 204–7
memory
allowing for narrativized loss, 42–43
archeology of, 182–83
creation of public memory, 197–98
figures of memory, 100–102
historical amnesia, 32
historical genre and, 119
imbued in handicrafts, 182
"Istanbul-centric" remembrance, 165, 167
Jewish memory practices, 157–58
mnemonic literature, 12–13, 26, 32–37
mourning as act of, 115
multidirectional memory, 137
reactivated through form, 178
resurgence in Jewish memory, 2
storytelling and, 183
trauma and, 136, 142–43
virtual discourse, xii–xiii
worldmaking and, 147–48
See also *Exiles: A Dialogue with the Museum of Moroccan Judaism* (exhibition); Jewish memory in Turkey; Kurdish-Arab-Jewish Memory
Memory-Sequential Movement in Darna (exhibition), 187–88
Merchant of Venice, The (Shakespeare), 85
messianic and apocalyptic themes, 122–23
metallurgy, 178, *180*, 180–82, *181*
Middle East, immigration to Maghreb from, 52–53
"Middle Eastern turn" in scholarship, 2
Middle East Studies Association, 3
Midnight Orchestra (film), 14
Mikhael, Sami, xi
Miliani, Driss, *Casanfa*, 34
Minister of Antiquities (Egypt), 69
minorities, 36, 137, 143–50
mirror-artistic investigations, 172, 173–74
Misgeret (Framework), 66

Mizrahi, Togo, 14
mnemonic literature, 12–13, 26, 32–37
modernity and religiosity, 85
moneylending, 82
Mordechai Kriaty Foundation, 165
Moroccan Other-Archives (El Guabli), 8, 26
Morocco
  Alliance Israélite Universelle, 5
  desires for normalization of Israel, 17, 45n7
  dominance in cultural production, 9, 13–14
  Euro-American interventions in, 4
  mnemonic literature, 12, 32–37
  See also *Exiles: A Dialogue with the Museum of Moroccan Judaism* (exhibition); loss as catalyst
mourning, 31, 115
"Mourning and Melancholia" (Freud), 10, 31
multiculturalism
  cultural homogenization, xiii, 8, 36, 118, 192
  Egyptian interest in Jewish heritage, 69–70
  interfaith marriage, 77–78, 89n39, 123
  Jewish imaginaries in Egyptian literature, 71
  minority identities and language, 137, 143–50
  multiethnicity of Maghreb region, xi–xii, xv, 48, 53
  new-consciousness novel genre, 72, 84, 88
  shared religious-cultural sphere, 75–77, 200
  See also Kurdish-Arab-Jewish Memory
multidirectional memory, 137
Muqri, Ali al-. See *Al-Yahūdī al-ḥālī* (The handsome Jew) (Al-Muqri)
Murad, Laila, 14
Murad, Munir, 14
Museum of Moroccan Judaism (MMJ)
  described, 171–72, *172*
  remodeling of, 175–77
  See also *Exiles: A Dialogue with the Museum of Moroccan Judaism* (exhibition)
music, xii, 27, 100–102, 161–62
Muslim Brotherhood, 106–7, 110n55
Muslims
  Algerian-Israeli relations, 48, 66
  Amazigh ancestry, Algeria, 50
  Arab-Israeli conflict in Egyptian novels, 80–81
  guards attending to Jewish ruins, 33, 44
  impersonation of Jews by Muslim characters, 82
  interfaith marriage, 77–78, 89n39, 123
  Jew as "professional stranger" and, 39
  Muslim-Jewish solidarity, WWII, 56–57, 64–65
  replacing Jews as enemies, 106–7
  reshaping of Arabic literary field, 30–32
  Turkification policies, 155, 160, 162
  See also Jewish-Muslim relations

Nafisi, Azar, 192
Nakba (catastrophe), 113–14, 141
Naksa (setback), 30
names, depictions of Jews and, 76
Naqqash, Samir, xi
Nāṣir, Abdul-Jabbār, 29–30
Nasr, Mostafa. See *Yahūd al-iskandariyyah* (Jews of Alexandria) (Nasr)
Nasser, Gamal ʿAbd el-, 71
nationalism
  Egyptian interest in Jewish heritage, 69–70
  Egyptian literature and, 71, 73–74, 88
  Egyptian television and, 94–95
  exile and nationalist sentiment, 186
  Jewish indigeneity to Maghreb, 51–55
  language and national identity, 50
  Muslim resistance to Gallicization, 6
  new-consciousness novel and, 72
  superseding religion, 104–5
  Syrian emigration and, 140–41
  TV as national pedagogy, 108
  unifying national symbols, 102
  See also Algerian literature; Egyptian television
National Liberation Front (FLN), 57–58
Nedjma (Kateb), 51, 52
neolachrymose narratives, 194
new-consciousness novel, 72, 84, 88
newspapers, "imagined communities" and, 71
nomadism, 128–29
"nonplacement," 186
North Africa
  Algeria, 4, 6, 18, 49, 57–59, 66
  early Jewish immigration to, 52–53
  Jews in cultural production, 25
  Tunisia, 4, 29
  See also Algerian literature; Arabic literature in Egypt; Egyptian television; loss as catalyst; Morocco
nostalgia
  al-zaman al-gamīl (the "beautiful age"), 96–99, 108
  and conflict, binaries of, 16–17

postcolonial nostalgia, 114
See also memory
Not Without My Daughter (Mahmoodi), 192
novels. *See* literature
Noy, Orly, 197

objets-valise (suitcase objects), 184
Of Links and Exiles (exhibition), 188
Okbi, Cheikh al-, 64
On the Banks of the Tigris (film), 27
Operation Magic Carpet, 118, 121
Orientalism, 1, 37, 179, 192, 197, 199
other-thought *(pensée-autre)*, 38
Ottoman Empire, 4, 7, 115, 117, 140, 155, 156
Ouarzazate, Morocco, 33, 34
Ouettar, Tahar, 48, 49, 50, 54, 61–64
Ouissaden, Mohamed, *ISRAE, Elle . . .* (ISRAE, she . . .), 35

Pahlavi period, Iran, 204, 206
Palestine
1967 War, 30, 32, 136, 139–43, 155
articulations of loss and, 10, 16
authoritarianism and, 36
Egyptian literature and, 86–87
experience of exile, 177, 183–84, *184*, 185
Israeli proestablishment politics, 6–7
Jewish immigration to, 117–18
and scholarship on loss, 11, 25, 29, 45
See also 1948 War
"Paralogismos" (Abraamidou), 127
Passover, 202–3
Pearlman, Wendy, 142, 146
pensée-autre (other-thought), 38
Persian Brides (Rabinyan), 196, 198–200
"placehood," 176
pogroms against Jews, 57, 58, 63, 64, 169n3
politics
in Egyptian literature, 80
political power, 79
religion and, 84–89
of translation, 197–98
postcolonial readings, 113–14, 128–29
Postcolonial Witnessing (Craps), 142–43
presence-absence, 172, 173
professional stranger, the Jew as, 38–39
Prussin, Labelle, 178, 182

Qamishli, Syria, 135–36, 141, 151n1
See also Kurdish-Arab-Jewish Memory
Quddūs, Iḥsān ʿAbd al-, 78, 90n42
Quincentennial Celebrations, 155, 158, 165
Quincentennial Foundation Museum of Turkish Jews, 158, 164, 166

Rabinyan, Dorit, 196, 198–200
Ramirez, Francis, 182
Ramses, Amir, 14–15, 109
Rāshīdī', Ḥamad Ḥamīd al-, 29
Reading Lolita in Tehran (Nafisi), 192
religion
cosmopolitanism and, 103–5
interfaith marriage, 77–78, 89n39, 123
politics and, 84–89
shared religious-cultural sphere, 75–77, 200
Syrian national ethos and, 143–44
Riyāḍ, Ḥasan, *Awrāq ʿibrīyya* (Hebrew papers), 34
riwāyah siyāsiyyah (political novel), 80
Rolot, Christian, 182
romantic transgression, 123–24
Rothberg, Michael, 137
Ruhayyim, Kamal, 12, 29

Sabbateanism, 123
Sabri, Nadia, chapter by, 18, 171–89
Said, Edward, 186
Salāṭah balādī (An Egyptian salad) (film), 14, 109
Salt Research Center, 158, 164
Ṣannūʿ, Yaʿqūb, 14
Saper, Jacqueline, 195, 196, 204–7
SAVAK (Organization of National Security and Information), 201, 203, 205
Sayegh, Said, 10
Saʿdāwī, Ahmed, x–xi
Schönfelder, Christa, 147
Schroeter, Daniel, 194
Secret Armed Organization (OAS), 58, 66
Sekkat Hatimi, Hanane, 9
Sénac, Jean, 51
separation
Jewish-Muslim relations, historical context, 1–8
loss as conceptual framework, 10–17
narratives of, 1–2
See also emigration
Serfaty, Abraham, 8
sexuality and sexual transgression, 123–25
Shabazi, Shalom (Salim), 120
Shakespeare, William, 85

Shamma aw Shtrit (Shamma or Shtrit) (Hariri), 34–35
shapes, mystical power of, 182
Shemer, Yaron, 80
Shohat, Ella
  authors' approach and, 2
  on colonial interventions, 4
  Eurocentrism in Jewish histories, 169n3
  memoir as analytical framework, 192
  Orientalism and Jewish-Muslim enmity, 1
  on Sayegh's *L'Autre juive*, 10
  on Umm Kulthum, 102
  on writings on Iraq-Iran war, 10
Shokor, Majid, 27
Shuker, Edwin, xiv
Si je t'oublie Istanbul (If I forget thee Istanbul) (film), 154
Simmel, Georg, 38, 43
Sivil Düşün (EU program), 157
siyāsat al-tamṣīr (policies of Egyptianization), 84
soap operas. See *H. ārat al-Yahūd* (The Jewish quarter) (soap opera)
socio-cultural habitus, 182
Somekh, Sasson, xi, 76
Soto-Crespo, Ramón, 115
space
  representations of, 165–67
  spatializing historicization, 187
Spain, 48, 53, 54
Starr, Deborah, 83
State of Israel
  Algeria-Israel relations, 48, 66
  authoritarianism and, 36
  Egyptian interest in Jewish heritage and, 70
  in Egyptian literature, 80–81, 86–87
  establishment of, 5, 6–7, 81, 113–14, 129–30, 141
  immigration to (*See* emigration)
  interest in Jewish-Arab identity, 197
  Iran-Israel relations, 193
  Iraqi Jewish archive, xiii–xv
  Morocco-Israel relations, 13
  normalization of, 17, 28, 45n7
  War of Independence and, 49
Sternfeld, Lior B., chapter by, 19, 190–210
Stillman, Norman, 4, 85, 136
superstition, 182
Syria
  1967 Arab-Israeli War and, 139–43
  Jewish emigration from, 136
  See also Kurdish-Arab-Jewish Memory
Taklā, Naʿīm, 71
Tamazgha, North Africa, 25–30
  See also loss as catalyst
Tangi, Myriam, 173
Tapis et tissages du Maroc (Moroccan tapestries and weaving) (Ramirez and Rolot), 182
Tazi, Mohammed Ezzeddine, 34
Taʿm aswad, rāʾiha sawdāʾ (Black taste, black smell) (Al-Muqri), 118
television. *See* Egyptian television
Thābet, Kamel Amin, 141
theater, in preserving language, 162
They Were Promised the Sea (film), 13
Tinghir-Jerusalm (film), 13, 26–27
Tizgui N'Barda, Morocco, 33
Tobi, Yosef, 122
Tofigh (satirical magazine), 201
toponyms reflecting Jewish heritage, 32–33
Touati, Émile, 59
Toufic, Jalal, 126
Toshavim (natives), 53
translation, politics of, 197–98
trauma
  literary language of, 138–39, 147
  memory and, 136, 142–43
  study of, 31
Treaty of Lausanne (1923), 155
Trees Cry for Rain (film), 154
Trevisan Semi, Emanuela, 9
Tunisia, 4, 29
Turkey
  Ankara, 158, 159, 162–64, 167
  Turkification policies, 154–55, 160, 162
  See also Jewish memory in Turkey
Ṭuyūr al-ʿanbar (Birds of ambergris) (ʿAbdelmegid)
  introduced, 71
  Jewish departure from Egypt, 81–82, 83–84
  as new-consciousness novel, 72
  religion and politics, 84, 88
  representation of space, 74

udāyn (Jews), 32
Ulus Private Jewish School, 166
Um Hārūn (Harun's mother) (soap opera), 28
United Arab Emirates, 17, 28, 45n7
United States
  expatriation of Iraqi Jewish archive, xiv–xv
  immigration of Iranian Jews to, 195
  interest in Jewish-Arab identity, 197
  US-Iran tensions, 193

urban setting, 72–73, 74–75
US National Archives and Records Administration, xiv

Vichy government, 56–57
Villa Empain (cultural center), 188
visibility and invisibility, 171–72, 175–77

Wagenhofer, Sophie, 171
Wailing Wall, Jerusalem, 177
War of Independence (Algeria), 18, 49, 57–59, 66
Wazana, Kathy, 13
weaving, 178, 180, *180*, 182, 183, 188n13
We Crossed a Bridge and It Trembled (Pearlman), 142
Wedeen, Lisa, 152n57
Weiss, Ulrike, 173, 175, 177–83, *179*, *180*, *181*
Where Are You Going Moshé? (film), 14
White, Hayden, 187
Wilad al'Am (Escaping Tel Aviv) (film), 109
Williams College, 2
women
- imposed wearing of hijab, 205–6
- interfaith marriage and, 77–78, 123
- patriarchy and women writers, 193

worldmaking, 147–48
World War II
- Algerian-Jewish relations, 56–57, 64–65
- "era of the witness" following, 28
- JDC operation in Iran, 194
- Jews in Egypt following, 81

Yahūd al-iskandariyyah (Jews of Alexandria) (Nasr), 71
- bequeathing of wealth, 83
- economic and political power, 79–80
- impersonation, 82
- interfaith marriage, 78
- Jewish departure from Egypt, 81
- as new-consciousness novel, 72
- religion and politics, 84, 85, 88
- representation of space, 74–75
- shared religious-cultural spheres, 77

Yawmiyyāt muslim yahūdī (Diary of a Jewish Muslim) (Ruhayyim), 29
"years of lead," Morocco, 36
Yemen
- *Al-Yahūdī al-ḥālī* as Yemeni novel, 119–21
- Jewish emigration from, 6–7, 114
- southern Arabian historical context, 115–19
- See also *Al-Yahūdī al-ḥālī* (The handsome Jew) (Al-Muqri)

Youngs, Richard, 157
Youssef, Mary, 72, 84

Zaoui, Amin, 12, 48, 49, 50, 51–52, 53–55, 58
Zaydi, Khdair al-, 12
Zeidel, Ronen, 19
Zenner, Walter, 136, 139, 140–41
Al-Zilzāl (The earthquake) (Ouettar), 48, 49, 50, 54, 61–64
Zionism
- Alliance Israélite Universelle and, 5
- Arabic literature in Egypt and, 73, 85–87, 88
- conflation with Judaism, 1, 2, 11, 86
- exclusion from cosmopolitan genre, 80
- Sabbateanism and, 123
- Syrian emigration and, 136, 140–41
- Yemenite Jewish emigration and, 6–7, 118

Zola, Émile, 56

Printed in the USA
CPSIA information can be obtained
at www.ICGtesting.com
CBHW030809241024
16252CB00002B/3

9 780271 097558